# a TOLTEC path

A user's guide to the teachings
of don Juan Matus, Carlos Castaneda,
and other Toltec seers

# a TOLTEC path

## path

*A user's guide to the teachings
of don Juan Matus, Carlos Castaneda,
and other Toltec seers*

# Ken Eagle Feather

HAMPTON ROADS
PUBLISHING COMPANY, INC.

Cover art by Rosemary Crocker
Cover design by Matthew Friedman

For information write:

Hampton Roads Publishing Company, Inc.
976 Norfolk Square
Norfolk, VA 23502

Or call: (804)459-2453
FAX: (804)455-8907

If you are unable to order this book from your local
bookseller, you may order directly from the publisher.
Quantity discounts for organizations are available.
Call 1-800-766-8009, toll-free.

ISBN 1-57174-023-6

10 9 8 7 6 5 4 3 2 1

Printed on acid-free paper in the United States of America

Dedicated to—

The Blue Ridge Mountains

"Even writing and speaking, whether didactic or poetical, have as their ultimate aim the guidance of the reader to that knowledge of perception from which the author started; if they do not have this aim, they are bad. For this reason, the contemplation and observation of everything *actual*, as soon as it presents something new to the observer, is more instructive than all reading and hearing about it."

—Arthur Schopenhauer,
from *The World as Will and Representation*

"Be a warrior; shut off your internal dialogue; make your inventory and then throw it away. The new seers make accurate inventories and then laugh at them. Without the inventory the assemblage point becomes free."

—don Juan Matus,
from Carlos Castaneda's *The Fire from Within*

# Contents

# 1
# Stepping Off a Flat Earth

This book finishes one of several tasks given to me by don Juan Matus (*don* is a Spanish appellative indicating respect), the Indian seer many of us have come to know through the books of Carlos Castaneda. In them, Castaneda presents don Juan's philosophy and practices to enhance perception. I first met don Juan while walking down Speedway Boulevard, a main avenue in Tucson. Late for class at the local university, I simply gawked at him and continued a hurried pace. When I arrived at class, a flood of energy swept through me, indicating that the very poised Indian I had passed was don Juan. A couple of days passed and I saw him again, this time standing near a small market on the outskirts of town. I approached him and held a very short conversation; I was too intimidated to remain long in his presence.

Over the next few years, our paths crossed many times. Each time, he offered a lesson regarding the mysteries of awareness. When I later moved from Arizona to Florida, his instruction continued during dreams and visions. My first book, *Traveling With Power*, offers a full account of how I came to be his apprentice.[1]

Meeting don Juan marked the end of one journey and the beginning of another. Prior to meeting him, I had totally immersed myself in Castaneda's books. Rigorous, daily practice of the techniques offered in his books was the only way I could secure relief from a bleeding ulcer. The balance I learned from this regimen eventually led to healing that disease. Then, through don Juan's instruction and continued daily practice, I embarked on another sojourn as I learned to stand firm within his tradition of exploring consciousness. Don Juan later charged me with writing two books that would elaborate on Castaneda's material.

In the course of this task, I changed some of Castaneda's terms. These changes are entirely in keeping with don Juan's teachings. Indeed, he mentions that his teacher, Julian, changed terms to suit himself. The only guideline is that the changes have to be verified through *seeing* (*Fire*, 60).[2] In this light, changing terms allows us to view his concepts from different angles. As Clarissa Estes writes in her book *Women Who Run With the Wolves,* terms create a territory of thought and feeling.[3] They give us a place to live, she says. In other words, terms shape what is perceived. The trick, however, is to learn how to handle the territory so the boundaries don't become barriers.

Instead of the term "sorcery" to describe the system don Juan teaches, for instance, I call it the Toltec Way. A practitioner, therefore, is a Toltec rather than a sorcerer. Two compatriots of Castaneda who have also published accounts of their interaction with don Juan use Castaneda's term "sorcery." Florinda Donner, in *Being-in-Dreaming,* and Taisha Abelar, in *The Sorcerers' Crossing,* refer to sorcery as a means of expanding perception.[4] Thus sorcery is an entirely abstract endeavor, and the evil connotations often placed on that term are automatically voided. No argument. But using the term "Toltec" also voids erroneous connotations, and it acknowledges a particular way of unfolding perception, as well. Any time you have a worldview and techniques designed to bring awareness of that world into view, you have specific influences shaping perception. The term is also in keeping with don Juan's references to his predecessors as Toltecs.

Another change is from "stalking" to "tracking." Here, too, I wanted to remove the negative connotation "stalking" sometimes carries. Also, while the implication of tracking down an objective or prey applies, the term also reflects the pursuit of aligning energies. Proficient alignment between oneself and that which is sought produces that awareness; hence, the goal is realized. To adjust a video cassette recorder's tracking, you tune the heads until you align them with the cassette tape and receive the clearest picture and the best sound. Accordingly, humans have the ability to align with, or track, a host of perceptions. For example, think how you feel when you are in touch emotionally with someone you care about. At those times, you know you are connected in some way. You have achieved an alignment with that person. The quality of alignment then determines the quality of what is perceived.

By far, changing the term "warrior" to "ranger" has prompted the most response. Analogies to war and preparedness for war are scattered throughout Castaneda's books. However, the term "warrior" may prompt images of hostile activity, and the change to "ranger" provides a demilitarizing tone. Additionally, I wanted to remove connotations of regimentation, of having to behave in a certain manner. But I also felt the need to offer a term which portrays the training, the struggle, and the devotion to freedom-fighting that Toltecs exhibit. Thus, paradoxically, this change represents a tribute to U.S. Army Rangers and other Special Operations elements of the armed forces. Over the years, my associations with this particular breed of warrior have shown that they are well-trained, competent, dedicated, sober regarding the realities of war, and confident. In short, they invariably meet don Juan's conditions of "going to knowledge or war" (*Teachings,* 58). In a Toltec sense, a ranger reflects a basic level of discipline. And this personal integrity is what enables further evolution.

Within the Toltec Way, there are a number of Toltec paths, with each path defined by a particular lineage. It's as though there is a Toltec world, and that world has a number of countries with different cultures. Just as humans have racial and cultural differences while sharing common features, Toltec lineages have differences while sharing common features.

While *A Toltec Path* relates specifically to the lineage of don Juan and Castaneda, I've occasionally drawn from other sources. Doing so provides a greater context, and shows that Toltecs don't reside in a vacuum. Furthermore, that their work can be related to the work of those who are not Toltec indicates that Toltec teachings apply to human perception in general, and thus are neither exclusive nor aberrant.

To complete this task, I outlined all of Castaneda's books and took volumes of notes detailing the effect of placing his material into practice. I then measured this against don Juan's personal influence. I found that Castaneda had successfully rendered don Juan's core teachings.

With *The Teachings of Don Juan,* Castaneda entered the popular counterculture in the late 1960s. Pursuing graduate-level anthropology at UCLA, he first investigated don Juan's use of psychotropic, or mind-enhancing, plants. He also participated in other Toltec practices such as the gait of power, erasing personal history, and using his death as his advisor.

He later broadened his research by presenting an extensive accounting of don Juan's teachings as a "seer," or one who has matured beyond the need for a system. Rather than dogmatic adherence to a system, a seer is concerned with handling perception. His or her use of a system is intended only as leverage to foster that pursuit. A seer's evolution centers around a mode of perception don Juan refers to as *seeing.* As it refers to achieving an alignment of energies, *seeing* provides direct insight into a person, event, or awareness itself. It bypasses the symbolic, indirect qualities of the rational intellect.

I wasn't aware of Castaneda until the publication of *Journey to Ixtlan*. Retitled *Sorcery: A Description of the World*, this third book served as Castaneda's doctoral dissertation. In part due to the novel-like style of his books, Castaneda remains controversial. Many think his books are fiction. Offering a strong counterpoint to this, Donner and Abelar have associated with don Juan and Castaneda. In fact, they are members of Castaneda's team, and therefore are in a position to offer first-hand accounts. Their books provide hard evidence for Castaneda's—hence, don Juan's—legitimacy.

When considering Castaneda's books, it is important to acknowledge a few factors. First, don Juan spoke to Castaneda, not to us. We are not privy to don Juan's voice inflections, facial expressions, nuances, or the complete context of his endeavors with Castaneda. Moreover, don Juan took Castaneda's personality into account. For instance, don Juan regarded Castaneda as having an affinity with the old cycle of seers, which at times placed his interests more in line with ancient, sorceric concerns. (*Dreaming*, ix, 39.) Hence, Castaneda's books carry a flavor that fulfills certain tastes and answers certain questions, while leaving a hunger for more and different connections. Yet it's clear don Juan knew the impact of his teachings. He assigned Castaneda the task of writing several books about them. Castaneda proved equal to the task with his relentless questioning, courageous participation, and his superb rendition.

Second, it is inappropriate to take one thing don Juan says and expand that as conclusive evidence for a particular point of view. For example, sometimes people say don Juan is sexist. This view is often based on a conversation between don Juan and Castaneda, when don Juan likens the female aspect of datura plants to a woman. He says datura sneaks up on a man and gives him cravings (*Teachings*, 74). In other references, however, it is clear don Juan holds the highest regard for women, usually considering them better than their male counterparts (*Fire*, 142).

Third, in his doctoral dissertation abstract, Castaneda clearly indicates his work is emic anthropology.[5] Emic methodology looks at knowledge from the perspective of participation, of membership within the culture one is studying. Etic methodology, on the other hand, is the more traditional, non-participatory, objective-observer approach.[6] Therefore, Castaneda's material is presented from participation rather than from observation. As a result, his manner of reporting varies from more conservative academic presentations.

The basis of this book, then, is the exploration of Castaneda's books and verification of their teachings through personal experience. In doing so, I developed the knowledge as my own and have produced an autobiography of sorts, where presenting the knowledge is presenting myself. Which brings us to another consideration: while striving to investigate a system, a person encounters the danger of becoming locked within the system. This state automatically interdicts growth, which is the thrust for getting into it in the first place. Thus a central theme is to not get lost in *any* teachings. Only by remaining steadfast can you trim your sails to the seer's wind.

It is not my intention to present the definitive statement about the Toltec Way. It has been accumulating momentum for thousands of years as men and women explore the most intricate aspects of the human condition. As a result, there is vast knowledge—most of which could not find itself on the pages of a book. Nor do I consider this a substitute for Castaneda's work. There is simply no replacing the accounts of his interaction with don Juan.

What I have tried to do is distill Castaneda's work in order to present features of the Toltec Way that 'most anyone traveling it crosses. Just as Castaneda's work is influenced by his personality, this distillation is based on my experience, interests, and goals. One goal is providing sufficient context so that you don't lose your bearings, or can quickly reclaim them, if you travel past the known boundary markers of your reality—in essence, keeping your pouch of perception open to the mysteries of self and world.

The first glimmerings of this openness led me to Tucson. Moving from Florida to Arizona, my highest priority was meeting someone of don Juan's stature. It was beyond my imagination to think I might actually meet him. But I did. With my physical ailment, he served as a healer. He seemed to possess the attitude of "You have a problem with balance? Well, here is an example of what balance is."

Elderly, robust, and self-assured, don Juan seemed the quintessential example of how to live well. To me, he appeared stern until the last time we met. While I always felt intimidated by him, I never distrusted him. I found him to be the kind of person you seek out year after year for guidance and knowledge. Don Juan gave himself completely to life as a seer, as he gave himself completely to life. He could be as lofty as a university philosophy professor, or as down-home as a rural woodsman. He adapted to any situation, teaching not so much how to become a Toltec as how to fully develop innate human capacities, including a full and complete life. I once heard him say, in the midst of teaching an apprentice how to use visions, "You act like a boy of 14 during early spring, when his blood drives him wild. I'm not asking you to ban this feeling. But train it, discipline it, so that you'll have it even when you're an old man."

By repeatedly contrasting the ordinary world I grew up in with the nonordinary Toltec world, don Juan kept pushing me off balance. When I regained it, he pushed again. He created a dynamic opposition which eventually split my world in two, leaving me to restore wholeness. For example, he used dreaming as a means of communication. In the ordinary world, dreams are not considered to have great purpose, let alone be used as a vehicle for deliberate communication. But as a skilled seer, he entered my dreams and controlled them for his purposes. Or during dreaming I sought him out to help solve a riddle. He also stimulated my waking-life perceptions. Once, for instance, I *saw* his head turn a bright crimson. *Seeing* his head aflame and his body remain normal reminded me of a candle. On other occasions, I *saw* his personal energies blend and delicately harmonize with the world at large. His balance with the world was not only out of the ordinary, it was extraordinary.

Through sophisticated modes of perception such as dreaming and *seeing,* don Juan used Toltec methods to further split my perception. By contrasting these perspectives with ordinary reality, I learned to balance between two worlds. Free to pick and choose pieces of either, I found I could also stand apart from both. This ability to step out of and aside from a reality is perhaps the first significant step on the quest to become a seer. I call it, therefore, the seer's first essential maneuver.

Fully incorporating *seeing,* the Toltec Way is an ancient tradition where men and women have labored to construct a philosophy and a way of life enabling them to extract the most from life. As a philosophy, it is a method of inquiry, a system for learning. As a form of knowledge, it is a form of power. The value of a system is in providing context, channel markers that guide one not only through the unexpected, but through daily life. People tend to separate their thoughts from their behavior, so what they say, feel, and do are often different things. Toltecs work to integrate thought, emotions, and behavior, leading to a complete integrity of personal energies. Thus it is a way of life.

For good and ill, a system determines what is perceived, understood, and realized. On the down side, instead of being used as a tool for learning, it is molded into what eventually becomes perceived as the ultimate, unequivocal reality. The person then remains lost within it. On the high side, it engenders a personal transformation in which the expression of personality reflects the essence behind and beyond personality. Behavior emanates from an intimate connection with all creation rather than from the social conventions of ordinary or nonordinary realities.

The features of a system provide a map of perception. Maps orient us to our location, offer a direction in which to proceed, and facilitate movement in that direction. For example, principal features of a Toltec map are the luminous body and the focal point (which Castaneda refers to as the "assemblage point"). The luminous body surrounds and permeates the physical body. When *seen,* the physical body floats inside this egg- or ball-shaped luminosity. Emanating from the luminous body is the aura, or auric field. Likening this to an incandescent light bulb, the physical body is the filament, the luminous body is the energy within the glass, and the aura is the emitted light.

In his later work, Castaneda refers to the luminous body as the "energy body." Since the physical body is also energy (albeit of a different form), this offers a slight semantical problem. But I think "energy body" is more graphic, and suits the overall purpose better. So that term is used here as well.

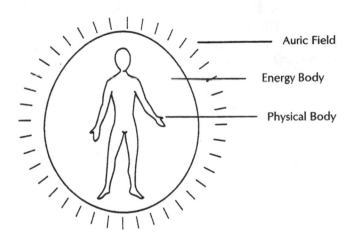

Auric Field

Energy Body

Physical Body

### The Energy Body and Auric Field

The energy body is the greater portion of our nature, a portion we have neglected to develop. Energy emanating from the energy body is the auric field.

The energy body connects directly with the world. It offers a sense of knowing our natural place in the universe. But as our evolution has thus far developed, we now interact with the world through another field of energy which principally uses symbols—rather than direct communication—to structure reality. We develop this field through our thoughts and familiar feelings about our world. Hence this field generates a reflection of reality. The conditions of reality we place in it echo back to us. There is yet a third energy field which exists outside human awareness.

Castaneda refers to these energy fields as the "first, second, and third attentions" (*Fire*, 46). These attentions may be perceived as energy, which makes the term "energy field" a practical step to the more abstract qualities "attention" connotes. The first energy field relates to what we know. It is everything in our known world. The second energy field concerns what we don't know, but what can be learned and incorporated into our known world. It is the unknown which waits for discovery. The third energy field extends beyond human perception. It is the unknowable which rests well beyond our grasp. An alternative way of viewing the three attentions holds that the first field is the physical world, the second field is the nonphysical world, and the third field is a completely abstract, or formless, energy. Later we examine both views and the effect each view has on perception.

In *Traveling With Power*, I referred to the first and second fields as the "first and second reflexives," and I referred to the third field as "Spirit." Those terms were intended to generate an awareness of how we form reality. "Reflexive" meant that the meaning we load into a term reflects right back to us. For example, by defining the first attention as our known world, we remain vigilant to perceive anything that verifies that definition. As a result, whatever we recognize is automatically categorized as part of the first reflexive. Use of the term "Spirit" was intended to foster an awareness that energy exists beyond human form, beyond human definition, beyond human knowledge. The mystery of Spirit suited that purpose. For the purpose of this book, I have shifted those terms to indicate energy fields. With this shift, we add a new perspective to Spirit; as well as a mysterious force, it is the binding, unifying force of all energy fields.

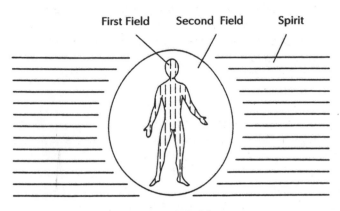

First Field     Second Field     Spirit

## Energy Fields

First Field:     Physical energies, thoughts, feelings, personality, the familiar.
Second Field:   Dreaming and psychic energies, personal essence, the unknown.
Third Field:    Worlds beyond human awareness.
Spirit:         The binding, unifying force of creation.

On or within the energy body is a soft glow. It's a little brighter than its surroundings. The intersection between energies external and internal to the energy body produces this glow. This intersection also reflects how the energy fields have been stabilized. Stabilized energy focuses awareness; hence, the focal point.

Don Juan says that the location of the focal point is a reference point for everything we think and say (*Silence*, 109). Turning his statement around, we can say that everything we think and say stabilizes the focal point. One objective of this book, then, is to provide insights and techniques to help you reclaim the awareness of your complete energy body, and especially reclaim the power gained from purposefully aligning and realigning your energy fields. In other words, you're exploring how to shift the focal point.

Don Juan says that a Toltec is anyone who can deliberately move the focal point. From this ability, you "can do all kinds of good and bad things" to others. Thus being a Toltec is the same as any other vocation. Don Juan adds that a Toltec seer goes beyond moving the focal point. A seer, he says, is concerned with establishing proper relations with others and with the world (*Silence*, 102).

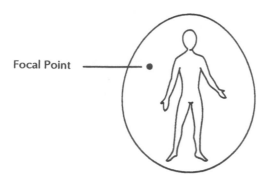

Focal Point

### The Energy Body and Focal Point

As energies external to the energy body pass through it, the focal point forms. The focal point also indicates the type of energy pattern formed by this intersection.

To establish a point, let's for the moment refer to these energy fields as the known, unknown, and unknowable. For instance, the notions that the Earth is round and that Earth revolves around the sun was for a long time unknown. When proved and accepted, the worldview of a round planet which sails around the sun then entered the known world. Perception evolved. In a like manner, knowledge of the energy body is nonexistent for many people. Developing the intricacies of the energy body is exploring the unknown in order to increase awareness of what can be known.

While exploring nonordinary realities, people often pull up short and limit their investigations. Due to the vastness of the unknown, it's easy to lose track of yourself or think you have found the core of knowledge. Don Juan, however, stresses the need to recognize where you are and what you're dealing with. In fact, this is one distinction which separates what he refers to as the old and new cycles of seers. Toltecs with old-cycle tendencies use the unknown to bewitch, whereas new-cycle Toltecs concern themselves with freedom (*Fire*, 20). Old-cycle practitioners enter the unknown and bring back self-indulgence. New-cycle adherents continue exploring beyond their current fences. In doing so, they turn their back on marketplace power plays, and focus on unfolding awareness.

To fit together the pieces of an ordinary or a nonordinary worldview is a stupendous accomplishment. But it is not, itself, freedom. Freedom lies beyond a worldview or any world. Its pursuit is the only way to match your heart with the heart of creation. The subtlety of this point is enormous. It requires a continuous openness, a never-to-be-forgotten awareness that whatever we do know suffers pale in comparison to that which we can never know. This is the seer's second essential maneuver.

In relation to ordinary reality, Toltecs have stepped off a flat earth. In much the same manner that we grow and leave superstitions behind, Toltecs have left the ordinary world behind. To then, once again, step out—away from the new reality—is the mark of a seer. This step is off a nonordinary world, not an easy task. Nonordinary worlds tend to be considerably larger. They have more inhabitants and more complex terrains. Thus they are more captivating. To increase the very slim chance of gaining freedom from the constrictive influences of any reality, new-cycle seers developed and refined the strategy and tactics of tracking, dreaming, and intent (*Fire*, 20).

Tracking emanates from the first field. It is the art and craft of stabilizing and directing perception. As such, it concerns managing energy and knowledge. Thus it brings to bear a systematic and calculated quest for personal growth. While its tenets govern behavior in the everyday world, it is also a way to maintain your gains in other worlds. For example, dreaming consists of activities in and of the dream world, or in parts of the energy body outside of ordinary human activity. Purposefully entering dreaming, and holding that awareness steady, is tracking. Orienting yourself toward further growth is also tracking.

Dreaming, in turn, is not your ordinary variety of dream activity. It deals with the second field; thus it is a way to tackle the unknown. Engaging the dreaming body represents a significant shift into the second field. In contemporary literature, using the dreaming body is often referred to as an "out-of-body experience." By entering the unknown, dreaming stretches the boundaries of the known. Whereas tracking offers continuity, dreaming offers multi-dimensional expansion.

Tracking also consolidates travels into the unknown, thereby bringing them into the known. Tracking may be developed through dreaming, just as dreaming may be developed through tracking. When trying to figure out which is which, there comes a time when you leave the terms and method behind. They have served their purpose of pointing out a direction, and now you just want to travel the road.

Intent consists of focused or condensed energy. It embraces the essence of a person, place, or thing. It exists beyond desire. It is quiet certainty. It is the energy of alignment, the energy required to shift the focal point. Thus it is the energy which controls what we perceive. Proficiency in shifting energy and moving the focal point determines what you manifest, or what you bring into conscious awareness. Manifesting your core nature leads to *being,* a state of balance and harmony with the world. It consists of present-centeredness, an innate sense of direction, and feelings of completeness and joy.

Throughout all of this is Power, which I also define as Divine Will, or the Spirit governing our steps. Power supersedes all forms of personal power because all forms of personal power flow from Power. We all want power. We all want a sense of relation, meaning, and control. Usually, however, this desire is expressed as power over or against others and the environment, rather than as a deepening of awareness. Plants, animals, Earth itself, all emanate from Power. So everything has its own power. Through expanding awareness, personal power increases.

How personal power is utilized separates the old and new cycle of seers. The old cycle crammed personal desire into their pursuit of powers. The person demonstrating the most control over something was the top banana. So they remained locked within themselves. One key the new cycle introduced was ethics. Rather than the accumulation of power for show, this new refrain included an overriding bent to use personal power to enhance perception, to gain freedom. In these terms, personal power results from how a person and Power coincide. The better and deeper the connection, the more personal power.

Hooking into Power, you subordinate yourself to a higher awareness, a higher knowledge. This is the seer's third essential maneuver. If you can implement the three essential maneuvers, you have established a primary orientation for your continued evolution. These maneuvers are addressed from different angles throughout this book.

The Toltec Way offers a means to develop a unique relation with the world. Your life is then between you and Divine Will, not how a culture or another person thinks your relation should be. This path has shown me that there is Spirit in all people, places, and things. The entire world is alive and this makes the Toltec Way something good to write about. On its path I have found beings of different makes and models, worlds of different form and substance, and treasures of different hue and texture. It is indeed like stepping off a flat earth and falling into worlds of other makings. Then again, perhaps we step off only to find the earth was never flat after all. The only thing flat was perception.

Following a Toltec path gives form to something which is, in essence, formless. To travel it, there are no standardized steps. The order of this book is for coherency, to help you use a system which Castaneda has called "extremely sophisticated" (*Gift*, 7). Since the system deals with the abstract, part of its rendering is abstract. As don Juan says, for a Toltec the abstract is something with no parallels. It can't be conceived of, but it can be handled (*Silence*, 58).

The difficulty in designing a tool (such as this book) is directly proportional to the complexity of how the tool is to be handled. For example, in their book on virtual reality, *Silicon Mirage,* Steve Aukstakalnis and David Blatner compare a hammer, a photocopier with 50 different buttons, and computers.[7] One of the questions they deal with is how to design an interface between tools and the humans who use them. As a limited tool the hammer has a simple design. More complex than the hammer, the photocopier has a more complex interface, or method of use. Even more complex than photocopiers are computers. Their complexity, the authors mention, prevents some people from even trying them out. They also point out, however, that virtual-reality technology makes the user part of the technology rather than external to it. Thus while it may be an even more complicated computer, its interface has been simplified.

Therefore, the detail of this book is to help you conceive and handle Toltec sophistication. But, as you'll discover, it is designed to deliver you into the system itself, to make you part of the technology. The challenge then is to handle it, and make it work for you—even if you don't understand it. This requires one thing: practice. It is the doing of it that stimulates the energy body. And this process is what sets the stage for growth.

Also, while its premises have been tested and explored by other Toltecs as well as by me, keep in mind that what works for one may not work for another. So try the techniques and examine the perspectives. Observe, test, and measure the results. Don't assume truth.

No one can tell you what you'll find by learning to take stock in your perception, other than that you'll most likely find an interesting time. Nonordinary worlds may prove unbelievable to some. They may go against the grain of all that has been taught and learned. Keep in mind, though, that experience follows from what has been taught. One hundred years ago, someone introducing aerospace engineering would be considered nuts. Yesterday or today, it is the same prejudice against expanding our comfort zone of knowledge and traveling new landscapes of awareness. As unusual as Toltec perspectives and experiences might seem, they are still a human endeavor.

This book is for those whose wish to increase their practice of perceptual evolution. In essence, *A Toltec Path* is about how to engage, and then to transcend, method en route to a seer's freedom. Even if the Toltec Way is not your natural path, engaging it will further crystalize your path. And remember, while terms and concepts of any system hold power by giving perspective and direction, there comes a time when they lose their effectiveness. Technique and method should always rest subordinate to a personal relation with Power. So when they lose their power of keeping you with Spirit, it's best just to let them dissolve and go about your business of living. Let them dissolve into growth, however, not from lack of effort. The work is always your—the individual's—responsibility. And it's not simply to realize in understanding, but to realize throughout your being.

# Part I
# The Toltec

# 2
# Places in Time, Places in Mind

Like much of the Toltec Way, its history resembles a herd of cows. You know it's there but the form keeps shifting about. Maybe this is due to its oral tradition of handing down bits and pieces of its past. Maybe its history has been intended only to serve liberating people in the present, and so almost anything goes. But whatever the situation has been, the continuity Castaneda started with his books now offers everyone a standard reference to one of its lineages.

Julian prepared don Juan for the assignment of grooming Castaneda, and, as a result, Castaneda's books. Julian required that don Juan read and study because someday he would be called upon to explain Toltecs and their ways (*Silence*, 206). As such a teacher, don Juan personifies thousands of years of an evolving system intended to break the shackles of ignorance.

Don Juan lived his knowledge. Like a top-notch scientist, he learned to remain an unbiased, passive observer, knowing that the quirks of his own nature influenced whatever he perceived. This stance of participatory nonattachment reflects a major turn in Toltec history. Its inclusion in their tool kits heralded an evolutionary leap, a leap he called the new cycle.

While fulfilling his task, don Juan often commented to Castaneda on Toltec history. Castaneda's books, particularly *The Fire From Within* and *The Power of Silence*, contain many of these insights. For example, he told Castaneda that one of the core features creating the new cycle of seers was the addition of the knowledge that something exists beyond human perception: a complete unknowable (*Fire*, 48). Until this point, Toltecs reckoned that all elements of the universe could be reduced to and included in that which can be known. They hadn't counted on having to come to grips with something greater than their perception. As you'll discover later, this arrogance highlighted their downfall.

The brand of Toltec history presented here is not currently found in the encyclopedias. Don Juan defines Toltecs as people of knowledge (*Fire,* 18). Yet he recognizes a connection with at least a strain of the cultures known as Toltec, Mayan, Aztec, and other Central American peoples. The difference is that the nonordinary practices of Toltecs place them outside many of the currents of mainstream society, and most reference books offer versions of history that reflect mainstream views. While Toltecs are often ingrained within a culture by, for example, offering their wares in the marketplace, their overall worldview and behavior place them outside most cultural endeavors.

To avoid wishful thinking and a conjuring of history, don Juan always charged his students to verify his words for themselves. He also indicates that *seeing* is an advantageous way to do this. For example, a few years ago I actively studied Toltec history. Following his advice, in order to *see* certain periods I used the thoughts and feelings I had about the time for an initial reference. Before *seeing,* however, I entered dreaming. I did so because I had verified his teaching that dreaming reduces the strain of pushing harder at perceptual boundaries. Once in dreaming, I focused my thoughts on the destruction of the Toltec world: the Indian Wars, the Spanish Inquisition, and the resulting changes. These formed into what felt like cubes of energy, one inside another. My feelings about Mexico, don Juan's struggles, and the new cycle added flavor and a texture within the boxes. This, though, was merely the setup, a preparation.

The real work began when I engaged *seeing.* My thoughts and feelings often changed into something unexpected. At first, I expected to *see* Toltecs engaged in ritualistic magic. Instead, I *saw* constellations of thought. It was like having the energy of a history book tumble toward me, then break like a wave over and through me. My preliminary thoughts did, however, help me latch onto a specific intent. By directing my intent into each box, I perceived mental pictures and gestalts of intuitive energy which created a remembrance. Boxes within boxes then appeared, each one delving further back through time. The boxes remained loosely connected as they telescoped into history. I then *saw* actual scenes of marketplace activities, of wars, and of Toltecs' renewed deliberations.

Thoughts and feelings bias all perception, and *seeing* is not exempt. It requires tuning. We're all familiar with the occasional odd feeling or jittery edge after someone says something. Perhaps what was said just doesn't feel right. In a similar manner, thoughts and feelings influence *seeing.* They can either enhance or detract from what is perceived. With practice, discipline, and an unbiased attitude, however, *seeing* provides increasingly accurate and direct information. Used well, *seeing* can take you beyond the thoughts which created the box, the box from which you view your world.

Since I have a natural curiosity about my lineage, using dreaming and *seeing* to explore it was enjoyable. From a seer's perspective, using nonordinary perception to obtain and verify knowledge is no different than a scientist using professional journals and a laboratory to acquire knowledge. In this light, I offer the following viewpoints regarding Toltec history. Please keep in mind that what I refer to as the second cycle, don Juan refers to as the old cycle, and what I refer to as the third cycle, don Juan calls the new cycle. Each cycle has its own energy. Don Juan states that periods of history determine how and what humans perceive. He refers to this as the "modality of the time" (*Silence*, 10). The modality of the time is a package of energy fields generated by the Eagle's emanations which shapes our perception.

## First Cycle

The first cycle was a most primitive period. There was no sophistication of thought, no approach to the world other than through the beginnings of myth. Yet the stirring of a new relation to the world edged forth. Somehow a split occurred within awareness from which the recognition subject-object relationships developed; that is, an individual's sense of separateness from others and from the world manifested. A sense of innocence was lost, and humans were no longer instinctively part of the world. In his book, *The Origin of Consciousness in the Breakdown of the Bicameral Mind,* Julian Jaynes addresses this shift in consciousness.[1]

As people sensed their loss of union, rituals were born. Rituals connected people with their visions, visions of gods and spirits that were deemed to exist beyond the human world. The first indications of another order occurred as their thoughts and rituals became more detailed, organized, and shared.

## Second Cycle

Complexity ushered in the second cycle. Rituals became so elaborate that it seemed the goal was to develop intricacy rather than to explore perception. As they became lost in their grandiose schemes, their fabricated sense of invincibility became the tragedy of second-cycle Toltecs. This sense was laden with competition and self-importance (*Fire,* 166).

One of the most observable features of this cycle was what we typically think of as sorcery: the use of personal power to manipulate people and things. In the marketplace sorcerers innocuously sold potions to aid lovemaking, remedies for healing, and psychic readings for advice. But behind the scenes, sorcerers fiercely competed to accumulate powers that eventually turned one against another. Furthermore, rituals were seen as the source of powers rather than as supportive agents for focusing awareness. Balance of self and of craft were shunned. Emphasis rested on manipulating their physical bodies into nonhuman forms, seeking personal glories by summoning creatures from beyond this world, and holding sway over others.

These Toltecs did, however, push through barriers and expand awareness into unequaled dimensions. Perhaps the best indication of this expansion resulted in what don Juan calls the "death defiers" (*Fire,* ch. 15). Toltecs gained the ability to remove their physical bodies from the physical world and fully place their awareness in other dimensions. This feat remains a part of Toltec tradition. Indeed, Castaneda's doing so marked the end of his apprenticeship. After he hurled himself off a cliff, his physical awareness dissipated as he vanished into thin air. He says his perception then re-stabilized in other dimensions. Days later, he returned to physical awareness (*Second Ring,* 7).

The second cycle was also a time when Toltecs were entwined within society. People did not think twice about witnessing marvels such as someone jumping as high as the treetops, or tossing boulders in a herculean manner (*Teachings,* 75). On the high side was raw adventure. On the low side, Toltecs' relation to people and to the world in general deteriorated. Don Juan says the second cycle is 10,000 years old, and its practitioners ruled central Mexico 7,000-3,000 years ago (*Dreaming,* 59).

Although enmeshed within the culture, Toltecs were too caught up in their own affairs. This paradox of being part of society yet oblivious to all except their own machinations reduced its practitioners in thought and awareness. Even though they thought they saw the big picture, they didn't know the picture at all. They had no fortitude, no real understanding because they couldn't get past themselves. This left them wide open for obliteration during the Indian Wars.

# Transition

Second-cycle Toltecs thought spells, charms, and incantations could protect them. Yet they offered no protection from invasion as foreign armies moved relentlessly through their land. Since Toltec leaders had the biggest ideas of themselves, and hence the least flexibility and adaptability, they were the easiest to spot and remove. Without leadership, Toltec society fell into disarray and was easily conquered. With the world as they knew it demolished, the remnant found themselves in a prison of their own making. To survive, they went underground. They also took refuge in the unknown, the only freedom available.

The shock of having an external force crash down and obliterate their world forced a total reevaluation. They strove to remain unbiased as they examined the tragedy. Doing so tempered their desire to ruthlessly expunge their self-important ways. They systematically cultivated a new order, trying to account for and eliminate the excesses of their past. As foolhardy as they were before the destruction, they were able to pool their resources and adapt to meet and to exceed their conquerors. It was also during this time that the Toltec Way split into lineages that were never to intersect. This split was necessary so that, should a lineage be destroyed or fail to flourish, others remained to carry on the teachings.

By the time of the Inquisition, when it was the Spaniards' turn to invade, the Toltecs had reduced or eliminated many of their former practices. Still, their review continued. Now at hand was the burgeoning third cycle. They recognized that their imbalance resulted from their lack of harmony with their environment, particularly with the people who were once viewed as objects for personal gain. During the Spanish occupation, the remaining Toltec contingent *saw* that the foreigners echoed their own imbalance. And so they chose to do nothing overtly and watched with detached interest. From those observations a refined set of practices known as tracking evolved further. Sobriety of purpose replaced wanton excess (*Fire*, 19).

This struggle away from oppression also led to a more objective view of the world. They *saw* perception resulting from the alignment between internal and external emanations. Perhaps resulting from an external force demolishing an internal world, the third cycle saw the interaction of external and internal influences as the principal determinant of perception. This view was corroborated through *seeing* the energy body. They witnessed external patterns of light matching identical internal patterns of light. They deemed that this alignment produces perception.

At the same time, they began to recognize that the perception of movement is only a device, an invention of mind. Don Juan addresses this when he tells Castaneda that what the second-cycle seers viewed as depth, those in the third cycle viewed as a realignment of energies within the energy body (*Fire*, 110). This discovery collapsed a main pillar holding up their world. A three-dimensional view fell way to acknowledging that depth is a perception, not an actuality. In addition, a materialistic view of the world was deemed only a point of view, only one of an infinite number of energy alignments.

One result of striving for objectivity was having more fun with the world. It became something to frolic with. Tracking practices such as "controlled folly" are examples of this light side as a Toltec strives to manage only personal energy and allow the world to have free reign (*Silence*, 102). Giving the world freedom further enhanced objectivity.

Looking back at this transition, what is amazing is that even though they practiced the heights of uncontrolled folly, they still carried the spark of brilliance which led to a renewed cycle. The heartbreak is that it took such destruction to cause them to act. Modern Toltecs remain in debt to their courage in tackling the boundaries of awareness. And we should feel humbled by the cost of their excesses. But the devastation left its mark. The necessity of dealing with integrity with those who are not a part of the Toltec order was faced, and the rigorous discipline of tracking was fully incorporated (*Fire*, 172).

This tumultuous heaving to and fro is not unique to Toltecs. There have been other instances of systems' failures, such as in ancient China where pure or spiritually-oriented Taoism fell head-long into sorcery. Like the Toltec Way, it also reemerged stronger and more deliberate.[2]

We can also relate this kind of failure to our contemporary world. Just as the Toltec second cycle got wiped out because the participants ignored what was at hand, we are now our own invaders as we destroy our lives, our planet. Our weapons against ourselves are laziness, greed, and apathy. On a personal scale, it seems easy to lose oneself in second-cycle competitive energies. On a wider scale, the Toltecs of old fascinated themselves with complexities, just as we get wrapped up in ours. The effect is that we don't realize we have created an Inquisition of monumental proportions as we gradually squeeze the life from our planet. Perhaps it will lead us en masse into a new cycle where we have learned to govern ourselves better. Perhaps we will never recover. The outcome rests in our behavior, now.

## Third Cycle

Out of the storms of the Indian Wars and the Inquisition grew the third cycle. The intensity of the subjugation provided a springboard for a leap to higher, more sober, realms. Whereas the second cycle was mesmerized by their findings, a feature of the third cycle was understanding (*Fire*, 249). And part of this understanding was recognition of the limits of understanding.

One of the more stabilizing forces of the third cycle resulted from a death-defier known as "the tenant." Don Juan states that the tenant has lived for thousands of years (*Dreaming*, 61). Seeking energy to remain alive, and to escape from an inorganic world, the tenant met and took energy from a Toltec leader named Sebastian. In return, he gave Sebastian a gift of power, a second-cycle Toltec skill.

According to don Juan, third-cycle seers had rebelled so completely against their predecessors' aberrations that they forbade all second-cycle practices. However, through the tenant, Sebastian rediscovered them. Don Juan says that since 1723, when the tenant met Sebastian, portions of those ancient techniques have been passed to a team leader from each generation, thereby establishing the continuity of a specific Toltec line (*Fire*, ch. 15).

In a sense, the difference between the second and third cycles is like the difference between the Vietnam and Persian Gulf Wars. In Vietnam the thinking seemed to be that a massive, raw display of power would wipe out the resistance of a small Third World country. A missing ingredient was a cohesive strategy: an overall purpose, clearly defined orders of engagement, and a national commitment. Vagueness permeated the air; single-mindedness was the casualty. Learning from the past, the leadership in the Persian Gulf War insisted on painstaking preparation and a well-defined mission. In addition, substantial efforts were made to bring the national *will* of all allied forces to bear. The effect was an overwhelming military success. In short, this scenario echoes the conditions for *unbending intent*.

In a similar manner, Toltecs learned from their downfall and produced a more viable strategy. Whereas the second cycle aligned behavior with greed, manipulation of power, and personal aggrandizement, the third cycle aligned behavior with more abstract qualities of balance and freedom. They also realized that lack of character, and not the practices themselves, resulted in the second cycles' destructive accumulation of personal power (*Fire*, 109). The following chart lists a few key differences between cycles.

| Second Cycle | Third Cycle |
|---|---|
| Preoccupation with nonordinary powers | Focus on developing perception |
| Accent on unknown | Accent on knowable |
| Focal point equates with perception | Focal point reflects alignment of energies |
| Enhance self-importance | Reduce self-importance |
| Morbid pursuit of powers | Refinement of goals |
| Increase personal power for show | Use personal power to gain further knowledge |
| Control and manipulation | Cooperation with the natural order |

Tracking innovations increased the odds that Toltecs would not get hung up in second-cycle activities such as the bizarre practice of turning into a tree (*Fire*, 169). Rather, the discipline was to remain steady on course for higher, more refined attainments.

A dance, similar to the movements of a martial artist, depicts the advances of tracking. This dance is similar in nature to the one don Juan taught Castaneda. He was to groom it throughout his life, as it would reflect his victories and defeats (*Journey*, 188). In the throes of death, he was to perform it in its entirety.

I once had the opportunity to watch and *see* a Toltec perform a portion of the tracking dance. It began with the person standing upright, at relaxed attention. His right arm was bent upward at the elbow, his right hand even with his right shoulder. The fingers were together, the palm open and facing outward. This side of his body symbolized the initial and unwavering posture of equanimity. The left arm hung loosely on the left side of the body, and the left hand was in a fist, representing the power of dreaming. The right hand then descended and crossed over the chest as though it were chopping something with the edge of the hand. This movement represented tracking (the right side) should command dreaming (the left side). It was meant to show the necessity of using the quest for freedom to rule the powers derived from the journey into the unknown, dreaming side. In the next movement, the left fist curled upward, hooked the right wrist, and both hands came upward. This motion meant that dreaming should uplift tracking, and that it should be used to enhance freedom. The hands then came to rest as the arms formed an X over the heart, indicating that both were joined in the heart and should be used for purposes of the heart.

Indeed, a culminating influence of the third cycle was the recognition that strength doesn't lie in the accumulation of powers. Strength rests in the clear assessment and refinement of yourself, permitting you to launch yourself into the unknown unfettered by the strings of greed and abuse. You learn to relinquish yourself to a universe which is quite beyond human awareness, but which completely incorporates it. The quest is to live fully the essence of your life, a path of continual self-discovery.

## Before Anything. . .

The brutal loss of his culture, the Toltec world, and his parents led don Juan to the conviction that, before anything else, we are human (*Separate,* 175). His teachings, therefore, are geared to common denominators of what that meant. Rather than teaching a red, white, yellow, or black way of looking at the world, he taught about perception, and about the alignments of energy which enable perception.

A distinct advantage of this view is that, regardless of philosophical or spiritual orientation—such as whether or not one regards himself as having a soul—"human first" grounds experience in the here and now, in this life, in this world. This concept doesn't negate God or spirituality. Rather, it can be used to enhance spiritual awareness. Instead of defining our experiences by occupation, vocation, or nationality, for example, "human first" offers a stable, concrete reference point for all to connect with. With that awareness we can utilize different spiritual orientations to increase everyone's quality of life.

Part of the Toltec tradition maintains that an aspect of the human condition is that of having energy bodies, and that our initial condition is that of being aware. This tradition led don Juan to think that our place in the natural order was simply to learn (*Teachings*, 72). This attitude causes an ongoing examination of oneself, and of one's relation to society, the world, and beyond. Doing so brings to life the fullest potential in each person by building harmony in all spheres of activity. It also provides an orientation to uncover the unknown. Otherwise, there is no true learning. There is only repetition and enhancement of what is already known. When you realize that you are not separate from the world, for example, you create a new reference point. Rather than strive to be an individual, you may find your individuality by allowing all life to express itself through you.

"Human first" is a predilection of Toltecs, a dream they share from which other dreams emanate. Making it possible to handle the immensity of infinite perception, it furnishes a reference from which to explore. It is a practical tool. The lesson of not losing themselves in their dreams was hard-won. And it is that very discipline which generates evolution. I believe don Juan generated much of his consistency from his "human first" orientation. It was a consistency that helped him effortlessly maintain a delicate balance.

In its entirety, the Toltec Way is but one path weaving through infinity. Like Zen Buddhism, Sufism, Taoism, and a host of other systems, it requires that, to follow it in earnest, you must make it your principal path. This doesn't mean you can't participate with other philosophies. It means that you must fully traverse its corridors in order to know it, and then to be able to leave it. To use its boost, you must use it. Within Toltec corridors, a "human first" attitude balances priorities. It pulls you away from dogma into actual experience. Rather than locking you into self-reflection, or simply continuing to validate your own thoughts, it enables you to tap new avenues of information. While a system may support that endeavor, it cannot, by itself, generate total freedom. The knowledge gained would always reflect the views within the system, a more elaborate form of self-reflection. If a system requires de-emphasizing psychic abilities, for example, its adherents will work to do so. As their skills in handling psychic abilities atrophy, they may well issue decrees that all psychic functioning is fraudulent. One of the most appealing things about the Toltec Way is that it requires its practitioners to take things further, deeper, wider. The Toltec Way simply will not rest within the status quo.

If someone offered you a path better than the one you now travel, would you recognize it? Whether you're a Toltec, a scientist, or a truck driver, the challenge is not to escape into a seemingly secure world of dogma but to seek knowledge. And part of doing so is understanding that knowledge often fits within the parameters of the method used to claim it. Perhaps this is part of what led Sam Keen, in his book *Fire in the Belly,* to reflect that we must break free of habitual thinking and define ourselves by our own experience.[3]

## Fourth Cycle

The fourth cycle sprouted during the turmoil of the 1960s. During the time of free love and rampant drug use, Castaneda began delivering books detailing a sophisticated way to accumulate knowledge. He spoke to the disenchanted and provided context to make sense of their nonordinary experiences. Since only his first two books deal with drugs, or power plants, he has since gained a wider audience. Through his books, Castaneda has spun the tradition once again, in much the same way that the new seers spun it into the third cycle.

Since it contains the essence of the third cycle, and since it is just a generation or two of age, mentioning a fourth cycle is basically acknowledging that significant change is occurring. By offering the core features of the system, Castaneda has provided a stable reference to anyone who wants to use it. His books, however, do not account for all of don Juan's instruction, and so some of the flavor is lost. This has the effect, though, of once again streamlining the craft.

The new strategy of harmoniously blending with people has also brought the Toltec Way back into mainstream metaphysical thinking, perhaps creating a blending with other nonordinary philosophies and possibly further enhancing the teachings. The Toltec Way is also now part of a highly technological world, and subject to those influences as it continues to adapt. Therefore, the beginning of the fourth cycle offers fertile ground for almost any result.

For instance, somewhere in the fabric of existence there is The

Church of the Don Juan Tribe. It seems that don Juan had such an impact that an entire religion was formed. Much to his consternation, he was given far too much reverence. There is also a version of reality in which don Juan, his peers, and his apprentices maneuver Castaneda into learning their ways and set him up to write his books. This scenario breaks down into different versions. One view constructs Castaneda into a somewhat bumbling, naive apprentice who reports his experiences with an unusual bunch of people. His work is deemed fiction, and no different or more important than other fantasy novels. In another version, Castaneda is a masterful anthropologist who plucked the core teachings from years of instruction, then offered it to anyone interested in his experiment.

While we see strains of each scenario, from a seer's perspective all of these scenarios are true. Each has its own intent, its own energy. Don Juan speaks of this when he says that "pure understanding is an advance runner probing that immensity out there" (*Silence,* 136). He refers to a seer's conviction that, somewhere in the universe at large, a storyteller's story is an actuality. The binding energy to live in a storyteller's universe is knowing that how a person relates to the world is a force that selects which world the person lives in. It is as much a matter of living in one continuously evolving world as it is a matter of continually changing paths which lead to another world already in existence. Part of the storyteller's pure understanding is an understanding of how perception works; again, a third-cycle emphasis.

Don Juan says that the modern seers' emphasis on the abstract includes applying its practices to concrete social functions. He says this means "you'll never catch them being the official seers or the sorcerers in residence" (*Dreaming,* 2). In other words, Toltecs don't lock themselves into specific stations within society. This does not mean, however, that seers withdraw from society. Tracking developed so that seers may participate in society, but on their terms, terms that allow them to continue their quest for freedom. Hence, they deliberately structure their lives for maximum pursuit of their goals. If seers automatically excluded themselves from ordinary society, we wouldn't have Castaneda's, Donner's, and Abelar's books. Their publications—their work for hire—place their activities in the mainstream. I think, therefore, that what don Juan means is that seers don't trap themselves within ordinary cultural standards. Creating a Toltec bureaucracy would only hinder the work of evolving past form of any kind.

From his own story, we find that Castaneda is a different breed of Toltec leader. His energy body is comprised of three compartments, not four as leaders such as don Juan possess. Don Juan considers this circumstance to indicate change and revitalization (*Gift*, ch. 12). Upon discovering his condition, Castaneda says don Juan had to establish a new team more suitable to his three-prong energy. As a result, the women and men we read about in *The Second Ring of Power* and *The Eagle's Gift* were replaced by Abelar, Donner, and Carol Tiggs, Castaneda's female counterpart (*Dreaming*, x).

Donner takes the idea of change so far as to say that Castaneda represents the end of his line and there will be no new teams.[4] Perhaps. Or perhaps she senses the interdiction of normal affairs. Or perhaps Castaneda has spun the system so anew that he is the end of a cycle. And perhaps there are other forces at work. For instance, there is at least one report that Castaneda and crew have found a "new nagual," a new team leader.[5] If this report is true, the person will assume a position in relation to Castaneda that Castaneda has with don Juan, a situation which would indicate a continuance of the lineage. Inconsistencies such as this can be accounted for in terms of don Juan's instruction. Accordingly, maybe Donner is just covering her team's tracks, erasing team history. Then again, it might reflect Castaneda's unsettling, three-prong energy and so his team's efforts in finding stability is a constant challenge which sometimes produces inconsistencies.

At the same time, there is other evidence that don Juan's lineage will survive, and that Castaneda is only playing his part in its evolution. I have heard reports from Mexico of people not mentioned in Castaneda's books who claim that don Juan is their teacher. I've also corresponded with Norbert Classen, author of *Das Wissen der Tolteken (The Knowledge of the Toltecs).*[6] Classen is a team leader of a Toltec team assembling in Europe. All of these people are outside of Castaneda's team yet continue to work with don Juan's teachings. This leads me to conjecture that don Juan may have set up the fourth cycle as a response to finding Castaneda's nature too volatile. Since Castaneda's tumultuous predilections would not ensure survival of the system, perhaps don Juan seeded other groups. Just like cactus fruit is cram-packed with seeds so that one might take root, maybe don Juan taught others in various locations to provide for the survival of the teachings. Or it might also be that the Toltec river is forging new tributaries.

As Castaneda's books provide a reference for the latest cycle, perhaps this uniformity will act in a manner similar to that of the consistency provided to the third cycle by Sebastian and the tenant. But the advent of the fourth cycle does not mean that second-cycle practices are forever gone. They're not. Anyone following this type of path long enough has to deal with them in some manner, at some time. However, it is the third cycle's realignment of energies which offers the chance for freedom. Through unrelenting discipline, its practitioners must never lose third-cycle gains. But they must also continue to tackle complacency and challenge those gains, while retaining the sense of adventure life itself offers.

Using other-dimensional creatures for sorceric gain, for example, is characteristic of the second cycle. Don Juan and the third cycle grew directly out of that kind of world. So when he finds those kinds of practices objectionable, he is responding to his cycle's quest to harness and redirect those pursuits. With an enhanced perspective granted by time and experience, perhaps those activities can be seen with an even greater understanding of their effect. This evolution will allow certain practices to fall by the wayside and others to be viewed in a different light. And the different light is what signals the emergence of the fourth cycle.

# 3
# Toltecs Have Their Way

This chapter presents a few major components of the Toltec Way. At first glance it may seem like a religion. It is not. It demands neither worship nor reverence. It is a philosophy, a way to obtain knowledge. It is also metaphysics, which in its classical sense means it is a branch of philosophy dealing with the nature of reality.[1] For you to get anywhere with it, it must be applied and lived, not simply discussed.

A feature of the Toltec Way is that the lineages within it provide views, methods, and techniques which work together, enabling you to perceive more than ordinary reality. These elements are verifiable. All you need do is earnestly and persistently practice. As a result, you automatically cultivate the awareness that our physical world is but one of numerous worlds, and that our relation to these worlds continually changes and evolves. Regardless of the specific path, then, the Toltec Way is a tool. While it may help you perceive that which is considered sacred, it is, itself, not sacred.

The Toltec Way embraces different personal attitudes and approaches. Accordingly, it encourages—no, it demands—that people groom and harness their individuality. But the fight not to harden the terms of what a sense of self means is what gave rise to don Juan's words: "War, for a warrior, is the total struggle against that individual self that has deprived man of his power" (*Silence*, 170).

For this reason, we find don Juan incessantly teaching his apprentices the value of losing self-importance. At the core of self-importance is self-reflection, or continually reflecting to ourselves about what the world consists of. Hence, a Toltec tradition continually pushes past the limits of any view of the world. As don Juan teaches, what matters is not adhering to a system, but arriving at the totality of yourself, arriving at your complete nature (*Tales*, 240).

It is when one forgets that systems and lineages are techniques that dogma enters, and the hard-won gains are lost. To deal with this problem, don Juan required that I recognize his behavior as stemming from his participation in another reality. He didn't want me to think that he offered a new and greater, and therefore "the true," reality. He wanted me to regard ordinary and nonordinary realities on equal footing, balance them in relation to each other, and then slip between them in the hope I could free myself.

Through don Juan's instruction, there came a time when I achieved partnership in the Toltec world. It occurred when I commanded a sufficient number of elements of that world. Doing so generated a force which organized my perception into a nonordinary framework. I then had at my disposal the means to slip between two realities: the ordinary reality I grew up with, and the Toltec world. By going between them, I took my first step toward freedom.

## Heightened Awareness

Simply put, heightened awareness is perception elevated beyond the ordinary. The rules of what is "normal" change. Accessing nonordinary realities occurs more easily. The supernatural becomes natural. Heightened awareness occurs through balancing the first and second energy fields. This balance is a keystone of Toltec endeavors.

Florinda Donner refers to this state as "dreaming-awake."[2] This term is fitting, as heightened awareness brings dreamlike qualities to life. Inanimate objects possess vitality. Messages on billboards abruptly and magically change. Paintings hanging on walls spring to life as the features in them move about. Trees gesture, often showing which way to proceed. And rocks glow, illuminating narrow paths at night. This may seem as though reality has slipped beyond repair, instead of having grown. But in practical application, heightened awareness makes physical senses keener and intuition more accurate. It enhances the ability to deal with people and magnifies your sense of adventure and fun. You possess more vitality.

As with most states of consciousness, heightened awareness comes and goes. The slightest thing may trigger it. Or it may be the result of long, hard work. You may enter it for five seconds, five hours, or for the rest of your life. A Toltec goal is to reach and sustain it.

Don Juan often slapped Castaneda between the shoulder blades to produce such a shift. Much of don Juan's teaching occurred while Castaneda was in it. Don Juan later explained that only his presence was needed to shift Castaneda's awareness. The slap was a trick, a ploy to divert Castaneda's attention (*Silence,* 139), permitting don Juan's unbending intent—laser-focused energy—to produce the shift.

You can also enter heightened awareness through artificial means, such as by using the sound technologies pioneered by The Monroe Institute. Located near Faber, Virginia, the Institute was founded by Robert Monroe, author of the classic *Journeys Out of the Body* and the more recent *Ultimate Journey.*[3] In essence, the Institute's technology uses sound to assist in balancing the electrical activity of the right and left hemispheres of the brain, which correspond to the left and right sides of the body. This balance produces heightened awareness.

## The Eagle and Its Emanations

The Eagle is the source of creation (*Fire,* 51). In contemporary terms, some say this is God. It is not an entity, and yet it is. It is a force, or perhaps a condition. It is beyond limitation, and therefore beyond definition. At best it can be alluded to or briefly described. Extending from it and through all creation are emanations of energy. These emanations carry the impulses and patterns for life, matter, and any other manifestation. Our energy bodies exist as part of an emanation that defines human awareness. The containment of energy within the energy body gives rise to self-awareness.

The emanations issue commands in the sense that natural laws command our behavior. For instance, gravity, inertia, and other laws influence our behavior. As part of this energy, we can issue our own commands. It is by doing so that we can build aircraft and utilize laws which offset other laws, such as gravity. Don Juan says human awareness occurs within a very narrow spectrum of the emanations (*Fire,* 162). We can therefore issue commands only within stringent limitations. The remainder of the Eagle encompasses aspects of creation far exceeding human comprehension or realization. From this, questions arise: Do we actually command the emanations, or are our commands part of an Eagle command which gives us the sense that we issue commands? Is the sense of command an actuality, or a reflection which creates an illusion of self-determination? Here rests the essence of that age-old question regarding whether or not we have free will.

In terms of reaching out for knowledge, the human awareness emanation is like one small eagle feather. Our familiarity with the feather is the known. What we have yet to learn about this feather, its relation to other feathers, and what "feather" consists of, is the unknown. The rest of the eagle's emanations comprise the unknowable. We can perhaps glimpse it because we feel its influence, but since it has more and different properties than a feather, we have nothing to relate to. By our very nature we lack comprehension.

Don Juan says that while recognition of the Eagle is universal among seers, how a person relates to the emanations is individual. "In other words, there is no pat version of the emanations, as there is of the Eagle" (*Fire,* 57). This openness to interpretation gives rise to varying metaphysical traditions. Each tradition offers views based on the ideas of its leaders as well as cultural influences in general, or what the population can relate to and accept. Individual practices aside, they often share the recognition of a single, unifying force. For example, the major religions of the world are monotheistic. Christians, Jews, and Muslims have different orientations, but share the view that there is one all-powerful creator.

On occasion I have *seen* the Eagle. After reading about it in Castaneda's books, I felt a keen desire to do so. Don Juan says second-cycle seers described it as "something that resembles a black-and-white eagle of infinite size" (*Fire,* 51). Eagles played an important role in their mythology, so for them it's practical to describe the source of creation from within their worldview. While portraying an abstract force as an entity skews understanding, it also offers a way to relate.

The times I *saw* it were similar in that during meditation I felt propelled into a dimension of vast proportions. There was no landscape as one might ordinarily think of. A nondescript field of light gave the sense of infinite luminosity. I perceived many colors: orange, pink, blue, violet, peach. But they all seemed part of one color. There was no separation between them, and yet there was. A blackness emerged in the center of my field of vision. It grew until it towered beyond sight. It reminded me of the Sears Tower in Chicago. It was as though I was standing half a block away from it and bending backward, craning upward to take it all in. Each room was like a distinct world, and the entire building rose into infinity.

I then understood don Juan's words that *seeing* the Eagle is an emanation acknowledging itself. When this greater self-awareness occurs, he says, it results in "a vision of the Eagle and the Eagle's emanations. But there is no Eagle and no Eagle's emanations. What is out there is something no living creature can grasp" (*Fire*, 53).

## Inorganic Beings and Spirits

Don Juan says there are innumerable inorganic beings. Most are useless to humans; only a very few can be utilized. This utilization, says don Juan, is a "fair exchange of energy" (*Fire*, 109). It occurs when energy from the being and the human align. Aligning with a human's energy, inorganic beings can materialize into this dimension. Aligning with an inorganic being's energy, humans can augment and keenly focus their energy, as I reported in *Traveling With Power*.

These entities are not considered alive as we think of flesh-and-blood alive, but alive as in possessing awareness. As with human awareness, their natural habitat is within a particular spectrum of the Eagle's emanations. But they occupy different bands, and therefore different worlds (*Fire*, 161). Different systems offer varying accounts about how many worlds exist. Traditional Western metaphysics often ascribes five levels, or planes, of reality: physical, etheric, astral, mental, and causal. Each level may have sublevels, such as the lower and upper astral. Don Juan's sidekick, don Genaro Flores, says there are ten levels to the other world (*Separate*, 123).

According to don Juan, one of these worlds is a black world. He thought it was important because it is a world in its own right, not a twisted reflection of this world (*Fire*, 288). One of its features is extreme density. He thought he had aged ten years while visiting it for only a couple days. I first experienced the black world several years ago. While dreaming, I felt rocketed into another world. Once there, I felt as though I weighed a ton, as though gravity pulled me from every direction. I then noticed six objects that looked like pencils filled with light. Looming in the distance, some had two or three colors, others only one. They danced lightly as they approached me. As they drew nearer, I knew they were alive. But their light was steady; it didn't have the movement of energy as *seen* within humans. When I recognized that they were alive, one of them backed away. My awareness then returned to my physical body. I felt tired and worn out. I felt I had been there about half an hour. The clock indicated only a few minutes had passed.

I learned more about these creatures after Castaneda published his ninth book, *The Art of Dreaming*. In it, don Juan says they are projections of energy from inorganic beings (*Dreaming*, 86). He taught Castaneda that dreaming opens avenues to different dimensions, and maintained that these foreign energies send scouts into our world. Dreaming is one place to perceive this intersection of worlds. *The Art of Dreaming* offers a good account and analysis of the inorganic beings' world.

In addition to the light-stick entities, I have encountered other beings, or spirits, if you will. In one instance, I stood in front of a large, very old tree. Its trunk reached about eight feet high before sprouting branches. Its limbs were thick and long. I deliberately entered dreaming-awake. I then *saw* an apparition of a woman superimposed within the tree. She stepped out of the tree and stood before me. She was five and half feet tall, seemed about in her mid-thirties, and wore a white, flowing gown. She had brown hair and blue, ageless eyes. In a telepathic manner, she said she was the spirit of the tree. I had had previous encounters with nature spirits and so wasn't taken aback. I asked her about elves. She said that while she and they had a friendly bond, elves also were not necessarily life forms. Rather, they had lives which reflected the spirit of the elements within nature.

A more dramatic event with inorganic beings took place one afternoon while sitting in the showroom of a custom glass shop. I worked for a cabinet maker and was on an errand to pick up a piece of glass. While waiting, I noticed an unusual configuration of mirrors on the far wall. A large bronze mirror was flanked by standard, mercury-coated mirrors. Enraptured by the effect they created, I gazed into the bronze mirror. I laughed at myself as I thought about don Juan and Castaneda pulling an other-dimensional entity out of a mirror (*Fire*, ch. 6). I wondered if I could do the same.

After several minutes of gazing into the mirror, I *saw* a man-like figure step out of it and into the showroom. He was a little more than medium height and stocky. I remember thinking that he seemed a little taller and slightly less muscular than don Juan. Why I even thought of don Juan I don't know. Perhaps it simply resulted from associating Castaneda's story about the mirror and this occurrence. Perhaps it was because I fleetingly recognized don Juan's energy stepping out of the mirror.

The creature had large bumps on its head and was slightly hunched over. This aspect of the image created a marked contrast with don Juan, who was the epitome of health and stature. At times, however, I had witnessed don Juan present himself in different forms. Once I encountered him in the guise of a drunkard, and yet another time as a woman. But then the thought that the being wasn't don Juan jolted me. Only then did I realize that I had no idea how to respond. I felt like Mickey Mouse in the film *Fantasia*, when the sorcerer's apprentice unwittingly unleashes great power. In a mild panic, I simultaneously shifted my vision away from the being and stood up to walk around, dispelling the image. I still felt its presence, however. I went outside, got in my car, and drove off. To this day I wonder if that creature still roams about, looking for the person who summoned it. I behaved quite irresponsibly in this episode.

## Power Plants

Don Juan says that Toltecs first started on the path of knowledge by consuming power plants (*Fire*, 17). *The Teachings of Don Juan* and *A Separate Reality* offer detailed accounts of Castaneda's experiences with several plants, including peyote, datura, and mushrooms. He found that each plant carries its own intent and thereby produces specific shifts in consciousness. For example, don Juan views mushrooms as offering sober, nonpassionate awareness, while datura is more volatile. A common denominator among power plants is that their energies force perceptual shifts, reflected by the focal point moving to nonordinary locations. They lessen the constraints of the first field and thus provide glimpses of the second field.

In doing so, they provide temporary heightened awareness. Hence their value lies in providing insight into the unknown. Their cost is the distortion of energy produced by the forced shift. To accentuate the seriousness of using power plants, don Juan always had Castaneda engage rituals to focus his attention. The rituals also made him step out of an ordinary framework regarding their use. Don Juan insists power plants are for education, not entertainment.

Don Juan also makes it clear that not everyone needs them, and that he gave them to Castaneda because Castaneda was slow to catch on to other teachings (*Tales*, 12). In fact, don Juan says that third-cycle seers deliberately de-emphasize them due to their distortions (*Fire*, 19). This is not to say that what one experiences while under their influence is necessarily garbled, but that their use affects the energy body detrimentally. On several occasions I have *seen* the energy bodies of Toltecs who regularly use power plants. Instead of a harmonious blending between the edges of their energy bodies and the environment, their energy bodies contort. This malformation makes their energy bodies look like cauliflower, rather than a vibrant sphere of energy. Warping the energy body then distorts perception.

Using power plants is like running 75 watts of power through a 60-watt light bulb. You boost the power but strain the filament. In other words, power plants also place strain on the physical body. Their optimum use requires directing their energy for specific results. As a result, don Juan established goals before, during, and after he gave them to Castaneda. If you use power plants, the trick is to head in the directions you've thereby glimpsed, but under your own power.

I also think we miss the point if we don't acknowledge their value. For instance, in the desert of southeastern Arizona, under the influence of marijuana, I once experienced the humble nobility of being "human." Perched atop a desert mound, with the summer sun beating down, I ingested a small quantity of marijuana. In a few minutes, I had a vision where I *saw* the struggles and victories of humans. As I returned my focus to my physical body, I felt the sun's heat change into another form of energy. I no longer felt it as heat. It was now something I could ride or surf. Connecting with it, my senses stretched out and touched the surrounding hills which were bathed with clarity. I *saw* my place as a bi-ped walking the face of this planet. Rather than feel the dread of our existence as we are often taught to, I felt illuminated that we all carry the seeds of greatness within us. We need only learn how to make this energy sprout, rather than how to tread on it.

In addition, during the one occasion I ingested peyote, I recognized that the physical world is not what it seems. I *saw* that physical objects were just dense energy. This experience drove home don Juan's lesson that the world is first comprised of energy. Material objects only reflect that energy. Both of these drug-induced experiences lifted me out of a conventional, ordinary world, and into a world where visions, beauty, and harmony between humans and Earth abide.

But people often use power plants in lieu of discipline. At times I know I have. Having learned their limitations, I now prefer to rely on my own abilities. The results feel stronger and clearer. I keep in mind a third-cycle tenet proposing that a certain lifestyle

automatically leads to enhancing awareness. The heightened awareness a Toltec path generates is far more substantial and longer-
lasting than that offered by power plants. For long-term growth,
it is essential not to let a temporary boost replace the commitment
of personal discipline.

# Omens

Omens utilize a special language, a unique set of agreements
between an individual and the world. Just as symbols create
alphabets, words, and sentences, so do signs and symbols known
as omens provide information, direction, and guidance. Colors,
the behavior of people and animals, compass directions, and almost
any occurrence can play a role in this form of communication. If
nothing else, omens make you pay attention to the world about
you. Omens also reduce the wear and tear people plagued by
doubt face if they have not yet learned internal guidance.

Omens are manifestations of Spirit, messages from the abyss of
creation. For example, one building block of omens is color. Through
systematic study, I learned to isolate my beneficial and negative
colors. To begin, I noticed which colors I wore and how I felt as
the day progressed. I also gazed at colors, allowing their energy to
pass through my eyes and into my body, and then took note of how
I felt. I found that for me, green indicated positive, and orange
negative. In essence, I had come to an agreement with Spirit that
these colors held particular meaning. I had "yes" and "no" symbols.

In practice, they work something like this: several years ago,
I applied for a job making tofu. The walls of the work space were
orange. I knew this indicated something negative, but I needed
money and so took the job. Within two weeks, my sinuses flared
up in violent protest to the large quantities of salt needed to make
the soybean derivative. I quit the job. A day later I had to take
an airline trip. The changes in cabin pressure exacerbated my
discomfort so much that I had to consult a physician. The medical
bill took all my earnings, plus more.

A single omen can mean different things to different people.
On day, while I was out for a drive with a friend, an orange car
swerved in front of us. We both knew to take heed rather than
just get upset at such recklessness. Using her intuition, my friend
said she thought it meant her son was upset. Returning to her
home ahead of schedule, we discovered her son had come down
with a sudden case of flu.

In turn, I had been contemplating either continuing my graduate studies in religion or relocating to Virginia. Since the first three letters on the car's license plate were "PHD" (which I associated with graduate-level schooling), I tentatively figured on leaving the university. On my way to class a couple days later, I passed a green motorscooter with a Virginia vehicle-inspection sticker. I now had two omens pointing in the same direction. After finishing that semester, I left school and moved to Virginia. Over the next few years I landed jobs with The Association for Research and Enlightenment and with The Monroe Institute. From these organizations, I experienced hands-on approaches to what I had been studying. These experiences proved essential for further development.

Correct interpretation of omens relies on the ability to step outside of your thoughts. Continually thinking about your needs, wants, interests, relationships, and whatever else that feeds your thinking, acts to conform omens to your thoughts. Therefore, intuition plays a critical role. Feeling serves to direct awareness, and thus interpretations, into new dimensions.

Just before moving from my residence at the Grand Canyon, I decided to take a night hike into the canyon. I wanted to say goodbye. About a hundred yards down the trail, I was assaulted by a bird. If I backed up to a certain point, the bird left me alone. One step beyond an imaginary line, the bird attacked. From experience, I've found that a bird defending its nest usually stays on the offensive until the trespasser is headed away. This one seemed possessed by purpose. It ended its attack at precisely the same spot more than half a dozen times. Taking the incident at face value, I felt it was a sign I should not hike further. Reflecting on the event later, my decision made sense since at the time I was at a point in my apprenticeship where I was open to stray influences. So perhaps I was not up to venturing into the nighttime power of the canyon alone. If so, the omen served to alert me. The point is that this is nonordinary decision making, which reflects participation in a nonordinary world.

With practice, the meaning of omens may become self-evident. A noisy bird may mean something in particular to you. Another key element in learning omens, however, is to remain open. Continually use your feelings to prevent too much standardization. And don't make your interpretations too quickly. Build an extensive dictionary. Pay attention to colors, behavior, directions. If a bird flies quietly from the south, what happens later? If you're about to enter a building and crows start to make a fuss, what are the short- and long-term effects of having entered that building? Especially take note of unusual happenings, then watch carefully. Try to match symbols with actual occurrences. Don't lie to yourself. And don't try to make something arbitrarily fit your views. That won't get you anywhere. Stay loose and open, and you'll discover an intimate dialogue with the world.

## Nonordinary Healing

Here we deal with a common practice in the Toltec world: healing. This discussion is intended neither as medical advice nor as a replacement for orthodox medical treatment. It is a recognition that physical well-being hinges on mental, emotional, and spiritual dimensions.

Don Juan maintained that there are no diseases, only indulgences (*Journey,* 291). In one sense, indulgence is the squandering of energy resulting from an imbalance among personal energy fields. Too much distortion of the first field, for example, and second field energies can't feed the individual. Physical symptoms or manifestations of illness reflect the indulgence.

From this basic premise, don Juan further addresses nonordinary healing. After listening to a story about a psychic healer, don Juan told Castaneda that the healer's art rested in shifting others' focal points (*Silence,* 142). That is, the healer's abilities hinged on realigning another's energy. Don Juan also thought that a healer's power emanated from serving as a conduit for Spirit. Hence Spirit, not the healer, realigns the energy. This exquisite balance found by releasing oneself to Spirit is a seer's hallmark, perhaps explaining why healing is prevalent among seers.

A few years ago, during a seminar I was presenting in Massachusetts, a participant I'll refer to as Carol complained of a headache. She also said she had pain in her left knee. During a break, two women co-participants (whom I'll call Betty and Marge) said they routinely practiced nonordinary healing, and with Carol's permission they went to work on her. I sat back and gazed at their efforts. I soon entered *seeing.*

Betty kneeled in front of Carol (who was sitting) and placed her hands over the troublesome knee. Marge stood in back of Carol, placing her hands slightly over Carol's head. I could *see* energy pouring from Betty's energy body into Carol's knee. It seemed that Betty was summoning her own reserves, then pumping them into Carol. Marge, on the other hand, stood calm and cool, and worked seemingly without any effort. From about four feet over Marge's head, a beam of white light came down and entered the top of her head. This energy flowed through her, out her hands, and into Carol's head. After about five minutes, Betty and Marge stopped. Betty appeared slightly fatigued. Marge looked vibrant. Carol reported an easing of the pain in her leg and said her headache was completely gone.

Over the years I've found that many medical doctors and most alternative healers share don Juan's perspective. Still, healing is a vast arena. And there is a variety of approaches and techniques. One of Taisha Abelar's teachers, Clara, gave her a number of "sorcery passes," or specific physical movements which were intended to restore or maintain health.[4] In addition, one of Donner's associates, Delia, told Donner that cures are easy in dreaming, in the dreams that have purpose.[5]

Dreaming also offers potential in healing at distances far removed from the patient. For example, given only a name and address (often from a medical doctor's referral), Edgar Cayce, a twentieth-century American psychic, entered a trance, which is a form of dreaming. He then psychically located the person and provided diagnosis, treatment, and prognosis. Cayce's readings are located at the Edgar Cayce Foundation in Virginia Beach, Virginia, and are available to the public. The Foundation is a sister organization of The Association for Research and Enlightenment.

## The Rule

Among the Eagle's commands is the Rule. The Rule is the intent, the consolidating energy, the dream of the Toltec Way. Used as a map, the Rule accounts for all facets of the Toltec world. It provides guidance for worldview, techniques, and even the personalities of the practitioners. Toltecs' increasing awareness of this emanation accounts for the evolution of cycles. Emilito, another of Abelar's mentors, says the Rule is vital in that it prevents one from "becoming arbitrary or whimsical."[6] In other words, learning to shift the focal point automatically provides numerous options. Thus it's easy to get lost exploring the unknown. Preventing this is another reason that modern seers possess unyielding resolve for staying on track to freedom. The Rule provides a map to do so.

Just as different highway maps are produced by different companies, so do metaphysical traditions offer different directions.

Each system has its own Rule, its own way of relating to the cosmos. Each Rule provides the logic—the building blocks of knowledge—that maps out the specific tradition. Each map points out what to look for, and how to get from point A to point B. Saturating oneself in a system's energies constricts awareness in one way, yet offers freedom in another. By focusing your awareness on what you deem essential, you screen other perceptions. But by following a well-drawn map, you get to where you want to go.

The Rule has core abstractions, abstract because they deal with an undefinable Spirit. One of the abstractions found in the Toltec Way is that Spirit makes itself known, as with omens. The Rule itself manifests from Spirit. Another abstraction is that you can communicate with Spirit. Through internal, nonverbal dialogue and through omens, you may enter into dialogue with Spirit. Accordingly, the Rule offers guidance for participating with Spirit. In *The Power of Silence,* Castaneda presents other abstract cores.

## Tracking and Dreaming

Part of the Rule is dividing energy into tracking and dreaming. Donner refers to these as nearly indivisible units.[7] We all possess both, yet accent one or the other. Although they may appear indistinguishable, the manner in which a person uses or deploys energy highlights the difference. Tracking relies on convergence, a channeling of intent. Dreaming employs a more dispersive, expansive approach. Therefore, the emotional texture of each as well as the skills of focus vary.

The following chart offers perspectives regarding this division of energies.

| Dreaming | Tracking |
|---|---|
| untamed | reserved |
| unsettling | purposeful |
| expansive | flexible |
| leaping | practical |
| outrageous | disciplined |
| balanced with nonordinary worlds | balanced with the ordinary world |
| reactive | reflective |
| highly energizing | supportive |

As an attainment of the third cycle, tracking incorporates a world-of-people orientation. As it deals with this narrow band, it utilizes small shifts in the focal point, giving more time to adapt and to incorporate knowledge into daily life (*Silence,* 265). It offers sobriety and direction. Dreaming, in turn, provides the adventure of greater, often mind-boggling shifts and thus adds immense stimulation to exploring the energy body. As a result, tracking and dreaming supplant the need for power plants.

While tracking often refers to first-field activities, and dreaming to second-field activities, they are not always exclusive. For example, dreaming-awake is dreaming applied to physical, or first-field, pursuits. The idea, then, is to work with both. The power of dreaming is necessary to ensure dramatic and significant shifts of the focal point. Tracking is necessary to direct those shifts into productive avenues. From one perspective, tracking is a form of dreaming where the dream intersects the world of humans. From another perspective, dreaming is a tracking maneuver to provide greater orientation and generally to expand awareness. Both serve to focus your energies. Harmonizing them heightens awareness.

## The Seer

Evolving out of the Toltec Way is the seer. The mark of a seer is the ability to step outside the Toltec world and continue unfolding perception. In a sense, the difference between a Toltec and a seer is the difference between the second and third cycles. Both the second and third cycles had seers; hence they were able to come to terms with the Eagle and its emanations. But second-cycle Toltecs stayed within the system. Seers work with the system long enough to step beyond it.

Remaining locked within a system keeps people locked within themselves, enhancing the self and reducing awareness. Don Juan says that the second cycle's forays into the unknowable were governed by greed and self-importance, producing marked changes in their energy bodies. Rather than maintaining human-shaped energy, they became something altogether different than the human condition. Don Juan says that while he admires the immensity of their thinking, he detests their morbidity (*Dreaming,* 14, 2).

While the second cycle achieved remarkable journeys into arenas outside ordinary human perception, they thought the unknowable could be reduced to the known. To save the day, third-cycle innovations orient the seer to the unknowable's purely abstract qualities. Viewing the unknowable as an abstract force places the unknowable into a realm of total mystery. This serves to keep perception open and flexible.

## Earth's Boost and the Death Defiers

Don Juan advised Castaneda not to confuse the world with what people do (*Separate*, 264). For don Juan, the world consists of dimensions within dimensions and holds unimaginable opportunities. When he guided Castaneda to perceive himself as a crow, for instance, he showed that human awareness was only one option available to us (*Teachings*, 188). He also teaches that constant and varied manipulation of the focal point enhances awareness of other life forms, including Earth.

He indicates that as one progresses, a Toltec's relation to Earth automatically becomes more exquisite and intimate. Toltecs connect points within personal awareness to Earth. This alignment grants additional power for entering other universes. By aligning intent with other emanations and then hooking into Earth's vital energy, don Juan maintains that you can propel your complete awareness into realms beyond normal life and death. He thinks that seers at this level, the death defiers, have the ability to die only when they want (*Silence*, 228).

Don Juan also regards seers with third-cycle orientations as the quintessential death defiers (*Fire*, 295). To him, they seek true freedom rather than elaborate and bizarre flirtations with the unknown. They seek liberation through the Fire from Within.

## The Fire from Within

Don Juan's impeccable control of his focal point gave him some very nonordinary options. If confronted with imminent danger, for example, he says he can move his focal point and thereby, in the twinkle of an eye, place his physical body in another location. He also says he can choose to burn with the Fire from Within (*Silence*, 228). Either action removes him from the danger.

According to don Juan, the Fire from Within produces total awareness; hence, total freedom. It occurs when one deliberately stretches awareness across the entire energy body. Tracking and dreaming enable you to engage, explore, and energize different regions of the energy body. Sufficient stimulation enables a stretch of awareness throughout the entire energy body. Don Juan says that the physical body then evaporates from the world, and yet a form of individual awareness remains (*Fire*, 295, 291).

To provide another reference, the Fire from Within occurs when the first and second fields unite as one. The limitations of the first field give way to the second field and to the total energy body. Yet the influence of the first field permits the individual's sense of self to remain. Awareness is then propelled into the third field. The abstract qualities of the unknowable become concrete. Don Juan thought the only requirement to obtain total freedom was having sufficient energy (*Fire*, 295). He taught the Toltec Way as a means to harness that energy.

# 4
# A Toltec Team

Over the years I have associated with Toltecs scattered about the United States, Mexico, Canada, and Europe. They consist of men and women, with some of each gender oriented to tracking and to dreaming. Diverse in ages, preferences, tastes, styles, backgrounds, and abilities, their common bond is an unrelenting quest for freedom. As such, they reflect the personalities of a "nagual's party," as outlined in Chapters 9 and 10 of Castaneda's sixth book, *The Eagle's Gift.*

The profile of a nagual's party, or what I refer to as a Toltec team, is an aspect of the Rule. Toltecs use the Rule as energy for stability and growth, not for mindless adherence. Thus there can be individual interpretations within its overall scope. Plus, not every team need mirror another. There is plenty of room for variations while implementing the overall theme. The guiding light is for each member to deal with what actually unfolds rather than forcing compliance with preconceived notions. In turn, each team must find its own way. Pressures and requirements change with time and locale. While guided by the Rule, this chapter, then, is based on my observations of, and my interactions with, these people.

## The Sexes

Donner states that males and females relate to reason differently. These differences, she says, make females more flexible.[1] Don Juan says that while men possess sobriety and purpose, females have the talent (*Fire,* 142). He adds that due to their nature, women have a marked edge over men in the general pursuit of knowledge (*Tales,* 144).

This kind of thinking blows most twentieth-century models out the window. But it is also interesting that this division of labor is consistent with archetypes of masculine and feminine energies. Masculine energy is thought to provide direction and thrust. Feminine energy is often considered open, pliable, and nurturing.

It is also important to note that males and females are generally regarded as having both masculine and feminine energies.

Donner extends don Juan's thinking about women by saying that our survival as a species depends on giving women time to evolve. Rather than align with procreation, she feels women need to align with evolution.[2] By using the womb (a dreaming organ), she says the dream of another intent—another reality—may be latched onto and expressed. One effect would be leading the entire species in another direction, from which women would give birth to another species. This is not leadership in the traditional sense. It is leadership in radical transformation.

There's no question that in recent history male perspectives have ruled. We have few monuments to women. We have relatively few female political representatives. Thus it's obvious that our society has refused to recognize the validity of their views, their power. Now, however, women have had their fill and seek to claim their freedom. There is even a growing discourse on patriarchal versus matriarchal societies. Quite often, I hear that patriarchal societies are contriving, power-dominated, and subversive of human rights. Matriarchal societies, on the other hand, are viewed as embracing, nurturing, and protective of the highest ideals.

A concurrent theme is that patriarchal societies (hence, men in general) don't have the comprehensive view women do. Men are deemed to harbor natural limitations. This view often becomes implicit, not needing expression, and therefore the flip-side of a drive for domination surfaces. This time by women. Women who exhibit this attitude arbitrarily and systematically demean men. By doing so, women commit the very grievance they wish to correct.

For instance, I remember a kitchen-table conversation with friends where one woman spoke endearingly of her affiliation with the sisterhood. This connection provided strength and helped her focus her resolve toward liberation. One of the men spoke of how he felt the same way toward men; he sought to encourage their evolution, their empowerment. He spoke of men capitalizing on the women's liberation movement in order to better free themselves. The woman said it was too bad he just couldn't see people as people, not as sexes. So while it was fine to espouse virtues of sisterhood, like-minded male activity was seen as boys being boys.

Her remark does carry great meaning, however. For a time men were considered by many as superior, the breadwinners. Now a growing number say women are superior, the saviors. Perhaps the pendulum needs to swing in the opposite direction to generate more awareness and balance. Perhaps humans simply seek to dominate. Perhaps, however, we can even step beyond patriarchal and matriarchal concerns. Perhaps if we find a common ground of equality, we can move on to a higher ground. As don Juan says, the fact that we all face death makes us all equal, leaving us no time for anything less (*Journey*, ch. 4). Using this advice as a guide, perhaps we can elevate ourselves beyond the so-called battle of the sexes, and into the rhythms of universal consciousness where the drama of masculine and feminine energies is but a stage play.

## The Four Directions

The Rule divides individuals into four groups or directions: north, east, south, and west. The directions reflect a natural balance of orienting oneself on a path. Furthermore, each direction embodies a particular intent. Arguments of male or female superiority aside, a defining Toltec view is that women carry within them the intent of the directions. By their nature women are therefore connected with intent, whereas men must learn to make the connection. It is this difference that led don Juan to give women an edge in pursuing knowledge.

The following categories reflect forms of energy. The idea here is not to define types of behavior as much as it is to direct awareness into another frame of reference.

**North**. This direction concerns itself with knowledge. A person from this direction seeks and gains highly specific knowledge in a particular area of inquiry. It is the intent of the scholar. While vital to almost any endeavor, north inhabitants often carry an aloof, domineering arrogance. Resting too comfortably within their domain, they are easily blinded to the unknown and thus run into trouble by a reluctance to continually break the boundaries of their current knowledge.

**East**. Optimism and humor bubble forth from this intent. Often having gentle dispositions, people with this orientation make perfect messengers and scouts. Although a little fickle, they efficiently scout the road in front of you, making sure you don't run into something you'd rather avoid. An east-oriented person usually requires direction from without. They need instigation, but once in motion are more than up to a task.

**South.** A very nurturing, soothing direction. As though sealed in a protective cocoon, this person's energy body automatically produces a sheen which shields them from the *seeing* of others. It is harder to *see* into them and their motives than it is to *see* into the other directions. This makes them suitable for behind-the-scenes work. For example, this person enjoys the control derived from getting a political aspirant into office rather than personally seeking the office.

**West.** Power. Those centered within this direction are prone to action, doing instead of talking. They possess a very aggressive demeanor. Their raw energy provides fuel for propulsion into almost any endeavor. However, they also tend to be volatile, boisterous, and contemptuous. The natural power lurking within continually challenges their sense of balance with the other directions.

The following chart offers male and female perspectives regarding the four directions. It offers views on orientation and function, plus a positive and negative trait of each. Again, it is to provide perspective, not to confine behavior.

## 1. Direction/Type
## 2. General function
## 3. Positive trait
## 4. Negative trait

|  |  |  |
|---|---|---|
|  | 1. North<br>2. Knowledge<br>3. Insight<br>4. Conceit |  |
| 1. West<br>2. Power<br>3. Thrust<br>4. Volatile | **Females** | 1. East<br>2. Peace<br>3. Optimism<br>4. Fickle |
|  | 1. South<br>2. Nurture<br>3. Soothe<br>4. Flaccid |  |

```
                    1. Scholar
                    2. Specialized knowledge
                    3. Makes knowledge functional
                    4. Too aloof

1. Man-of-action                          1. Courier
2. Act, not talk        ┌──────────┐      2. Messenger/Scout
3. High energy          │  Males   │      3. Easy-going
4. Arrogant             └──────────┘      4. Requires Direction

                    1. Behind-the-scenes
                    2. Organizing
                    3. Stealth
                    4. Manipulative
```

These are not exclusive categories. Other descriptions of the directions may fit just as well. Also, I find a typical reaction is, "Oh, but I am all of those!" Correct, we all have each direction within us, including male and female perspectives. Yet some people are moody, timid, or aggressive. Some have marked tendencies toward scholarly work, arts and crafts, or human services. The directions serve only to account for different temperaments, not limit us to them. For example, a southern direction does not preclude action, just as an action-prone person is not excluded from refined knowledge. It doesn't mean males can't be conceited, or females can't be manipulative.

The directions also provide a model so we may accept variations in others, as well as understand how different personalities influence us. For instance, north-directed people may use well-crafted, authoritative arguments as a subterfuge to cover the fact that they don't *see* all that well. I also know south-directed Toltecs who, as a result of their nurturing bents, carry with them (and inflict upon others) their pervasive understanding that they know best. Some of what they consider nurturing is just an attempt to bend others to their wishes. Rather than get in an uproar over these kind of excesses, it is sometimes easier to tolerate their behavior by placing their individual tendencies into a larger context.

Moreover, we can use the elements of each direction to measure our strengths and weaknesses. By understanding various components of our personalities, we stand a better chance to integrate and balance the energies of each, making us better equipped to get on with any task.

## Trackers and Dreamers

There are many facets to tracking and dreaming. In a manner, dreaming is awareness and tracking is the discipline to harness awareness. Both are necessary. As with the directions, we all carry both. Yet people usually lean toward one or the other as a matter of predilection or inherent self-nature. Those who lean toward tracking—trackers—tend to fare better in ordinary human endeavors, while those who lean toward dreaming—dreamers—find a natural home in worlds beyond the ordinary.

Trackers are usually down-to-earth, grounded in practical views of self and world. They are amenable and adaptable. They easily focus their energy toward order and stability. After all, tracking is the skill of stabilizing perception. Trackers offer a team balance and support because they are at ease in dealing with consensus. They can also enter, use, and leave a social order with minimal difficulty as they ardently groom their knowledge of social interactions. However, they often lack raw imagination. While their discipline is essential for continued growth, their stability hinders dramatic ventures into the unknown. They have the ability to tackle the unknown, but lack the orientation and energy to enter its most elusive regions, as do dreamers.

Perhaps due to their affinity with other worlds, dreamers may have a hard time with earthly discipline. Their sense of order tends to come from how they relate to external authority. This gives them something to latch onto. They therefore tend toward fixations, however. In an attempt to internalize their sense of order, dreamers then envision that the world accurately reflects their thoughts. They often grab onto one or two pieces of evidence and then get lost along those lines of thought. Then they may expand their dreaming to think others share the same dreams, and thus have the same values and views. With their intense energy, this tendency has the effect of pulling others into their web-like dreams. Their fixations prevent adaptability and measured, directed growth. As a result, strength and stability supplied from a consistent external source is required to penetrate this barrier. Not always making solid connections between their inner world and what's occurring outside, dreamers offer a team workouts in abrupt, energetic change.

Quite often, stress results from working with these apparently opposite traits. Trackers may wonder if they are in the same conversation when talking with dreamers. They may feel frustration with dreamers' incredible mood swings and their seeming lack of discernment. Dreamers may feel upset over trackers' tendencies toward reflection and caution. As these counterparts work together, however, they begin to augment each other. As dreamers supply raw energy, trackers supply stability. Simply soaking up dreamers' energy by their mere proximity provides great dividends of energizing anyone's dreaming. For a dreamer, immersion in the often tedious tasks associated with running a business may feel draining and lifeless. However, conducting business is a good way to learn tracking.

Sometimes it is difficult to say which is which, tracking or dreaming. Their expression often blends as there are no hard-and-fast rules to indicate distinctions. Also, a child with a natural tracking bent who is reared by a domineering dreamer may at first glance appear to be a dreamer. It's not out of the ordinary that the child has simply adopted the mannerisms of the parent. In addition, every now and then you run across a person who possesses an equal blend of both. Whatever the situation, it's best to apply everything to the tracker and dreamer within you.

It's also best to approach this lightly, as the terms may blind you to their essence. They are meant to provide orientation. In a nutshell, trackers systematically point themselves into new domains of power and knowledge, whereas dreamers blossom through immersion in new domains of power. But to lock someone away in an identity precludes evolution of the individual, the team, and the path. Hence, the team model is best used only to assist self- and God-realization, not to define it.

## Team Leaders

The personality of a team reflects the temperaments of the team leaders. Like a business company's CEO, a team leader influences the behavior of the entire team. Based on personal predilections, each leader uses a different motif. For example, Abelar writes that due to Castaneda's "keen interest in formal academic erudition, [the team members] under his care had to develop their capacity for the abstract, clear thinking that is acquired only in a modern university."[3]

There is a male and a female team leader: the naguals, as

Castaneda refers to them. Don Juan says that to be a top-notch team leader, one has to love freedom first and foremost (*Fire*, 152). This, he adds, requires supreme detachment so that one doesn't revel in the known or unknown, and lose sight of the mysterious unknowable.

According to don Juan, initially what makes a team leader is the configuration of a person's energy body (*Silence*, 13). Typically, a team leader has four compartments, whereas other members have two. This configuration provides more energy as well as natural reference points for the four directions. Don Juan indicated that this balance allows the leaders to reflect Spirit better (*Dreaming*, 10). Elaborating on this, Castaneda says team leaders are not driven by normal desires. They receive "orders from some ineffable source that cannot be discussed."[4] It is this dance with the abstract that moves the entire team toward freedom.

While all members develop tracking and dreaming, doing so is especially important for the leaders. It is not that team leaders are more knowledgeable in each and every subject. Rather, they must be proficient in a variety of capacities in order to generate balance. As don Juan says, in addition to their energy, they have sobriety, endurance, and stability (*Silence*, 13). He adds that being a team leader is more far-reaching than having more energy. They are groomed to be leaders, teachers, and guides (*Fire*, 11). For instance, Castaneda tells us that Abelar was trained by Toltecs in Mexico, all of whom were under the guidance of don Juan.[5]

As Castaneda observed, the members of don Juan's team were equal yet different (*Silence*, 200). Yet don Juan also points out that team leaders have authority (*Fire*, 132). The dimensions of this authority hinge on the moment at hand, on whatever is taking place, on however Spirit moves the person. Providing a metaphor for team cohesion, Castaneda once remarked that he perceived don Juan as a military leader of a covert operation (*Silence*, 95).

From research on team behavior, I've found numerous parallels between Toltec teams and military special-operations teams. Commandos undergo rigorous training, develop a total commitment to their mission, and sustain prolonged activity under strenuous conditions. Additionally, in his book *Inside the LRRPS*, Michael Lee Lanning, referring to Army rangers, tells us, "Teams more often than not were a reflection of the team leader. His personality was mirrored in his subordinates, and while each LRRP was certainly an individual, he was foremost a member of the team."[6]

Don Juan says that leadership also stems from providing

situations for the focal point to shift. Given the intense individuality of the members, this often presents a formidable task. Almost everyone understands portions of the Rule differently. While this staunch individuality leads to arguments, it is also a team's saving grace since individualism helps prevent cult behavior. As Arthur Deikman points out in his book *The Wrong Way Home,* lack of autonomy is a defining feature of a cult.[7]

With a diversity of thought and experience provided by the team, the leaders can consolidate, refine, and implement the Rule. You might say that the leaders embody the Rule. In practice, this yields interesting results. For instance, to deal with the reality-shattering achievement of jumping off a cliff, physically de-materializing, experiencing other dimensions, and regaining physical form, Castaneda had to use the Rule for guidance (*Second Ring*). Indulging and fretting were taboo. Acceptance of possibility was the order of the day. In addition, Castaneda later had to divide the members of his first team into male-female pairs, where a tracker-dreamer balance was also struck (*Gift,* ch. 4). After this division, he scattered the team throughout Mexico. To do so, he used the Rule and abided by the directives of Spirit.

By participating with the Rule, Spirit influences the leaders to spontaneously create circumstances which place the members in different worldviews, different energies, and different landscapes of perception. In this manner, the Rule is imparted to the team. But when members run headlong into having to surrender pieces of their identities—their thoughts about themselves and the world—violence may erupt. For example, when faced with having to act without don Juan's presence, a group of his former apprentices angrily battled Castaneda about how to proceed (*Gift,* ch. 5). Each figured to have a correct bead on how things should shape up. Earlier, a group of female apprentices known as the Little Sisters had conspired to kill Castaneda in a deranged effort to spur him into action (*Second Ring,* ch. 2).

One goal for all members is to be centered within themselves without being self-centered, to lose individual identity without losing self-awareness. The ranger discipline is designed so that each member might wage this monumental struggle and transcend the ordinary balance individuality offers. Toltecs tend to find that part of their nature is that of being team members. Service to the team may then take precedence over service to self. Where individualism once offered a check to cultism, it might now get in the way of new and larger steps. The ranger's discipline leads away from constructing a social identity to handling awareness. Hence, the emphasis is always on freedom. And not all succeed. For instance, don Juan says that Julian succumbed to the liberties of the unknown and missed the connection to total freedom (*Fire*, 152).

Perhaps the greatest role of the leader is in emphasis. Don Juan says that we usually don't believe we can progress on our own. He added that a leader's energy-body configuration acts as a channel permitting energy to flow directly from Spirit (*Silence*, 181). It then follows that Spirit moves perception, not a person. What matters most for this shift is to reduce the amount of self-reflection and to increase the amount of mystery. This frees internal energy which permits new energy alignments.

## Leadership

Toltec leadership consists of implementing radical change. It requires continual development of energy coupled with continual refinement of context, or the terms that guide how energy is handled. Doing so takes years of arduous personal commitment and teamwork. In terms of challenging ordinary reality, all Toltecs are leaders. For a team, since the team leaders carry the Rule, through their behavior they convey a working model of that vision to each member. They require extra fortitude to withstand the disparities as individual members usually try to pull the team in various directions. As Donner states, to carry out this task team leaders receive extraordinary conditioning during their apprenticeships.[8]

The leaders do, however, rely on the energetic influences of the team. But it is almost impossible to say how the leader will be influenced. Although a member thinks he or she is providing a particular kind of influence, it might turn out to have an unanticipated affect of the leader. For example, a west-oriented female and a man-of-action were walking together in a suburban section of his hometown. As they passed a tree, they felt their energies shift and their focal points move. Both felt extreme fright and terror. They left the immediate area, regrouped their energies, and returned to the tree. They experienced the same shift, the same terror. They concluded that the energy of the tree produced those effects. Adhering to their responsibilities, they told their story to other team members, including a team leader. The leader regarded the report as valuable and was intrigued that trees might be used to shift the focal point.

As part of his training, however, the leader felt compelled to verify their report. He located the tree through dreaming. While he experienced a shift in his energy, he did not experience any negative reactions. Over time, he *saw* that both people had rigid energy fields. He concluded that their interpretation that the tree produced the terror was inaccurate. He found that their terror resulted from their fears of losing control—in this case, their reluctance to let their focal points shift freely into the unknown. To further illustrate, a friend told me he often felt extreme terror when he was by himself at night and in the midst of trees. He says that he outgrew the terror, however, by placing his experiences in the context of focal point shifts and then examining his fear. He now makes it a point to spend time among trees, and he no longer suffers deleterious reactions.

Thus, while the members wanted everyone to know of lurking dangers, something else occurred. Incidentally, at the time of this incident these people regularly used power plants, and they were among the people whose energy bodies resembled cauliflower when *seen*. Perhaps distortions in their energy amplified the distortions in their experience and subsequent interpretation.

Accepting the various influences of the team, the leaders aim to enhance personal clarity and clarity of the mission. Using a consistent theme in Warren Bennis's book *On Becoming a Leader,* leaders don't allow others to shape their lives; they take the influences of others and shape themselves.[9] In this pursuit, the team can either sink into second-cycle coercive influences of self-importance and power struggles, or rise to third-cycle freedom.

In ordinary situations, leaders have the most invested in the group they govern. They have invested in their group their ideas about this or that. This self-importance constricts their actions, and so they resist change, especially if they are no longer perceived as power brokers. Toltec leadership, on the other hand, requires ruthless adherence to ranger discipline. This discipline allows the flow of Spirit within each member and the team. There is no one in charge, as there is nothing to be in charge of. All ideas are looked at, inventoried, and then, as don Juan suggests, eliminated in order to expand knowledge further (*Fire,* 83-85). Unwavering devotion to the highest potentials regardless of the desires of any member gradually focuses the team. What is at stake is complete transformation of personal and group energies.

There are no steps to accomplish this. There is method, however. A method of Power. Again, the team leader follows Spirit rather than rational deliberations (*Fire*, 172). The fierce conditioning the leaders receive during their apprenticeships serves to open doorways through their own self-reflection. For the team to stand a chance of success, this discipline must be developed by each member. In pursuit of this ability, individual perception shifts away from reason to *will*, a more encompassing mode of perception.

Through *will*, an individual directly perceives a natural order, rather than the contrived and symbolic order of reason. This shift to *will* is explored in later chapters. For now, it is important to recognize that following Spirit requires unbending intent to follow something beyond personal thoughts and feelings. How a leader responds stems from his or her predilections. Don Juan indicated that some may choose to be more active than others. For instance, he often preferred to push a point, feeling that there wasn't always sufficient time to wait for someone to have a change of heart. He sought to convince part of his team not to foray into the inorganic world, for example (*Dreaming*, 188). In turn, reflecting on Castaneda's leadership style, Donner is told by her namesake, Florinda Grau, that Castaneda will help her, but not as she expects. He will only serve as an example.[10]

In essence, leadership involves guiding the team to follow Spirit, rather than getting the team to follow a leader. Judging by the amount of turmoil, hardship, and humor that Castaneda tells us regarding the two generations of Toltec teams with whom he associated, it's anybody's guess how a leader's guidance will unfold.

## Team Assembly

Don Juan told Castaneda that the minimal number under a team leader's direction is 16: eight women, not including the female team leader, plus eight men, which includes the male team leader (*Gift*, 181). The women represent each direction from tracking and dreaming perspectives. The female team leader, however, typically performs the Fire from Within and leaves with the preceding team. She then serves as a beacon for her team still in this world, while the male team leader is charged with leading the team to that beacon, as well as ensuring survival of the lineage.

Don Juan informed me that in addition to the leaders, a team of eight women and four men could succeed. The critical component, he said, was the eight women. Since women carry intent, all the elements within a team had to be covered, ensuring that the energies reflected by trackers and dreamers of each direction grow within the team. If there were only four men, they had to be four trackers, one from each direction. This would ensure stability in purpose and direction.

A series of checks and balances is used for the selection of members. Just as a company tries to avoid trouble in its initial selection of employees, so too can a Toltec team ill afford wrong moves. In true Toltec fashion, it is never a matter of individual tastes or preferences. The decisions are based on omens, the traffic signs of Spirit. Omens initially direct a team member to a person. Guided by Spirit, a determination is made whether or not to continue association with the prospective member. Castaneda tells us how don Juan regarded their first meeting as an omen (*Tales,* 229-230). Don Juan said they were introduced by a man "babbling inanities." Castaneda later had to find his beneficial area in front of don Juan's house in order to proceed with his apprenticeship (*Teachings,* 33).

Passing the sentry, as Donner refers to it, is a principal omen for member selection.[11] In her case, while Castaneda was driving her to the residence of don Juan's team, a young man appeared and waved at them. Don Juan told her that this was a sentry from the other world, and indicated Castaneda could continue his journey with her.

In my case, I was driving through the desert near Tucson. I had the afternoon to myself as there were no other vehicles on the road. As I rounded a corner, I saw a man standing a couple hundred yards ahead of me in the middle of the road. He was tall and lean and seemed physically strong. He wore dark brown pants and boots, a white shirt, and a dark brown cowboy hat that had a flattened brim. Strapped to his side was a long-barrel six-shooter. He looked ferocious but not mean. He reminded me of someone who was outside of the law but not an outlaw, perhaps an ex-sheriff who could no longer abide by the law and still be true to himself. I slowed down so I wouldn't hit him. As I drove past, he looked directly in my eyes. I thought maybe he was a local cowboy or an actor from a nearby movie lot. Almost immediately after passing him, I looked back. He was gone. I slowed down a little more and looked about. There was nowhere anyone could have gone that quickly. His appearance and disappearance were puzzling. A couple days later I met don Juan on the outskirts of Tucson.

Historically, leaders of well-established teams assisted the leaders of the next generation in assembling a team. Don Juan certainly provided Castaneda with a core team. Now, however, with don Juan having had to scramble about with the three-pronged Castaneda, team leaders might well be left more to their own devices. On top of that, Carol Tiggs returned from her jump with don Juan's team, which throws the prior order out of whack. Indeed, Norbert Classen and other Toltecs call for a new interpretation of the Rule. Perhaps this is a sign of the fourth cycle.

I once asked Donner what binds a team. She said, "Affection." I asked if this is human affection. She replied, "Affection itself." As this affection plays out, we find that a team is an extension of each member as each member is an extension of a team. Each member must align personal goals with the team's intent. While subordinating oneself often produces strong reactions, it also brings one to the threshold of a new domain of Spirit. So while the adjustment may prove cumbersome and wearisome, it is also uplifting. It remains important to understand that this is not a matter of subordinating personal *will* to a team leader's *will*. Personal *will* should be subordinated only to Power, the Great Spirit, Divine Will.

## The Mission

The mission for a team is to achieve freedom. Freedom is a very abstract notion; it means different things to different people. In Toltec terms, it means burning with the Fire from Within, the supreme death-defying act. Like Julian, many get waylaid. From a historical perspective, Julian never completely grew out of second-cycle practices. Remember, third-cycle seers sought to remedy second-cycle failings of short-sightedness, excessive self-importance, and tendencies toward domination. As remarkable as second-cycle accomplishments were, its adherents still fell head-long into a very deep pit.

To accomplish their mission, Toltecs must free themselves from all ordinary conditions. To spur this process along, each member provides a particular energy which other members can use to generate balance. For example, Vincente was a scholar on don Juan's team. His expertise was in herbs and medicinal plants. He used that knowledge to enhance the well-being of his team, as well as to produce sorceric visions (*Separate*, 47).

The transformation of personal energy fields is the work of a ranger. Within their daily lives rangers have, to some degree, balanced and integrated each of the four directions, as well as tracking and dreaming energies. For instance, one ranger I know uses north energy to develop her knowledge of ancient Greece, east energy to expand her writing, south energy to enhance her home, and west energy to explore dreaming. A four-direction diagram of her activities looks like this:

```
┌─────────────────────────────────────────────────┐
│                                                   │
│               Studies of Greece                   │
│                                                   │
│                                                   │
│   Entering          Ranger          Writing/      │
│   unknown           ──────          Storytelling  │
│                                                   │
│               Home life                           │
│                                                   │
└─────────────────────────────────────────────────┘
```

Gaining intricate knowledge of Greece is an activity of a scholar. It pulls in and amplifies north energy. Storytelling, a messenger's tales, develops east energy. It requires a light-hearted energy to follow the lead of the story itself. From the south flows energy to place her home in order. She has designed a very personal place to give her peace and serenity, thus nurturing her other endeavors. She also uses the powerful energy of the west to energize and evolve her skills. To me, she is a model of balance.

Each of these energies connect and work together. For instance, the balance and direction that north, east, and south energies provide keeps the wild energies of the west from getting out of hand. Thus, we again find tracking and dreaming energies working together. In this example, the north, east, and south energies offer direction and harmony: tracking. And from the raw energies of the west the ranger has a constant source of energy to develop her dreaming.

A team further amplifies these connections. Adjusting to numerous well-defined energies can significantly enhance your speed in finding your place in the world. Since the others' energies stretch you in different ways, you develop a remarkable integrity of personal energies. Furthermore, having a number of like-minded yet individual energies provides substantial momentum for everyone.

As a matter of practice, to complete the mission team members frequently trek into the unknown and report their findings to the team. Reports on, for example, inorganic beings, medicinal plants, how trees might affect perception, applying dreaming to daily life, or *seeing* the Eagle all go in to a team's evolution. A ranger's integrity allows the individual to withstand the pressures of drop-ping in and out of various dimensions.

Integrity also contributes greatly to the team, as the team is its own entity with its own energy. A lack of individual integrity from any member adversely affects the entire team. Therefore, a member must be first true to himself or herself. Only then can members let go to participate in something more expansive than themselves. And only then can an optimum amount of energy be delivered to the team. Members must know themselves, their places in the world, and their places on the team. Otherwise, a member sucks energy from the team for self-important purposes. After arriving at a workable balance, team leaders may then fuse the individual energies into one collective entity.

* * *

The Toltec Way as it stands today enables you to compare and contrast forms of energy, styles of behavior, and types of person-ality. In short, it offers a wide-ranging context. For example, *seeing* is part of a Toltec context. If you notice someone fixedly staring at you, and you didn't have this context, you might well enough think that the person is ogling you. However, if you're aware of *seeing*, you can determine if the person is rudely staring or *seeing*. From that point, you use another part of the overall context to determine your next action. In ordinary terms, you might get all huffed up and stomp away. From a Toltec perspective, you might use the occasion as an opportunity to *see* another person in the act of *seeing*.

I have endeavored to show that context is a model, a way of going about things. This does not mean that it is arbitrary or conditional to only a few situations. Success requires complete commitment. At the very least, it requires learning to handle its energies so you don't get gobbled up by the system. With luck, part of that commitment yields a personal understanding that the role of lineages is that of a tool for liberation.

To load conditions for success in their favor, third-cycle prac-titioners refined an almost separate form of training within the Toltec Way, that of the seer. A seer is more concerned with the nature of perception than with simply altering perception. This orientation leads to stepping outside of the second energy field and into the third field, a maneuver don Juan associates with the third cycle (*Gift*, 23).

Knowing the intricacies of systems helps accomplish this maneuver. Thus, while Toltecs study and implement the Rule to enhance perception, seers examine the ins and outs of perception itself. Just as the seers from other traditions have their guiding lights, the Toltec variety of seers use the Rule as a reference to get on with the mission. In this light, the next section explores influences shaping perception and examines underpinnings of a Toltec-seer's knowledge.

# Part II
# The Seer

# 5
# The Shape of Things to Come

A worldview is a principal force in shaping perception. By participating within a worldview, we gradually align our energies with that world. As a result, we actively condition ourselves to what we can and cannot perceive. As with anything else, there are costs and benefits. On the high side, by fashioning a worldview we have a world to view. The down side is that we tend to expand our snapshots into ultimate truth, thereby leaving other worlds out of the picture. Consequently, we readily cast aside new or opposing views since they challenge what we hold dear.

But worldview is not truth; it is technique. It helps us make sense of our experiences and allows us to interact with the world better. A worldview stems from binding together a host of elements, such as Earth's revolution around the sun, the nature of gravity, and views of God. A worldview guides our way. The energy placed behind it directs our thoughts, feelings, and experiences. Hence, it embodies and consumes a great amount of power. If it is a solid, well-constructed view, our experience matches it. This gives us a world to use. However, it also generates a huge self-fulfilling prophecy that limits what we see to its own boundaries.

This power rests in consensus, social agreements which bind together personal energies. These agreements produce an implicit contract from which we dogmatically determine what is real or not real. Due to the complexity of a complete worldview, a vast amount of a consensus typically rests below conscious recognition. We then assume that a reality is real. However, no worldview is all-inclusive. None can account for the sum total of creation; existence is simply too vast. Therefore, knowledge of how worldviews influence perception is important because of their power to limit or to expand perception. This chapter, then, focuses on a few influences which shape our perception and thus determine what is to come.

## Ordinary and Nonordinary Worlds

Any worldview is a coherent set of assumptions about reality. These assumptions are simply points of view, dots in front of our eyes. Even though we each have a distinct relation to the world, we share common tendencies. Culture, geographic environment, and the connections which result merely from being human, all work together to provide a consistency of perception. This consistency gives us the ability to communicate and to effectively interact with others.

Generally speaking, an ordinary reality focuses on the physical world, and a nonordinary reality brings into play other, often unseen, dimensions. Whether you are building an ordinary or a nonordinary world, the process of building remains the same. For instance, during the early stages of my apprenticeship I found no apparent consistency in the Toltec world. The new language enabling a shared outlook between don Juan and me hadn't been developed. Over several years, however, I worked with the techniques of different nonordinary disciplines, including Zen and Taoism but primarily Toltec. This work slowly expanded my worldview and I gradually developed the ability to communicate with other Toltecs. In a like manner, from birth we are taught the views and practices of ordinary reality. By employing these, we gain membership in that world.

Ordinary worlds tightly embrace the known, the familiar. Extending awareness into the unknown occurs slowly. While conducting experiments, an experimenter's worldview creates the boundaries of the experiment in terms of what can and cannot be tested. The conditions of what is allowed to exist determine what will exist. This capacity for distortion is referred to as "experimenter bias," or "experimenter effect."[1]

This bias affects not only what takes place during the experiment, but also how the experiment is evaluated. One difficulty with testing for psychic phenomena, for instance, is that experimenters often start from negative assumptions. Many scientists simply do not acknowledge psychic functioning. Worse yet, many do not allow for its possibility. To them, the terms of their world indicate it doesn't exist, and so they build that assumption into their tests.

Sometimes this bias produces even more complicated effects. For instance, say an experiment is to test if a person can have an out-of-body experience. During the experiment, the subject travels away from her body and perceives six numbers written on a piece of paper in another building. She returns to her body and correctly gives the experimenter the numbers as well as the layout of the other building. Critics who once said psychic ability doesn't exist might now say it was not her dreaming body, but some other form of psychic occurrence. As you might imagine, this manner of building reality takes a long time. Impeccably proving or disproving the results of others is a hallmark of the scientific method. Its rigorous nature offers strength; however, when you're aiming for the Fire from Within, relying on social consensus proves too tedious, too time consuming. Without sacrificing diligence, Toltecs step up the pace of their investigations.

Using a nonordinary worldview is one way to move the process along faster. For example, the dreaming body, various forms of *seeing*, and elementals are typically pre-established components of nonordinary worlds. Thus, if a person remembers his dreaming body, it won't be discounted as some kind of dream aberration. Or, if a person unexpectedly *sees* an elemental spirit, it won't be chalked up as imagination. In general, nonordinary views offer less constrictions on awareness, and so you don't require a longer amount of time to validate an unusual experience.

Nonordinary worlds also assist in expanding ordinary worlds. Dreaming abilities such as levitation or entering other dimensions act as scouts, as forerunners for expanding a reality's boundaries. Dreaming energy impacts ordinary reality and gradually aligns it with the greater options found in nonordinary worlds. Contemporary laws of interplanetary travel, for example, fall away as pure understanding grows. Where once researchers might think physical objects can't surpass the speed of light, they gradually recondition themselves to other potentials. They might then begin thinking about the notion of hyperspace, where current laws of travel are thought to evaporate. Their new thinking then aligns more of their energy with developing a technology that permits interdimensional, and therefore extended interplanetary, travel.

## Inventories

Don Juan refers to the combined elements of a worldview as an "inventory." He says that an inventory makes us invulnerable, which is why we go about making them in the first place (*Fire*, 85-86). It makes us invulnerable because it acts as a set of filters and mirrors, determining what enters consciousness. When don

Juan brought inorganic beings into a house, Castaneda couldn't perceive them. They were part of a Toltec inventory Castaneda had not yet learned. Since his inventory didn't contain that element, he could not purposefully align his energy with them. Therefore, he couldn't perceive them. As a result, he was protected from their influence. It's not that the beings were malicious. But just as in building the inventory of how to safely cross a heavily-trafficked street, a person learns in steps how to handle their presence.

Therefore, whatever type of world we're participating in, inventories shape what we view. An ordinary inventory contains man-made and natural laws: rules of the road—including the law of gravity and requirements for interplanetary travel—create the liberties and restrictions of that world. A nonordinary inventory often embraces what is considered supernatural. When the Little Sisters levitated and flew about their house, they tapped a nonordinary-world potential (*Second Ring,* ch. 3). Their Toltec inventory assisted them in developing this aspect of dreaming. Don Juan says that north-oriented scholars are knowledgeable in particular inventories (*Silence,* 185).

Inventories and culture reflect each other. Native American inventories, for example, support nonordinary reality more than western European inventories. Yet each has its own power. Bigotry occurs when we fight the power of the other. Native Americans are typically considered to have been conquered by Europeans. Yet today their teachings lead a spiritual renaissance. Hardly the mark of a conquered nation. Yet they were overrun and banished from their lands because they couldn't match the knowledge and power of the invading armies. Native American and European inventories each hold power. In the essence of Power, there is no white, red, yellow, or black truth. There is only knowledge.

## Conditional and Natural Energy

While nonordinary worlds may offer more room than ordinary worlds, both are conditional. They support a status quo, an existing order of what is considered meaningful. Reality is well-defined and participation in that reality is automatic. The conditions of a reality are projected onto the world and are reflected right back, thereby conditioning participants of that reality to a standard inventory. These boundaries then produce standardized behavior. By pointing the way to Spirit, however, nonordinary worldviews offer the advantage of helping you cultivate natural energy. Natural energy opens perception to potential, and thus to continual renewal.

There is no given behavior which automatically defines conditional or natural. Rather, it is the relation you have with the world. When faced with a decision, an automatic, reactive response is considered conditional. However, the very same behavior could be natural if it stems from an alignment between the person and Spirit, rather than from an alignment between the person and a social order. For instance, consider a person who watches a great number of foreign films. If the person does so to be considered cultured, the behavior is conditional. Behavior is directly related to conditions of how the person is perceived by others. If the person loves to attend foreign films to develop a better sense of culture, for the knowledge gained, for more freedom, then the person engages natural energy. Behavior is not tied to social requirements. It is done for its own sake. Natural is what actually works for an individual, not the way it is supposed to work.

By developing a natural field, you find your true self. According to a Toltec-seer's model, the major portion of that exists beyond ordinary individuality. To find your total nature, therefore, you need to connect with something outside of personal form. By *seeing* don Juan's energies, I discovered that, by releasing himself fully to Spirit, he had developed his core nature. By surrendering himself to something beyond his ordinary senses and beyond his ideas of himself, he arrived at his essence. Thus far, he is the only person I've *seen* whose energies evenly blend with the world at large. Paradoxically, he is totally an individual and totally blended into the world. Hence he had developed a natural field.

The following chart provides distinctions between conditional and natural energy. Notice "conditional" applies to ordinary and nonordinary worlds, whereas "natural" applies to nonordinary worlds and to *being*. This indicates that ordinary worlds automatically strap perception down. They exist solely from the conditions they place on reality. In turn, while nonordinary worlds may hold you down, they may also offer a bridge to natural energy. That is, if they are well-crafted, they temper perception, enabling a greater expansion of awareness. This expansion leads to *being*, a state common among seers. Remember, a consistent thread among seers is that they have earned so much knowledge that they may step aside from any worldview and still retain their balance. They don't lose their marbles when they break free from their inventories.

| Conditional | Natural |
|---|---|
| Ordinary / Nonordinary | Nonordinary / Being |
| what should be | what is |
| fixed | fluid |
| judgment | acceptance |
| social conditioning | self-actualization |
| habitual | innovative |
| dogma | mystery |
| static | evolving |
| reality through worldview | reality through experience |

Again, while nonordinary worlds offer more freedom, in an almost diabolical way this expansiveness can also hem you in. It carries the power to trap as well as the power to unveil. It can have you thinking you've discovered it all. The marked advantage of a nonordinary view is that it begins to channel perception into realms of Spirit. This is a learnable skill which all viable nonordinary systems impart. Learning to abide by Spirit offers the chance to encounter total freedom. Rather than structure your life around the conditional social agreements about what the world contains, you place yourself within the natural energy that created all worlds. Unless you open yourself to something greater than yourself, you can never experience your complete self. And so you remain hemmed in by the conditions of what you think the self is.

Another distinct advantage of a natural field is that it is not only flexible, but also fluid. With it you can gracefully shift from worldview to worldview, reality to reality.

## Energy Fields

As don Juan teaches, third-cycle seers discovered that alignments of energies produce perception. These alignments occur from the relationships among the known, unknown, and unknowable, or the first, second, and third energy fields. These fields extend throughout creation. They are part of a Toltec inventory.

For the first and second fields, we have personal bodies. The personal first field contains your physical body, your thoughts and feelings, and all the energies which produce ordinary individual awareness. It is what Castaneda refers to as the "personal tonal" (*Tales,* ch. 5-6). The first field generates perceptions of people, places, and things. In short, it is the portion of yourself with which you are familiar: the known. A diffuse field gives diffuse perceptions, causing you to walk around in a daze; a coherent field enhances your clarity of mind and provides greater depth to your experiences.

The first field holds your inventory. And the inventory focuses perception toward its own components. Business practices, courtship rituals, and common beliefs regarding an afterlife are part of one inventory. The Eagle, inorganic beings, omens, and the Rule are elements of another inventory. Combining them produces a third.

The entire energy body is the personal second field. It contains your essence, your completeness. It contains the known and unknown, and brushes against the unknowable. It is immersed within the human band of the Eagle's emanations. Even though it is but a part of those emanations, it contains infinite possibilities. Think of it: a circle is an infinite number of points which are connected. The energy body is spherical, and thus contains an infinite number of circles. This means that within the energy body there is an infinite number of possible perceptions. There is an infinite amount of unknown waiting to become known. And yet there are emanations known as the third field which exist beyond the scope of human awareness. Hence, it has no personal body, or form, relating to humanness.

The first field mirrors what is put into it. Our thoughts and habits lead our energy in certain directions, focusing perception but also distorting it. The objective, then, is to groom and temper it for the fewest number of distortions. To accomplish this, let's further distinguish between conditional and natural fields.

A conditional field is based on consensus, on agreements about reality. It requires many inflexible conditions about reality. It exists as a set of rules. From these rules emerge "accepted behavior." Through social conditioning, the first field becomes so static that it blocks perception of the second field. Thus the first field continuously mirrors itself, permitting little new awareness.

Reality becomes what we think it is, rather than an infinite mystery. A natural field, on the other hand, offers openness, flexibility, and adaptability. Whereas a conditional field blocks perception, a natural field automatically incorporates the second field.

Indeed, accomplishing the seer's three essential maneuvers is a matter of refining the first and second fields in order to acknowledge the third field. This precedence requires developing a natural field. By incorporating a complete unknowable in our inventory, we set the stage to move awareness beyond the human condition. This knowledge also permits us to remain open under all circumstances. The following diagram depicts the effects of conditional and natural fields.

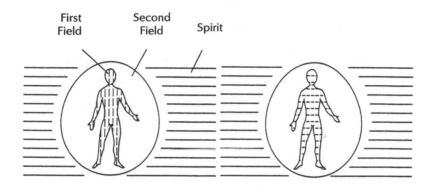

First Field    Second Field    Spirit

**Conditional First Field**          **Natural First Field**

The diagram on the left symbolizes how the first field might block awareness. On the right, the natural field yields to, and offers connections with, Spirit.

By experiencing the energy body, we can know that the second field exists; we can know parts of what it consists of, but not what it actually is. Interpretations of the second field automatically reduce awareness of it, making it part of our first-field inventory. Too rigid an interpretation produces a conditional field. An open, adaptable interpretation lets us take notice of it, and leads to a natural field.

Second-cycle Toltecs lost themselves in their well-defined version of reality. Their world enabled them to expand their perception, but only to certain limits. They possessed a very elaborate conditional field, and yet were equally possessed by it. Third-cycle Toltecs refined their worldview so that precedence was given to aligning personal energies with a natural field. At their best, nonordinary systems recondition the first field so that it may evolve from a conditional to a natural field.

Since the first field generates self-awareness, we don't want to get rid of it. We just need to temper it. An advantage of changing a conditional field into a natural field is gaining more awareness. Additionally, as it taps the second field, it also offers us more energy to use in our daily lives.

Realigning the first field into a natural field is where third-cycle ranger discipline enters. In essence, that discipline gives you the ability to go about your daily business while remaining aware of Spirit. You continually let go of conditions placed on reality in order to develop a natural relation with the world. Your openness permits more of your second field to influence you. You then discover more about yourself as you are sustained by your essence, requiring minimal self-reflection. Otherwise, you just experience in different ways what you already know. Don Juan says team leaders apply this lesson by not planning their actions. They let Spirit completely dictate their behavior (*Silence*, 172).

Donner takes this further as she relates a conversation from one of her mentors. In that talk, Zuleica, a member of don Juan's team, tells Donner that when a team leader is able to merge the face of self-reflection with the face of infinity, "the leader is totally ready to break the boundaries of reality and disappear as though he wasn't made of solid matter."[2] In other words, the person is ready to engage the Fire from Within.

Don Juan also says that team leaders must not have any points of defense (*Fire*, 52). Therefore, if they have reactive or conditional energy, they automatically remove their awareness from infinity and they are prevented from merging the face of self-reflection with the face of infinity. The question is how much a person can reduce his self-reflection without losing self-awareness. The greater the reduction, the greater the awareness beyond the first field. In practice, the team leaders' energies may then guide the entire team further through the unknown.

## Uniformity and Cohesion

Don Juan also says that the uniformity and cohesion of our energy bodies provide the key to perception (*Dreaming*, 40). Uniformity pertains to a standard shape of the energy body. Cohesion pertains to the pattern of energy within the energy body, and is also thought of as the dominant vibration.

In a sense, uniformity is like the standard physical shape of humans, and cohesion represents racial and cultural influences. Our physical structure molds the basics of how and what we as a species perceive. The location of our eyes and the vertical and horizontal partitioning of our brains, for instance, greatly influence how we perceive the physical world. Cultural influences act as filters and color our perception within the basic mold. Thus, cohesion paints the images of the world.

Cohesion also pertains to shifting energies within the energy body to alter uniformity. Evidently, second-cycle Toltecs stretched their energy bodies into straight lines (*Dreaming*, 13). That is, as they shifted their cohesion, the form of their energy bodies shifted, enabling them to perceive new worlds. As they achieved a new uniformity, they agreed on what they perceived. With the new consensus, they thought they'd arrived at the true reality. And so they closed off their awareness.

Since cohesion is the form of energy within the energy body, both conditional and natural fields reflect types of cohesion. For instance, a worldview consolidates energy into a conditional field. A natural field is more free-wheeling and less rigid than a conditional field; thus the cohesion is more supple and fluid. Perception is therefore permitted to entertain more insights and, indeed, entertain more worlds.

We fall into uniformity through birth. Each generation has its own uniformity which affects cohesion. As don Juan says, the shape of the energy body changes over time (*Dreaming*, 5). As a result, each generation has its own slant on reality. In other words, both uniformity and cohesion establish how perception focuses, thus bringing into focus what is perceived.

## Shaping Reality

Don Juan says that to make sense of our world we need to stay within boundaries (*Tales*, 190). The boundaries of any world are regulated by social consensus, or the social base, as don Juan terms it. An ordinary world usually has at its base the notion that physical objects are solid and separate. The base of the Toltec world holds that objects are different forms of energy, and that all energy originates from a single source. Indeed, a premise of don Juan's teachings is that the entire universe is made of energy first, form later (*Dreaming*, 3).

The energies from our geographical and cultural environments, associates, education and training, and goals, to name a few influences, all affect our cohesion. To establish how this energy formation works, the following is a brief outline of influences which create and maintain our boundaries and subsequently mold our perception. Therefore, each of these applies to energy body cohesion in sustaining ordinary and nonordinary worlds. Each can work for or against you. Knowing them helps you better manage your energies. Keep in mind that intent is always the predominant influence. Due to its importance, a complete section has been devoted to it.

**Selective-cueing.** Selective-cueing consists of emphasizing and de-emphasizing pieces of the world. Don Juan says that perceiving the energy body, dreaming, and perceiving inorganic beings result from stabilizing the focal point at specific locations (*Dreaming*, 69). The focal point shift occurs by first calling attention to something's existence and then reinforcing the experience through exercises designed to build and harness energy. The added energy then allows the focal point to move and re-stabilize.

In ordinary reality, we're taught to look for material items and to dismiss experiences with inorganic beings, for example, as imagination. Our ordinary definition of life hinges on life consisting of organic matter, whereas don Juan teaches that consciousness determines life, be it organic or inorganic (*Dreaming*, 45). Therefore, exactly what we are taught, how reality is selectively-cued to us, determines the extent of our limitations.

As don Juan groomed Castaneda, he selectively-cued what to look for and what to avoid. For instance, by stressing nonattachment and losing self-importance, he cued perceptual liberation rather than second-cycle power tricks. His teachings about Toltec history cued the differences between and the results of following second- and third-cycle avenues. In addition, his instruction on inorganic beings brought an imaginative concept into concrete reality.

**Projection.** A common definition of projection is "attributing one's own traits and attitudes to others."[3] In terms of energy fields, remember that energy body cohesion stabilizes the focal point. A stable focal point indicates sufficient numbers of elements within a given world have been consolidated.

The ability to develop a nonordinary conditional field is what don Juan means when he says we have the option of revamping our interpretation system. A system allows us to project and thus predict our environment. The drawback, he says, is that we continue to perceive in terms of a system, rather than from our senses (*Dreaming*, 97, 76). More to the point, we act according to our thoughts. And our thoughts are organized by a system, by a version of reality. Constant self-reflection binds perception to a system's conditional field. Recognizing these blinders, a viable system provides stepping stones for the shift to Spirit by instructing you to use all of your senses.

Don Juan also provides another option, that of disregarding systems. This significantly enlarges the scope of what can be perceived. But without a system, you may lose direction. If you approach the method with great care, however, not using a system might also speed your growth. With either approach, generating a natural field requires suspending all interpretations as any interpretation is conditional. It reduces potential to form.

This reduction is projection. It is interpreting the world based on a specific cohesion. That is, it requires fitting what is perceived into pre-established forms, and that process then establishes the conditions of your energy fields. For instance, how you interpret another's behavior stems from your cohesion. You project your awareness onto another and reduce what you perceive into categories meaningful to you. From this realization, we find that reality is a gigantic self-fulfilling prophecy. How we interpret our experiences, then, is determined by how we have consolidated our energy fields. An inventory produces a significant part of this consolidation. Thus we see the value of grooming our inventories in order to throw them away. Doing so, says don Juan, frees our energy fields and thereby frees the focal point (*Fire*, 256). We can enhance our world through inventories, then create room to enhance it further by throwing them away.

**Closure.** By throwing away your inventory, you set the stage to expand your perception. The flip side of expansion is closure. Closure relates to a human need to brings things into focus. When reading a paragraph with a word deleted, for example, most people automatically insert a word that makes sense, never noticing the blank space. Or, when talking about seers' explanations, don Juan says our need to explain is too great to rely on describing only what is *seen* (*Dreaming*, 8). Thus, we have an inherent need to provide context. Context offers multi-level perspectives; from context emanates personal and social meaning. We reduce what we perceive in order to focus, and then expand that into thinking it applies to everything.

Closure forges the paths you walk. If we didn't seek closure, we wouldn't learn. The idea here, however, is to keep your options open and your paths free and unencumbered. Otherwise, closure creates a prison for perception rather than an understanding for pursuing freedom.

**Entrainment.** Entrainment pertains to developing cohesion by following, or entraining to, specific influences. Innate predilections, environmental influences, and astrological influences, to name a few, all shape cohesion in some manner. For example, as we are fed a worldview by our parents, teachers, and peers, we gradually develop a cohesion which then stabilizes that worldview. We have entrained our perception to those influences.

Power plants temporarily entrain perception to nonordinary worlds. They offer glimpses of the second field. By using a nonordinary worldview to entrain and remold cohesion, the person can then learn to handle the second field without the use of mind-altering substances. Taking this further, as don Juan points out, the success of psychic surgery relies on the patient entraining to the cohesion of the surgeon. To accomplish this, the healer must remove all doubt from the patient's mind (*Silence*, 142).

Just as entire populations entrain to a worldview, entire populations can step off one path and into an entirely new reality. I believe this is what the tenant meant when he told Castaneda that whole populations have disappeared through dreaming (*Dreaming*, 232). For instance, popular mythology often portrays the lost continent of Atlantis as corrupt, with inhabitants whose misuse of power led to its complete destruction.

But what if they weren't corrupt, and didn't blow Atlantis apart as a result of misusing power? What if they were a race of Toltec-like seers who decided to step fully into another dimension? If so, perhaps the only way those who were left behind could comprehend this feat was to fill in the blanks based on their less-developed understanding. Destruction by a power they understood worked better for them than willfully stepping into another dimension. In less than a heartbeat, their interpretation created the actual destruction, which then left them to scatter to the four winds.

Then again, perhaps it was yet another scenario, a combination of the two. Perhaps when they *saw* the coming destruction, the seers were able to band a portion of the population together. Binding their energies, they achieved a sufficient mass of energy to step into another dimension.

Then again. . .

**Reality Consensus.** A conditional field is the entrainment of perception to social agreements, an exceedingly powerful form of closure. It produces a consensus of "reality." In itself, there is nothing terrible about this entrainment. We all have a need to make sense to ourselves and to others about the world. Difficulties arise when the consensus interferes with personal growth.

One of the more insidious effects of consensus is "groupthink." Groupthink is "thinking so dominated by the desire to maintain unanimity of thought in a group that critical thinking is suspended or rendered ineffective."[4] Groupthink is a form of peer pressure. Members reinforce among themselves what to do and what to think. Groupthink, therefore, creates a rigid cohesion.

As reality is an effect of groupthink, the complexity of social agreements at this level almost automatically precludes critical thinking. The scale is simply too vast and too energy-consuming for most people to undertake reappraisals. However, the ability to behave independently of peer pressure marks a significant step toward freedom. Keep in mind that the beginning of groupthink is the minor agreements that first bond, and then bind, us.

As don Juan says, in order to evolve we must first free ourselves from the bindings of the social order. Don Juan adds that in order for humans to survive, we must change our perception at the social base, at the level of common consensus (*Dreaming,* 176, 3). Rather than perceive a world of objects, for instance, he maintains we must first perceive a world of energy. Since the world would no longer be perceived as a material object for material gain, perhaps this shift in perception would lead to a greater and deeper harmony with the world. Perhaps this is why he thought the shift is so crucial.

Since we create our sense of the world by staying within boundaries, Toltecs use dreaming to step outside of boundaries. As Donner says, Toltecs are involved in "an abstract pursuit of re-making ourselves outside the parameters of what the social order has defined and allowed us to be."[5] Still, Toltecs develop agreements on a general worldview and ways to remake themselves. While these social agreements may be nonordinary, they are, nevertheless, social agreements. The trick is to use them as thrust to propel perception beyond any social base into decidedly unique and personal realms.

**Association.** Whatever is called to mind when you see, smell, hear, taste, or feel something is association. It acts as a form of entrainment. And it's how we build stereotypes. Through association you habitually isolate familiar components of your inventory. For instance, a flash of intuition reminds you of a trip to Paris. So maybe you think about how to return to Paris rather than about how to develop intuition. Whatever habits you have produce cohesion. If you're too habitual, you produce excessive closure. Your perception then whirls about inside a box. As a result, you merely validate and revalidate your world rather than step into new worlds.

Association also enables you to build categories such as dreaming and tracking. An element of dreaming, for instance, is traveling within dreams. If you have a flying dream, you can associate it with dreaming practices rather than with just having an interesting dream. With sufficient associations, you can learn to command dreaming. If you associate an unexpected cool breeze with elemental spirits, for another example, you can begin to focus on their world. With sufficient nonordinary experiences, you can associate yourself with an entirely different reality.

Not only does association help build realities, it also pertains to personal habits. For example, a person takes a drink of alcohol, relaxes a bit, and then has some clever insight. I think most people who have drunk alcohol can readily associate with this. Indeed, in *The Varieties of Religious Experience,* William James contends that people use alcohol because it offers glimpses of mystical realities.[6] Then seeking to gain more insight, the person consumes more alcohol. Through careful self-observation, the person then finds that whereas one drink may have assisted contemplation, repeated use has dulled it. Among the questions are: How long does it take a person to associate drinking with a lack of insight? And, how long does it then take the person to change his behavior?

**Expectation.** What you expect to perceive aims your intent, which then produces those results. If you expect to find a lower astral plane inhabited by negative entities, and an upper astral plane inhabited by good-guy entities, that's what you're likely find if you go out-of-body. If you expect people to walk all over you, you're generating the energy for that exact occurrence. If you expect to grow, you will. You view the world which is offered by your worldview and supported by your behavior. You find what you look for, and what you look for is based on what kind of options you give yourself.

**Contrary Evidence.** In our efforts to maintain cohesion, we tend to ignore perceptions which don't fit with the way we think things ought to be. For instance, on several occasions during conversations on male-female relationships, women have told me that women alone decide whether or not a woman and man will have sex. Men are viewed as totally reactive to women's desires. Overall, there is probably truth in the statement; people are influenced beyond reason by sexual energy. Yet to dispel this notion as all-encompassing, all we need do is witness a man turn down an invitation for a date or decline a sexual advance. Men, in turn, similarly trap themselves when they disregard evidence that women can't handle executive-level positions. There are simply too many good female executives and successful female-owned companies to harbor such prejudice.

Regarding nonordinary realities, we are often taught to ignore the substance of dreams as they are "just something we do during sleep." Dreaming-body activity is chalked up as imagination. A life-directing vision is mere imagination. As don Juan says, we interpret unknown expressions of the second field as something familiar (*Tales*, 190).

Also pay attention for contrary evidence as you investigate nonordinary teachings. At times, finding contradictions may suggest a fallacy in another's research. At other times, it may require additional research to understand what's going on. For example, Castaneda is told that to be aware of being in two places at once is the same as meeting his double (his second-field counterpart) face to face. Such a meeting results in death. "That is the rule," says don Juan. "That is the way Power has set things up" (*Tales*, 52). Now, compare this with don Juan being thrown into a river by Julian. As the river carries him downstream, don Juan observes his double running downstream with him. He lives to tell the story (*Silence*, 255).

At the very least these incidents hint at contradiction, and thus pieces of contrary evidence. So what's going on? Does it mean Castaneda's work is not valid? Or did he inadvertently distort don Juan's teachings? Or does it mean that don Juan used the threat of death to make Castaneda pay strict attention? After all, it is not unlike don Juan to trick Castaneda into learning. On the other hand, if the statement is in some way true, what exactly are the conditions of "face to face"? We have evidence that merely observing one's double doesn't mean certain death. But we also have another passage in which Castaneda finds himself observing his sleeping double. He says he "knew that it was deadly for me to awaken myself." If so, the question arises: Is *touching* one's double life-threatening? Through additional research, we find don Juan saying that "direct physical contact" with the second energy field results in death (*Tales,* 73, 185). As the second field is the double's turf, we come full circle to the initial question.

Just as in traversing any part of this path, assessing contradictions always rests in your hands. Just make sure you apply rigorous research standards. Whether you find fallacy, or flush out the details, you've benefitted. If you don't take the time to fully examine the situation, you're certain to remain within a conditional field.

By failing to recognize contrary evidence, at best we remain off balance with ourselves. We simply can't develop awareness by refusing awareness. At worst, failure to pay attention produces a false sense of invincibility—the same feeling that led to the downfall of the Toltec world. We must not arbitrarily dismiss evidence. At the same time, being onto something doesn't mean you've found it. You can't manage knowledge by taking a scrap of evidence, associating it with your interests, then generalizing the scrap into a broad-base conclusion.

**Cognitive Dissonance.** Cognitive dissonance is defined as "an uncomfortable psychological state in which the individual experiences two incompatible beliefs or cognitions."[7] It follows that the person has to ease the tension, reduce the dissonance. In general, if your energy fields aren't working in harmony, you experience discomfort. As Tiggs says, people have talked about the split and imbalance between mind and body. "But the real dichotomy is between physical body and energy body."[8] Ignoring the imbalance leads to dysfunction. Paying attention to it leads to conflict resolution, especially in Toltec matters.

To illustrate cognitive dissonance, in Castaneda's *The Art of Dreaming,* don Juan says second-cycle seers moved their focal points into the unknowable. By definition, this means that they placed their focal points outside their energy bodies. This movement is what altered their energy bodies, producing straight-line instead of ball-shaped uniformity. In the same book, he later says the second cycle concerned themselves only with shifts focusing on the human unknown (*Dreaming,* 12, 80). Again, by his definitions, this means they chose to stay within the energy body and the human band of Earth, shifting to various plant and animal forms.

I felt jolted by this apparent inconsistency. It struck me as a glaring contradiction and created a dissonance; I temporarily lost my sense of the continuity of don Juan's teachings. Almost as a setup, in the same book, don Juan speaks of losing your bearings. He says that when you lose your sense of direction, your worldview rallies to make the world anew (*Dreaming,* 76). So I set about further detailing the regions of the energy body. After months of tracking and dreaming the matter, I arrived at a scheme that achieved a more in-depth feeling of consistency. Once I reconciled the disparity, this struggle also reinforced my quest to adhere to Spirit as a means to approach the unknowable. I didn't want to rely too heavily on any teaching, including Toltec.

Considering a method, I felt that by completely following Spirit, rather than following social conventions, I could let Spirit unfold within me on its own terms. With time, this would naturally bring my essence to the foreground. Then, just as I outgrow phases of my life, I would gradually outgrow the entire domain of human experience as Spirit grew through and within me. I felt that this would be my way to experience the Fire from Within. I also understood better a teaching from Elias, don Juan's benefactor and Julian's teacher. He advised to seek the artistry in life, to gain freedom from any and all perceptual conventions (*Silence,* 285).

**Application.** Using as an example your quest to learn to use the dreaming body, here's how these elements work:

1. Through selective-cueing, you hear about the dreaming body.

2. Using projection, you can entertain what the experience might be like. You've also gained a structure to make sense of dreaming experiences.

3. Through associating your experiences with the stories you've heard, you hook onto something outside of your known world.

4. Expectation of results focuses your energies.

5. By regularly performing perception-enhancing exercises, you eventually entrain to and experience the dreaming body.

6. Since this interdicts your ordinary worldview, you experience cognitive dissonance.

7. Remembering lessons about contrary evidence gets you over this hurdle. You then seek to restore balance since you can no longer turn your back on the actuality of the dreaming body.

8. The more experience you have, the more you experience closure. That is, you've gained a new sense of stability with the dreaming body. Just remember that this is not the time to rest. Don't let closure turn you off.

You may apply these elements to different capacities. For instance, apply them to other nonordinary experiences, such as *seeing*. Then step by step watch yourself build another inventory and shape a new world.

# 6
# Awareness of the Self Beyond

Don Juan says that humans have the capacity to perceive many worlds. Our ordinary world, he says, "is only one in a cluster of consecutive worlds, arranged like the layers of an onion" (*Dreaming*, viii). He adds that other worlds exist independently of our awareness, and all that is necessary to perceive them is to have sufficient energy.

Metaphysical systems develop schematics to explore these worlds. These maps provide context and technique. Context is critical, as it provides reference points for the new terrain. When you glimpse a new order of knowledge, context enables you to capitalize on it. For example, a common reaction to *seeing* is to dismiss it as an anomaly of physical eyesight. Or a reaction might take on more significance. One person told me that after he began regularly *seeing* unusual light, he wondered if he were losing his mind. But by placing his experiences into a context that included their validity, he not only relieved his anxiety but found a way to develop his new perceptions.

A viable context must also contain provisions for stepping outside of its borders. When the schematic becomes too factual, too conditional, a system degenerates into dogma. Just as the maps of cities, states, and nations change with time, so do the landscapes of perception. As the known world expands, metaphysical maps must take new awareness into account and evolve as well. For instance, what the ancient occult maxim "as above, so below" tries to get across is today represented by the notion of a holographic universe; namely, that each and every part of anything contains the structure of all its other parts.

Technique, in turn, is equally important, as it establishes the actual awareness of the new terrain. The technique of gazing, for example, fosters *seeing*. Whereas context points the way, technique enables energy alignments that produce the shifts. By using an open-ended context, techniques then carry an additional payload of transporting you past the context. That is, techniques may then produce awareness beyond the system.

A Toltec schematic indicates that if we change the fixation of our awareness, we realize that the physical world was never really physical. It is another form of energy.[1] As for technique, dreaming and tracking provide ways to realize that viewpoint. But both context and technique are aspects of an inventory. To prevent the inventory from becoming dogma, don Juan suggests that we put in the time to make very accurate inventories, then laugh at them, knowing they are just schemes of our minds (*Fire*, 256). This freedom opens the gateway to a seer's domain.

## Energy Fields

A major portion of the Toltec scheme of things is selectively-cueing the first, second, and third energy fields. Each field is infinite. They are also intertwined and at their source—the Eagle—are one. (The Eagle, remember, doesn't really exist. Yet, as it can be *seen*, it does. It is everywhere and nowhere.) However, they are also separate. As each energy field exists as a result of having its own emanations, each field has its own properties. These fields may also be thought of as bands of energy. By stepping out of the first band into the second, for example, you step into worlds beyond the ordinary.

In the beginning stages of developing this model, the first field is often described as the physical world. The organ for perceiving this domain is the physical body. The second field is presented as a luminous, energetic world. Within this domain, the energy body is an individual's organ of perception. The physical and energy bodies are deemed to comprise human awareness. The third field is temporarily dismissed as irrelevant. Tackling it too soon only interferes with learning the basics.

Later, the terms shift and the first field becomes the known, the familiar, or order. The second field becomes the unknown, and the third field is deemed unknowable, as there are no points of reference for it within human consciousness. This change of terms radically alters the possibilities. Redefining the physical world as what is known opens doors to perceive it anew. Rather than lock away its potentials under a stream of thoughts about what "physical" means, it becomes the energy we're familiar with. As such, it becomes more malleable. It can be managed as energy, rather than as something concrete. This clears the way for the possibility of performing the Fire from Within, of making a leap in awareness where the physical body fully evaporates from this dimension. And by introducing the third field, you now know where to place your awareness. Through a death-defying maneuver, you enter an energy field outside the first and second fields. In short, you transcend the human condition.

## The Energy Body

The huge energy spent focusing on the known world ordinarily precludes development of the unknown. But dealing with the unknown is at the heart of Toltec craft. Since developing the energy body is the means to go about entering it, let's step further into that world.

Don Juan says that both the physical body and the energy body are energy, but the energy body is pure. He places added emphasis on the energy body by saying that it is responsible for awareness in general (*Dreaming*, 1, 8). The right side perceives the known world while the left side perceives the unknown. As seers expand the right side into the left side, the unknown is reduced and the known world is expanded.

We typically control an extremely narrow margin of the right side, indicating the cohesion of ordinary reality. Nonordinary abilities begin to form as we tap the left side. To gain "total perception" of a crow don Juan had to learn to use his left side. He tells Castaneda that he learned step by step to make a complete shift in his cohesion; a cohesion from which he fully perceived the world as a crow (*Dreaming*, 217). By agreeing with others about our experiences, we develop a nonordinary reality, thereby expanding what is known.

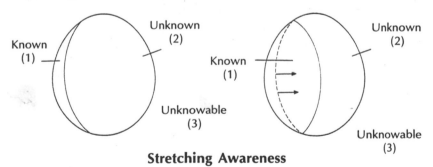

**Stretching Awareness**

The energy body contains the first and second energy fields. The right side of the energy body is considered the known, and the left side the unknown. By pushing your right-side energies into your left side, you expand your known world. The Fire from Within occurs upon stretching the right side completely through the energy body. Both fields then act as one, enabling you to transport your awareness into the third energy field.

Tracking and dreaming combine to generate deliberate cohesion shifts. Tracking characterizes right-side, first-field techniques; dreaming characterizes left-side, second-field techniques. Don Juan teaches that the second field needs to be tempered by the first field. Put another way, he says that to use the second field the first field must prevail (*Tales*, 253, 265). Otherwise we'd get lost meandering about in the second field and lose relation and meaning with our known world. Perhaps this is the fate of some people confined to psychiatric hospitals.

## The Focal Point

Cohesion gives you an angle on how to perceive the world. Changes in cohesion can be measured by focal point shifts. A coagulation of energy filaments (emanations) intersecting with the energy body produce the focal point (*Dreaming*, 7). An integrated cohesion produces a stable, or fixed, focal point. In other words, as you acquire cohesion you steady the focal point in place. With a stable focal point, you perceive a stable world. Shift cohesion and you shift the focal point. Consequently, you shift your world.

Tracking consists of procedures to acquire cohesion. Dreaming consists of practices to gather energy in order to shift cohesion. Applying both, we find that sustaining a dream is learning how to fix the focal point in a nonordinary location.

The content of any perception, says don Juan, depends on the location of the focal point (*Silence*, 165). That is, since cohesion is the pattern of energy within the energy body, the focal point indicates the nature of that pattern. As previously stated, the third cycle discovered that the focal point doesn't generate perception. It marks it. By using the focal point as a reference, seers have a way to make their cohesion shifts more exacting. They have a marker to define what kinds of shifts they pursue.

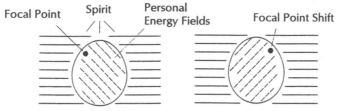

Focal Point    Spirit    Personal Energy Fields    Focal Point Shift

### Shifting the Focal Point

The structure of energy, or cohesion, within the energy body determines the location of the focal point. Shift your cohesion and you shift the focal point, thereby changing what you perceive.

There are also other indicators of cohesion. In *The Holographic Universe,* Michael Talbot reports on experiments by Valarie Hunt, a physical therapist and professor of kinesiology at UCLA. Talbot writes, "Hunt has discovered that an electromyograph, a device used to measure the electrical activity in the muscles, can also pick up the electrical presence of the human energy field."[2] Hunt has also correlated certain behaviors with specific frequencies. Psychics, for example, are reported to have energy fields vibrating at two to four times the normal rate of physical-body frequencies.

Another marker for types of cohesion is the color of the auric field. A color, as you know, is a certain frequency. Wiggle your finger quickly enough and you'll see color emanating from it. It turns out that Hunt also matched certain electrical-wave patterns with the findings of aura readers. Since several readers reported *seeing* the same color in a person's energy fields, Hunt was able to match patterns of electromyograph frequencies with specific colors. As a result, Hunt's experiments also provide evidence that people can learn to perceive another dimension of frequencies, or energy fields. *Seeing* auras is one result.

Therefore, the color of auric fields, physically measured frequencies, and focal point locations all represent a person's state of being. These markers are not the substance of cohesion. They reflect it, and thus can be used to measure or diagnose it. Perceiving the energy body itself is going a step beyond these indicators.

Excessive fatigue, stress, or anxiety can make a focal point shift. When the energy upholding a cohesion runs low, there's no energy to maintain it. A shift may then result. In turn, the first time the focal point shifts often produces anxiety or even fear. Losing your lifelong definition of reality is disconcerting. Anxiety often reappears as you shift into new realms. When Castaneda faced the inorganic world the first time, he experienced fear and revulsion (*Dreaming,* 39). He later dealt with that world smoothly and proficiently. The initial reaction of high anxiety is most likely what happened to the couple whose focal points shifted near a tree and they felt terror, which they attributed to the tree rather than to a significant focal point shift.

Do you see the effect these different interpretations have? On the one hand, experience with another dimension summons fear. On the other hand, a focal point shift produces a temporary disassociation from normal occurrences. The lack of familiarity produces anxiety. One interpretation conjures a hostile world, while the other examines processes of perception.

Examination of process provides a wider context to elevate perception. Becoming a Toltec requires immersing yourself in its way of going about things long enough to shift your cohesion. You then perceive a Toltec world. A seer, in turn, aims for more comprehension. Therefore a seer studies systems, cohesion, the focal point, and the forces shaping perception. Thus a seer acquires the freedom to develop cohesions that provide more context and comprehension than the cohesions systems offer.

In ordinary reality we have not only fixated the focal point, we have immobilized it. Thus we perceive no options other than those reflected by that reality. Participating with a nonordinary worldview, we find that it also molds our perception and behavior to the views and dictates within itself. As don Juan states, in both cases the world is perceived according to the system of reality rather than from the senses (*Dreaming*, 76). Seers, therefore, rely on their ability to shift their focal points fluidly. A system is then properly relegated to being a step along a more significant path. Not only does this approach prevent you from getting bogged down in a version of the world, it clears and frees other modes of perception.

## Cornerstones of Perception

The cornerstones of perception reside within the energy body. Each is a separate mode of awareness. Handling reason and the intellect, for instance, is different from handling the dreaming cornerstone. The manner in which the cornerstones are used determines whether a person remains in an ordinary world, develops a nonordinary world, or expands beyond both.

Don Juan says that the first field suppresses awareness of the second field by the obvious (*Tales*, 132). That is, any time the second field surfaces we make the occurrence fit into what we know. We rationalize it and produce a self-reflective, conditional world. As the diagram below indicates, the cornerstones reason and talking uphold self-reflective worlds. *Will*, on the other hand, taps additional modes and permits direct perception.

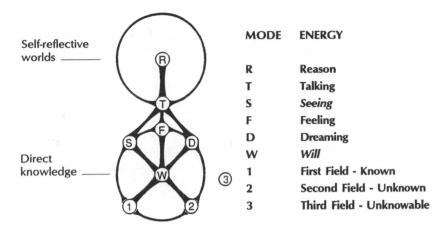

| MODE | ENERGY |
|------|--------|
| R | Reason |
| T | Talking |
| S | *Seeing* |
| F | Feeling |
| D | Dreaming |
| W | *Will* |
| 1 | First Field - Known |
| 2 | Second Field - Unknown |
| 3 | Third Field - Unknowable |

Self-reflective worlds ———

Direct knowledge ———

## The Cornerstones of Perception[3]

The cornerstones of perception are what don Juan calls
the eight points of the totality of one's being. He says that
we all have these modes of perception but the means
of presenting them varies (*Tales*, 98).

**Talking.** During the course of the day, watch yourself reflect on almost each and every thing that happens. This is like that, that is like so, and that ought to be something else. We go on and on, talking to ourselves about how the world is or should be.

As an agent of reason, talking helps stabilize cohesion. Mental energy directs other energies along its paths. Too much of this activity and cohesion calcifies. As don Juan says, "The new seers say that when we were taught to talk to ourselves, we were taught the means to dull ourselves in order to keep the assemblage point fixed on one spot" (*Fire*, 153).

To take advantage of this entrainment and to begin developing a nonordinary reality, you simply need to fill yourself up with a nonordinary inventory. In order to step beyond any worldview, you need to quiet and stop your talk. Since you don't reflect on ideas of the world, you don't maintain a view. You can then directly tap the world's energies.

**Reason.** Reason takes talking, synthesizes it, and produces a sense of order. How reasonable we are is a measure of how our cohesion matches the prevailing social consensus. The degree of success demonstrates how well we've molded ourselves to fit in.

But, again, this is projection in that by doing so we try to conform the world to the boundaries of our thoughts, a limited form of energy.

Seers are not anti-reason. Don Juan suggested that Castaneda cultivate his reason in order to avoid excesses (*Dreaming*, 8). Donner also learned that Toltecs need a well-developed rational side to leap into the unknown.[4] As a matter of course, teachers use reason to entrain their apprentices' energies. Selectively-cueing the mysteries of the world and the wonders of moving the focal point, for instance, aims energy away from self-reflection and toward new involvements. Through selective-cueing, reason also assists the forging of pathways to the other cornerstones. Discussing the rational value of dreaming, for instance, helps motivate a person to experiment with it.

All these maneuvers temper the first field, a major emphasis in a ranger's training. Through this discipline, there comes a time when the first field has been sufficiently buttressed, leading to letting cohesion shift into other patterns. During a Toltec apprenticeship, don Juan says, the sheer weight of nonordinary options reduces the fixation of the first field (*Tales*, 177). Reducing this hold automatically opens you to the second field. *Will* upholds this new relation to the world.

*Will.* An effect of the Eagle's emanations, *will* is the force of energy alignment. As though it were a umbilical cord, an individual's *will* connects directly with the emanations. It does not pertain to being willful. It is an impersonal force; yet it is the focus of your personal intent, or inner spirit. Located at the midpoint of your physical body, it also represents balance.

As the chart indicates, *will* upholds dreaming, feeling, and *seeing*. Talking indirectly connects with *will* through these cornerstones. While we can talk about them, they must be activated in their own right. Thus we can use them, but our understanding of them remains limited. Throughout this book, there are exercises that develop them just as reading, writing, and debating develop reason and talking.

*Will* also directly connects individual awareness with the first and second fields. Notice that these fields do not connect with talking because, in essence, they are mysterious. Whatever is said about them is just talk. But to get on with the program, their existence needs to be cued. We need to be aware that there is something there, and that we can deal with it.

Typically, *will* rests dormant as we rely on reason to carry us through our lives. Activating *will* means you can exercise deliberate control of your energy body and its alignments. At this stage, talking and reason only support these alignments. When you think of a reality, for instance, mental energy helps you participate in that view. But only partially. It is not a full-bodied experience because your experiences all go to your head (the brain being reason's abode). *Will*, in turn, enables full participation with the energies that are only described by a worldview: energies such as those associated with the dreaming body, psychic phenomena, nonordinary healing, and other dimensions.

Using *will* also renders asunder most worldviews. A three-dimensional view of the world gives way to other formats. As don Juan says, "When we perceive the world with our *will* we know that it is not as 'out there' or 'as real' as we think" (*Separate*, 181). Internal and external worlds mirror each other. Consequently, there is only what we perceive and how we relate to it. And depending on the pattern of your cohesion, there are a myriad of ways to relate.

Feeling, dreaming, and *seeing* each perceives energy in different ways. Feeling is like having a guiding light illuminating your path; dreaming allows you to explore and test new behaviors in this and other dimensions; and *seeing* offers comprehensive insight or knowing. With a functional *will*, these modes operate on command.

**Feeling**. Feeling is like water. It molds perception like a river cutting its way through the earth. Formless, it can also be molded. How you feel about something helps form your worldview. In turn, your worldview helps forge how you feel about things.

To begin educating feeling, don't always act on your thoughts. Within the limits of not bringing harm to another or to yourself, act according to how you feel. Regularly go out for a walk and follow your heart faithfully and fearlessly. Don't censor your intuition.

This exercise also liberates thinking. Since you're not going to act on your thoughts, you feel easier about exploring them. In the same manner, don't always act on your feelings. People tend to be swayed by talk laced with emotional vehemence. The certainty associated with emotional intensity is often misconstrued as a sign of truth. So a person might naively believe the other person knows better. More likely, this passion relates to self-righteousness and self-indulgence. And self-righteous doesn't mean right.

Ordinary leadership is often associated with swaying people along certain channels. And so a person with great charisma is often seen as a great leader. But this doesn't always equate with leading a person or a population to freedom. More likely it is intricate spell-casting and skullduggery designed to get people to follow a certain path for self-related interests.

Paradoxically, reducing emotional excitement develops intensity, or the density of energy. Holding waves of emotion in abeyance permits a more detailed assessment of your feelings. At the same time, too much caution dampens feeling. When saturated with feeling, such as frequently experienced during dreaming, don't fight it. Don't concern yourself with losing control. But don't necessarily act on it either. Experience it. Gain knowledge from it. Then act.

Furthermore, if you're not tracking the emotional communication in any situation, then you're missing a significant part of what's going on. You then reduce your ability to accurately interpret events. To do better, set aside personal biases. For example, if you align with another's energy and then feel angry, it doesn't mean the other person is also angry. Your perception must be clear to accurately assess if that is the case. Otherwise you're in the throes of projection.

In later chapters, there are several techniques which serve to educate and manage feeling. For now, to sense the energies of the first and second fields, try the following:

1. Attend to sensations on the surface of your physical body.
2. Attend to sensations and emotions within your physical body.
3. Attend to sensations of more subtle energy from the surface of your physical body to 2 feet away from it.
4. Attend to sensations of subtle energy within your physical body.

**Dreaming**. Dreaming grants direct access to the second field, which, in our day and time, is the greater portion of the energy body. Hence it provides a strong step toward knowledge. You actively use feeling while dreaming. In fact, emotions are the clay of dreaming. And intent is the molding of that clay.

As a mode of perception, dreaming involves no strategies, no processes. It just is. The cornerstone dreaming, however, differs from the technique of dreaming. Dreaming as technique incorporates tracking. Thus we can purposefully tap and use the second field. Since the technique relies on the cornerstone, and since it

is a fundamental part of the Toltec Way, a full section is devoted
to it.

*Seeing.* *Seeing* is the capstone of the cornerstones. Any good
metaphysical philosophy leads you to *seeing*, which then transports
you beyond the philosophy. Recognizing this power, don Juan
says that while a Toltec may have *will*, he may not necessarily
be able to *see* proficiently (*Separate*, 181). That is, a functional
*will* is the mark of a Toltec. A seer steps beyond this level into
an even greater sense of the whole.

*Seeing* obviates worldviews. Time and time again, to *see* you
have to discard what you think is true. To do this, you must
surrender your sense of self. Awareness of being a part of the
world is required for such an alignment. And as don Juan says,
to exercise *seeing* you must become nothing by becoming everything. You vanish but are still there (*Separate*, 186).

With *seeing*, you peer through the surface of the material world
and tune into the movement of energy itself. This process requires
keen dedication. One of don Juan's apprentices, la Gorda, remarked
that while we all *see*, we choose not to remember (*Second Ring*,
265). But, as don Juan says, *seeing* is not difficult. What is difficult
is breaking the retaining wall in our minds which holds our
perception in place (*Dreaming*, 9).

*Seeing* is not imagination. Nor is it visualization. It is gaining
knowledge without using words. And it takes on different forms.
It can be a particular feeling, a direct and sudden knowing, or a
display of light. You might *see* auric fields, energy patterns like
waves rising from hot asphalt, a soft rain of light, visions, elemental
spirits, or the Eagle's emanations. It requires a greater degree of
alignment than usual. For instance, seeing a coffee table results
from aligning the first energy fields of the table and yourself.
*Seeing* that same table requires alignment between the second
fields as well.

Everyone *sees* uniquely, making it often hard to come to terms
with the concept. One person might *see* wavy lines of energy,
while another *sees* the same thing as blue light. Having to
communicate through words what you perceive nonverbally also
adds confusion to verifying its validity. There are, however, some
common features. When you *see* during the day, for example, the
world often becomes dark. Conversely, when you *see* at night the
world may light up. The first time I *saw* an aura, a bright afternoon
day turned hauntingly dark. While I knew of auras, I had not yet

learned of the changes in light. So I probably would have panicked had I not begun to *see* the violet, blue, and yellow of a person's aura. I then knew I was *seeing* rather than going blind.

*Seeing* requires using the entire body, which is why don Juan stresses keeping the physical body in good shape. *Seeing* during dreaming also reduces the strain of developing it. You have more energy and less stress since you've already elevated your awareness. At times, *seeing* during dreaming works like this: After having dinner with a friend, I *saw* her that night while dreaming. Her energy body looked like a balloon filled with gently swirling light. Her surrounding aura gracefully shifted and danced as she approached. I noticed a deeper energy shift as she changed her intent. It became more focused when she physically moved, and relaxed when she talked. Then I suddenly "knew" she was focused on healing.

Upon waking, I experienced a double memory. I remembered *seeing* while dreaming. I also remembered *seeing* the exact thing during our evening engagement. A few weeks later she told me she had been in an intense period of physical conditioning. Soon after, she planned to hike the entire Appalachian Trail. During the hike she planned to work on prior emotional traumas in order to heal herself.

To get started with *seeing*, try the following exercise. The first four steps are also preliminaries of gazing. Gazing suspends conditional energy fields. Supplying the intent of *seeing* then moves the focal point, and paves the way to *see*.

1. Unfocus your eyes while looking at the physical world.

2. Pick one object. Look toward it but don't focus your eyesight on it. Gaze at it.

3. Relax.

4. To further align your energies with the object, feel your energy move out of your physical body and closer to the object. Then feel its energy enter your awareness. Become one with the object.

5. Listen with your entire body. Ease the stress on your eyes. Keep them unfocused and relaxed. Let them remain "soft."

6. Notice anything out of the ordinary. Attend to, but don't focus on, any spots, colors, images, or energy patterns. If you try to single these out too soon, they're most likely to disappear, as they're glimpses of the second field. With practice, you can maintain them. With continued practice, you move beyond them into deeper realms of *seeing*.

*Seeing* requires deep relaxation and intense inner concentration. This balancing act may be the hardest part to learn. To develop it, practice gazing. Extensively. Gazing opens pathways to feeling, dreaming, and *seeing*. Tips to develop it are in Chapter 10. In addition, Chapter 10 has precautions to use when you're by yourself and when you're gazing with others.

## Transition from Reason to *Will*

The shift from reason to *will* results from implementing a strategy and from plenty of practice. Strategy involves detailing your evolution to include the shift. Practice stems from exercising tracking, dreaming, and the cornerstones. These workouts tune perception into the regions outlined by the strategy. In this instance, the goal is to develop the entire energy body.

It's important not to fight reason. Let it be. Let energy flow to and from it. One way to exercise reason is to develop it so that it recognizes its limits. As it picks up data from *will*, it loosens its grip by learning that it simply can't account for everything.

Remember that reason is a major instrument in developing cohesion. Using it to develop a nonordinary cohesion makes you fluent enough to accept the possibility of focal point shifts. By making reason secure, it lets go. You then find that dipping into the infinite order of the first field offers a better, more comprehensive sense of structure than provided by reason alone. Rather than dominating, reason then works in partnership with the other cornerstones.

As you continue your practice, the second field begins to surface. As it does, you find new approaches to old tasks. While Donner was visiting don Juan's team in Mexico, she worked on some homework, a university term paper. While struggling to make it coherent, her second field surfaced. As though by magic, before her eyes "the entire structure of my paper emerged, superimposing itself on my original draft like a double exposure on a frame of film."[5]

You're also likely to find other unusual occurrences as the second field surfaces. As don Juan says, it is often accompanied by lapses of reason and memory, and with jolts that range from nervous tics to large movements of energy (*Tales,* 133). These incidents are fluctuations of the focal point produced by the person's awakening. Over time, the balance once found with reason is now found by working with the first and second fields. When this shift is made, the apprentice stage is over. Exercising *will* has become a daily regimen.

## Other Worlds, Reincarnation, and the Fire from Within

Stretching awareness into the unknown naturally takes you to unknown worlds. According to don Juan, a seer's strategy incorporates dreaming. By directly utilizing the energy body, dreaming integrates the second field so that it can be functionally used. Don Juan adds that there are three ways the energy body deals with energy. One is to perceive the world we ordinarily perceive. Another is to perceive energy flowing, which is *seeing*. And the third is to boost awareness into other realms (*Dreaming*, 31). *Will* commands these capacities.

One effect of developing your full nature is fully realizing that anything you perceive hinges on your cohesion. For instance, the view that the world is formed of material objects, and a common metaphysical view that the world is an illusion, are both valid in terms of their respective cohesions. Each and every view, therefore, is produced by a particular cohesion. And there is an infinite number of possible cohesions. Gaining this broader sense of reality allows you to deal better with any world.

Take, for example, the world of reincarnation. In most non-ordinary worldviews, reincarnation is deemed valid. Yet the topic is not directly presented in Castaneda's work. Possibly this omission is due to Toltecs striving to get their lives working in this life, and not passing the buck for troubles off to prior-life incidents. Don Juan does, however, offer a few indirect references which may indicate reincarnation-like experiences. For example, one reference occurs as don Juan piques Castaneda's interest in the focal point. Talking about the ordinary world, he proposed that "the fixation of our assemblage point is so overpowering that it has made us forget where we came from, and what our purpose was for coming here" (*Dreaming*, 197).

What is lacking from this allusion is some kind of supportive, experiential evidence. Several years ago, I had an experience along this line of inquiry. Shortly after I entered my regular afternoon dreaming session, I felt thrust into another dimension. There I met an entity I identified as my deceased father. It wasn't a mirage. It had the exact feeling as did my father when he was alive. After I made that connection, my body relaxed and I knew I had made a correct determination. We then traveled together to another entity. I *saw* it as a huge sphere, outstripping anything I had previously encountered. Its environment was pastel swirling light. My father then entered the sphere. He disappeared as though he were but one cell in a large and complex organism.

In a gestalt of intuition, I felt that my father was only one experience of the larger entity. Accordingly, reincarnation is a way to account for the larger entities' multi-dimensional experiences. Perhaps when the energy I knew as my father entered our ordinary world from this extraordinary dimension, a sense of his greater identity was shrouded. He had never addressed, with me at least, prior- or after-life issues.

Now then, don Juan also says that the focal point and "its surrounding glow are the mark of life and consciousness" (*Dreaming,* 8). Therefore you will not *see* an auric field or energy body around a corpse. About a year ago, I found supporting evidence. I was sitting on the porch of a farmhouse. It was late afternoon, and farmhands were cleaning up after the day's work. About thirty yards from me, one worker keeled over. Others rushed over to him. I froze in place, unable to move. I felt as though I had lapsed into a mild stupor. I then *saw* the workers' energy bodies superimposed over their physical bodies. As though I were watching an instant replay, I also *saw* the energy body of the stricken man begin to dissipate as he fell. It was like something within him was wired too tight and gave way. Chunks of his energy body spun away from him, then evaporated. By the time he hit the ground, there was no light about him. As I found out later, he had died on the spot.

So what does this say about reincarnation? If a person's light is snuffed out at death, what's there to continue on? Perhaps, though, the energy body is the focal point of another entity. Perhaps the large entity I met with my father placed its focal point in different worlds. Perhaps in this world its focal point was perceived as my father's energy body. Thus, when it shifts its focal point to another experience, the shift is perceived here as an energy body dissipating. And perhaps one life is perceived as gone, and a new life is born.

The Fire from Within, then, causing a person to retain luminosity, marks a point where ordinary life and death scenarios change. To accomplish this, don Juan says you have to place your entire physical mass into your energy body (*Dreaming,* 189). That is, if you're successful in hooking your first and second fields together, you retain complete awareness. The door again opens to many possibilities. One is that the person may then gain the ability to place his physical body back into this world. I think don Juan did so each time he met me. By the time I first met him, he had finished training Castaneda and had long since burned away from this world. By some quirk of fate, he returned to teach others.

Saying this in another way, don Juan's teachings enable you to consolidate your energies. Perhaps your doing so mirrors a larger entity stabilizing a particular cohesion. Perhaps this cohesion represents its experience of you. Upon death, that cohesion has unraveled and the experience "you" is gone. But say you perform the Fire from Within. In that case, the entity has gained control of that cohesion; therefore, that awareness is not lost. It is just not focused in the physical world. But when that cohesion re-forms, "you" return.

If this is true, the process mirrors what we do within our energy bodies. For instance, if you gain control of your dreams, you can return to the same dream time and time again. You have thus learned to control specific cohesions. Perhaps this is the mystery of "the dreamer and the dreamed" of which don Juan spoke in *Tales of Power* (ch. 2). Perhaps we are each but one dream of a dreamer who is dreaming many dreams.

# 7
# Ready, Aim, Fire from Within

In *The Fire from Within*, don Juan tells Castaneda that there are four steps on the path of knowledge: an apprentice, a ranger, a person of knowledge, and a seer (*Fire*, 36-37). In *A Separate Reality*, don Juan says that when a ranger activates *will*, the person has become a Toltec (*Separate*, 185). Taking into account the effect systems render on perception, I think it's necessary to regard the shift from a ranger to a Toltec as a distinct stage, as is stepping from a Toltec to a person of knowledge. Doing so provides a sense of developing the craft, what happens when the craft is consolidated, and where you can go from there. Therefore, this chapter offers a five-stage model for growth and radical transformation. In this model, "mastery" doesn't pertain to being another's master, a position don Juan shuns. It pertains to a standard educational method of learning for mastery.

## Stages of Awareness

Mirroring don Juan's instruction, the stages are (1) orientation, (2) training, (3) craftsmanship, (4) artistry, and (5) mastery. Keep in mind that in a holographic manner, each stage contains all other stages. Since you continually inquire about life in order to orient yourself, you never leave stage one. Then, through stage-two training, stage-one inquiry becomes the foundation from which to zero in on the other stages. Plus, since all stages are within us, we all have the capacity to develop stage-five mastery.

Each stage contains its own cohesion, its own order, its own meaning. Each is a different configuration of energy resulting from a multitude of influences. These energetic structures act as filters, affecting what we perceive mentally, emotionally, and physically. The filters shape our experiences, and our experiences shape our lives. Thus, to perceive more, we must put in the work to develop new cohesions. As we do, we find that at each stage we consciously incorporate and then transcend previous stages.

At the core of this work is reducing and eliminating self-reflection. As we tell ourselves what the world is like, defend our positions, and work too hard to become a part of a group that shares our views, we actively prevent new formations of energy. Therefore, each stage represents degrees of self-importance. Each stage therefore also reflects how much Spirit flows through our lives. Self-importance equates with imbalance. Balance is derived from following Spirit and thereby finding your natural path. The more you travel with Spirit, the less you need to reflect to yourself, as you *are* yourself.

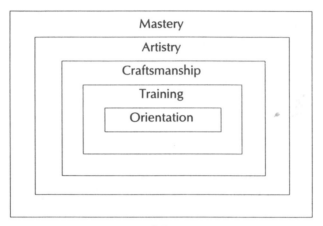

**Stages of Awareness**

Each box represents a major shift in cohesion. Together they represent the totality of human awareness. Outside of the boxes is the unknowable.

The first three stages consist of conditional energy fields. Within them is movement from an ordinary field to a nonordinary field. By reaching stage four, however, you have developed a natural field. At stage five you have attained mastery of your energy fields.

In addition, each stage reflects a balance between dreaming and tracking. Dreaming rapidly expands your awareness. Tracking tunes your attention and ability to focus. When a sufficient amount of energy within a stage has been integrated, you've stabilized that stage. Then on to the next.

As you sense the next stage, the tendency is to interpret it according to your current awareness. An apprentice might see someone behaving like a "darn fool," for example, while a Toltec might *see* the same person's behavior as the effect of excessive conditional energy.

Remaining aware that there are other stages, and keeping open to them, reduces fixations. Also keep in mind that there is the possibility of infinite expansion within each stage. Just as engineers continually add to their knowledge, you can stretch your knowledge of any stage from now into eternity. The idea here, though, is to get into it enough to learn it, then learn it enough to leave it.

While a standard model may facilitate growth, there is no telling what you'll find on your quest, or how you'll perceive the world at any stage. If the goal is to become pure energy and burn with the Fire from Within, how can you predict your thoughts and feelings at any step of the way? At each stage, you have to be willing to let go of all that you once knew. The changes are radical, which means you have no actual reference for them. You have only thoughts about them. So remember not to fool yourself into thinking you have stabilized a new stage, when you have only succeeded in peeking into it—even if it turns out to be a very long look.

## Elements Within the Stages

Within each stage there are consistent elements, although the dynamics of each element change. Accordingly, as we go through each stage, we'll look at how the elements evolve. These stages do not merely reflect mental adaptability. They indicate changes in all aspects of behavior. The following chart outlines what you can expect to find traversing a Toltec path.

| The Mastery of Awareness | | | | |
|---|---|---|---|---|
| **1** | **2** | **3** | **4** | **5** |
| **Stage** Initiate | Apprentice/ Ranger | Toltec | Person of knowledge | Seer |
| **Inquiry** orientation | basic/adv training | craftsmanship | artistry | mastery |
| **Engage** ordinary worldview | nonordinary worldview | energy body | Fire Within | total freedom |
| **Order** self (-) | self (+) | natural | mystical | |
| **Measure** random | life/day | one hour | moment | |
| **Interpret** good-evil | positive-negative | focal point | mind | |
| **Quest** conditions of going to knowledge | patience/ *will* | tasks | transcendence | |
| **Barrier** fear | clarity | power | old age | |

**Inquiry**. As an initiate you spend most of your time trying to figure out just what is going on. You have to decide whether or not you even want to travel this path. As part of finding your bearings, this stage also represents the focus within each stage. At the apprentice and ranger stages your focus is on training, albeit as a ranger you have more of a grasp on matters. So your training then engages more advanced practices of learning about the energy body, and how to manage its resources.

As a Toltec you deliberately practice your craft. You practice at each stage, but as a Toltec you have the ability to engage the teachings in the manner lawyers and doctors "practice." By now you're skilled at dreaming and tracking, and you work to refine this knowledge.

As a person of knowledge you elevate your practice to artistry. You can step out of the conventions of the craft and innovate. Once a seer, you elevate your knowledge to mastery.

**Engage**. Whereas the initiate works principally within an ordinary system of reality, an apprentice and ranger develop non-ordinary frameworks. Trying to step further out of conditional energy, the Toltec engages the energy body without locking the results into a particular reference.

As a person of knowledge, you concern yourself with journeys well beyond the ordinary. Seeking to deliberately fly past the force of the Eagle, you gain more awareness and control of your energy body. This awareness leads to control of the Fire from Within. You may then step in and out of dimensions, including the physical, at *will*. While a Toltec may experience this shift, a person of knowledge utilizes it, and a seer commands it. As a seer, by mastering this flight you enter another realm of vast proportions. A lifetime of work has delivered you to complete freedom.

**Order**. The initiate stage is a sluggish one. You deal with yourself as part of a prevailing social order, locked within its confines. Having been taught to define yourself as part of that order, you've automatically lost the natural drive toward freedom. The apprentice and ranger also deal with a sense of self but, as don Juan says, not selfishness (*Fire*, 37). Now the focus on self is from perspectives of positive evolution and liberation.

Since the Toltec cultivates a natural field, you find yourself dealing with the balance of nature, including what is considered supernatural. As a result, your sense of what the natural world consists of expands. Having developed a natural field, the person of knowledge deals with a mystical order and touches realms of pure creativity. What the seer encounters, I haven't a clue. So the remaining elements for this stage remain open, signifying that degree of personal freedom.

**Measure.** As an initiate, how you measure your life is random. Since you have no sense of where you're going, your life lacks sense. You strive to get oriented so your life gains meaning. Then, as an apprentice, you measure yourself according to how you'll build your life. Using your death as a measuring stick, for example, you tap the things in life that matter most to you. Having worked this through, a ranger uses that momentum to increase overall discipline. You now focus on the day at hand, accepting each event as a challenge.

A Toltec continues managing awareness, but now uses one hour as a reference (*Silence,* 262), reflecting increased discipline in much the same manner that an ordinary soldier must excel to become a commando. Having further refined awareness, which includes an innate sense of order supplied by the first energy field, a person of knowledge resides in the moment. You have learned to *be.*

The effect of this progression is learning to keep your mind on what you're doing. Emphasizing preceding or subsequent actions diminishes the importance of what is occurring at the moment. And a ranger "cannot possibly afford to do that," says don Juan (*Tales,* 108). By discovering what you want to devote your life to, letting that path unfold naturally, and participating with whatever is at hand, you gradually and keenly focus your attention.

**Interpret.** Based on social conventions, initially a person interprets the world as being good or evil. Social conditioning is a driving force of ordinary reality, and it especially influences the initiate. But, as Castaneda learned, only energy exists. The perception of evil, he says, results from the cumulative, deleterious effects of a rigidly fixed focal point (*Dreaming,* 238-239).

With training and experience, the apprentice and ranger learn to view the world as positive and negative, as in energy polarity, rather than as something good or bad. Taking another step, the Toltec interprets the world as the location of the focal point. As a person of knowledge, you step out of the Toltec model and view your experiences as a condition of "mind." Not as in rational mind, but as in a metaphysical condition of formless, creative energy.

**Quest**. To begin the quest for integrity, an initiate struggles to align with the conditions of going to knowledge. As we have seen, these conditions are fear, clarity, self-assurance, and respect. By developing a path with heart, the apprentice gains patience. You now know how you'll spend your life's resources. This step marks the beginning of advanced training. As a ranger, you make a true bid for power and awareness, and you wait for your *will*.

Having gained *will*, as a Toltec you concern yourself with specific tasks (*Tales*, 277). Learning tasks are crucial components of each stage. Your Toltec tasks, however, are designed to help you work your way through the craft toward natural freedom. They also serve as direction so you may balance yourself within the one-hour reference. By completing them, you earn such balance that you enter a new stage. As a person of knowledge, your quest centers on the flight to pure freedom.

**Barrier**. The barriers of perception are what don Juan refers to as "natural enemies" (*Teachings*, 93). They are fear, clarity, power, and old age. They are guideposts, giving direction on how to relate to and handle daily life. The barriers not only show how a person remains locked within a specific level, but also provide the means to aim personal evolution toward the next stage. Each barrier, therefore, is examined in conjunction with its specific stage.

## The Initiate

At this stage, you find your thoughts beginning to change. You're exploring new options, including new realities. But there are so many viable paths waiting that you may be quite perplexed about which way to proceed. Experimentation is the order of the day. The goal is to find which path resonates deeply within you. And then that's the way to go.

This is also a stage where the teacher and student find common ground. Castaneda says he knew don Juan a year before his apprenticeship began. During this time, he says they grew to know each other very well.[1] The teacher assesses which course to begin with; the student learns to trust the teacher. One of the most difficult aspects of this stage is redefining your sense of self. To let go of a lifetime of forging an identity, even if it is a poor self-image, strains your resources.

This stage also marks a crucial test for professional teamwork. To fully participate as a team member, you have to relinquish yourself without losing your integrity. Otherwise you might randomly flail at other members and arbitrarily latch onto their energies like a leech. And you might prefer your own agenda and never really come to terms with losing self-importance. Thus you never fully develop other stages.

Should you decide to follow a Toltec path, you begin by studying the fundamentals of a ranger. A core of this study is the conditions of going to knowledge. With clarity, you gain flexibility of thought and action. Your priorities are in order. With fear, you gradually temper yourself and refine your edge for survival. With respect, you don't dictate circumstances to others, nor will you be dictated to. With self-assurance, you allow your spirit to soar. With time, your training delivers you to a purposeful, deliberate life.

**Barrier: Fear**. How can a ranger use fear as a condition of going to knowledge if it is a barrier? As don Juan says, fear can be used as a spur to learn (*Fire*, 57). During his early days as a Toltec, his fear of losing his connection with Spirit kept him on the straight and narrow (*Dreaming*, 250). But fear, he says, only belongs to the Eagle's emanations of daily life (*Fire*, 243). Fear arises from encounters with other-dimensional emanations only because the first field hasn't sufficiently let go of mundane concerns. And so the issue of self-importance surfaces again. Forget yourself, says don Juan, and you fear nothing (*Dreaming*, 190).

But getting to that level of proficiency takes time. The guideline for initially handling fear, then, is simple. Each time you encounter a situation where the only thing keeping you from proceeding is fear, your decision is made. You proceed. Be fully afraid, but defy it (*Teachings*, 95). Seek not to avoid it or to control it. Abandon yourself to it. Use it to instill alertness. Doing so generates momentum toward freedom. And freedom is both contagious and frightening, says don Juan, but not frightening for those who have taken the time to groom their lives in preparation for it (*Fire*, 101, 268).

# The Apprentice

As an apprentice, you begin mapping Toltec terrains. Possibilities which stagger the imagination abound. In order to proceed, you learn the basics of tracking and dreaming. On the tracking side, you practice altering your routines, deliberately reducing your self-importance, using your death as an advisor to guide your every step, and a host of other exercises.

On the dreaming side, you first hear tall tales of escapades in this and other dimensions. You hear of adventures with inorganic beings, and you hear why the purpose of dreaming is to assist you in becoming a person of knowledge. Thus, you orient yourself to stages three and four right off the bat. At this stage, you have very few tales of your own. You are, however, breaking ground into the second field. And with that groundbreaking comes all sorts of joys and dreads. You are now beginning to develop another reality and naturally want to cling to the old one. That energetic shift, coupled with a lack of fortitude to handle new energy, keeps you busy with balance.

Your principal means of balance arrives from following a path with heart. You know what you want to commit your life to, and how to bring that about. The path with heart and other tracking skills are given additional consideration in the following chapters.

By the end of your apprenticeship, you realize you have been totally worked over by people whom you still don't know; yet a previous generation of Toltecs has extensively trained you. By witnessing your teacher's impeccability, you also realize that no matter where you are on the path, you're always an apprentice. There's always something else waiting to be learned.

# The Ranger

As an apprentice, you learned how to get going. Now you're learning how to pace yourself. A defining element of being a ranger is that you have established your path with heart. The pieces of your life form an integrated whole. As a result, you've learned the basics of letting go and working with the abstract, with Spirit. And now you aim to let Spirit rather than personal desires guide you. Keep in mind that to this end your training has educated feeling as well as the other cornerstones. Thus you're better equipped to journey with Spirit.

As part of this preparation, you've stabilized a nonordinary conditional field. In effect, nonordinary reality has become ordinary. You've collapsed a little more of the unknown into your known world. By now you've also realized that life holds many possibilities, and the most efficient way to respond to them is by working with the day at hand. Otherwise, you just get too far ahead of yourself.

Working more intensely with tracking and dreaming, you enter heightened awareness. But, in itself, this awareness doesn't mean all that much. It's the fortitude gained by the training that delivers results. On a newscast during the Persian Gulf War, a tank driver recounted what happened the first time his team entered combat. As the shells started flying, they all lost track of their actions. But he also said that their training took over and they conducted themselves well. From a Toltec perspective, the intensity of the situation shocked them into heightened awareness. And one effect of heightened awareness is losing track of the situation. I'm sure that with more combat experience, their temporary loss of awareness would cease.

As you tap second-field energies, you may experience this temporary loss of awareness. You enter heightened awareness and later forget what transpired. You also learn that without integrity, you just magnify your foibles. Even the consummate seers of don Juan's team labored for years before they recognized Castaneda's three-prong energy body. Thus, to think that a person in training can walk into a situation and handle it to perfection is not wise. The ranger discipline of sobriety and inner strength rectifies any personal or team imbalances.

As don Juan teaches, what matters to rangers beyond all else is getting to the totality of their being (*Tales*, 13), a state which doesn't seem as far-fetched as before. As a ranger, you embody Toltec discipline and have learned patience. You know how to wait and what you're waiting for: your *will* (*Separate*, 174). In the course of activating *will*, you continue to refine the core of your nature as you were created, rather than as socially conditioned. The elements of your path with heart sustain you.

Don Juan says that as you develop *will*, you may experience convulsions (*Separate*, 185). If you do, it will surely give you pause for caution and constraint. You must be able to recognize the difference between physical ailments and second-field reorganizations. Therefore you must become more astute at perceiving the differences between discordant and evolving energies. This is still a marvelous time, however, as the world springs forth fresh every day. So, as don Juan suggests, while you wait simply laugh and enjoy yourself (*Tales,* 282). Should you grow concerned about possible ill-effects, consult your physician. It has been my experience that following this path promotes health, and I have received calm assurances when seeking medical advice about physical anomalies.

**Barrier: Clarity**. After a long, hard struggle with fear, you develop clarity. By now you're pretty good at figuring nonordinary reality, and you avidly peer into everything. The physical world actually has sharper, clearer images. Your thoughts run trimly and smoothly. All of this demonstrates the certainty of your progression.

So why is this so bad? Clarity emerged from a greater degree of harmony in the first place; but it is precisely this fact that highlights a major trap along the way at each and every turn. You might well enough think you have gained a degree of knowledge, but most likely you've only seen the shroud of it. You haven't delved deeply enough to rightfully claim your new ground. By explaining your victories you close off the mystery. And you stop learning. Gaining insight and managing knowledge are different items on the agenda. Thus, the Mastery model demonstrates the value of building strength through steps.

Don Juan says that clarity makes you never doubt yourself. You're clear about everything. And so you act when you should wait, and wait when you should act. Do this long enough and you fumble away all your hard-won gains. Don Juan advises the use of clarity only to *see* (*Teachings,* 96, 97). Use the knowledge you do have for more intricate pursuits of aligning energy. Otherwise, pretend your clarity is almost a mistake. Make your decisions with great deliberateness before taking your next steps. And, whereas fear generated momentum, learning to handle clarity provides the restraint for controlling momentum.

## The Toltec

The bridge from training to craftsmanship is activating your *will*. Don Juan says this magic moment may happen at any time, under any circumstances. Castaneda and other apprentices jumped off a cliff into an abyss of pure perception. Don Juan, in turn, massaged a puma's tits (*Separate,* 262, 186). And don Genaro tackled the "ally" while standing in an ordinary field of dirt (*Journey,* 304). So you discover your own way when the time comes. A common feature for most, it seems, is gaining actual experience with the Fire from Within. Whether or not you return from your adventure is not something you can decide beforehand. Don Juan says *will* determines whether or not a person returns to again walk the earth (*Tales*, 277).

Using hours instead of days and years as your time reference means you have stabilized heightened awareness. It also means that your tracking and dreaming skills have developed to a refined resonance. Engaging your tasks continues this development, launching you from a nonordinary conditional field into a natural field. A common problem is thinking you've already established a natural field. Heck, you can talk with elementals and shift into other dimensions at *will*. But viewing your enhanced abilities as an indication of growth which is yet to come means you're still locked within yourself and traveling less with Spirit; reality just becomes a huge amount of projection. While you've partially awakened the energy body, there are greater feats yet to be accomplished.

**Barrier: Power**. Having jumped into creation's bosom, you've access to your totality. And don Juan says you now encounter power (*Tales*, 277). He says that, due to its seductiveness, this is the hardest of all barriers to transcend. Having worked through different conditional fields, you can now control those fields. Since you can control the energy body's cohesion, you can determine the focal point's location. You can therefore determine what you perceive. As a result, you can *will* anything you want. It's as though life has become a lucid dream, and you can control the dream. Fortunately, through prior training you've learned to trim your needs and wants.

Don Juan says that if you succumb to temptation, however, you'll never learn true control of your resources (*Tales*, 97). You'll remain isolated from your core nature and live only in the level of personal desires. So, as great an accomplishment as this is, don Juan advises not to use it under any conditions. This restraint proves difficult since your training has given you the skills and desire to test, measure, and validate everything for yourself. To suddenly apply the brakes requires immense effort. Your duels with fear and clarity, however, have provided the basics for managing this stage.

Because tracking and dreaming automatically carry powers, they require astute self-supervision. With tracking, you can maneuver in and out of people's lives, feeling and *seeing* their desires and motives, taking and leaving what you want. You can also entrain other peoples' energies to yours, thereby getting others to follow your wishes. Dreaming accesses recondite areas of your being, thereby adding to your personal power and enhancing your tracking abilities.

Some metaphysical lineages train their practitioners to refrain from any activity associated with paranormal abilities. Advanced dreaming practices are often included on the hit list. Toltecs, however, regard dreaming as natural. Thus Toltecs develop it, but use guidelines. The guidelines provide a strategy to evolve dreaming, and a dreaming task focuses your energies.

Several years ago, I was out and about during a lazy, warm summer evening. I paused to rest in the recreation area of the apartment complex where I lived. Leaning my back against a brick wall, I spontaneously entered a remarkable clarity. The surroundings seemed alive and held an extremely rich texture. I just relaxed into it. I soon felt my feet rise up. Looking down, I saw my feet and legs levitating upward. They rose about three feet and then dropped back down. I soon found that I could control the movements. I then *willed* my legs up and down three more times. Each time it was as though my shoulder blades were hinged to the wall, and a mysterious force moved me like a puppet.

As though you were an unwitting participant in the film *The Ten Commandments,* unexpected and unsought experiences with power will occur. They pave the way to learning how to handle it. The previous example is quite mild, even though levitation is considered refined dreaming. Currently, a specialized dreaming task enables me to place experiences such as this into a craftsmanship context. As a result, levitation becomes secondary to learning a broader picture of human capacities.

To hold manifestations of power in abeyance requires you to marshall all your skills. But this restriction is not perverse; you don't achieve something just to have it continually thrown in your face. Don Juan says that if you can keep yourself in line, there comes a time when you know how and when to use power. But first he says you must realize that it was never really yours in the first place, and that without control over yourself, using it is worse than a mistake. By then you have become a person of knowledge (*Teachings,* 98).

## The Person of Knowledge

The apprentice, ranger, and Toltec stages are degrees of participation and proficiency with the conditional field of a nonordinary reality. By rigorously following your path with heart, you've further developed your intent, allowing you to let go even more and producing a one-on-one alignment between you and the world; thus you can now sustain a natural field. Having disengaged self-reflection, you no longer place conditions on reality. Consequently, you engage a most intimate and complete dance with Spirit.

Don Juan says that to perform Toltec skills, it's not necessary to *see*. A person just needs *will*. However, a person must *see* to become a person of knowledge. Indeed, if you can *see* proficiently it's no longer necessary to live as a ranger since *seeing* offers sufficient guidance. If you can *see* that well, you're able to sustain self-awareness without having to hold onto an identity. Then, as don Juan says, nothing is more important than anything else. The effect is that a person of knowledge "has no honor, no dignity, no family, no name, no country, but only life to be lived. . ." (*Separate*, 240, 20, 182, 107).

Another interesting reference point for having attained this state is that in no instance can a person of knowledge cause injury to another. Don Juan says that if trouble is not foreseen, and injury befalls the person of knowledge, the person accepts this ill turn of fate without recrimination (*Tales*, 64). While this stance may reflect traditional spiritual perspectives of not harming another, it also indicates that the person has simply lost interest in people by virtue of having significantly redefined himself. And having reduced self-importance to nil, the person contains no feelings for retaliation.

By adeptly balancing tracking and dreaming energies, you evolve beyond the craft. Your domain is now the artisan. The patience you developed earlier expands, and exquisite timing between you and Spirit is in your grasp (*Fire*, 37). With a continuous starting point of *now*, you don't anticipate beyond the moment. This lack of anticipation indicates unwavering flexibility. Unwavering from your link with Spirit; flexibility in flowing freely with sudden changes in your path. By now, you realize that life holds so many dimensions that residing in the moment is the most practical, efficient way to behave.

This is extremely complex behavior. When you dance, for instance, you coordinate a number of physical, emotional, and mental activities. While *being*, you coordinate not only your immediate behaviors, but you're automatically aligning with the necessities of future actions for survival. Just like a creature in the wild, you hone your instincts to unsurpassed levels.

Don Juan says that becoming a person of knowledge is a

temporary state (*Teachings*, 94). In this case, I believe he refers to how a person of knowledge feels momentarily inundated with knowledge and energy, a feature of mystical experiences. The knowledge arrives, passes through, and leaves. Enhanced awareness remains. To be able to handle this degree of energy and allow it to work its magic, you need to stabilize a natural field. In these terms, being a person of knowledge is constant, an effect of having diligently labored for so many years. Without a natural field, the knowledge gets translated into the terms of a conditional field. Measuring the mystical experiences I've had and what I've read about them as compared with don Juan's anecdotes, I regard becoming a person of knowledge as the quintessential mystical experience, if not of an even higher order.

**Barrier: Old Age**. Old age is a time when we naturally enter higher abstractions and sense a more expansive picture of life and death. One problem is that culturally we've never adequately explored this time of life; hence, we don't know how to capitalize on it. Since we typically regard the world of human activity as the complete world, don Juan viewed old people as usually having exhausted the world of people, but not the world itself (*Separate*, 264).

As a result, the elderly are often left with a sense of unfulfilled dreams, when, in fact, old age lends itself to dreaming and venturing beyond societal concerns. The elderly have literally spent a lifetime working their way through a maze of social requirements. But as a society, we don't have a Toltec-like context with which to develop the fullness of life. Therefore, we can't reap dividends accrued by extending the ordinary conditions of what is considered a natural life.

Don Juan says that, by studiously following a Toltec path, you will find old age to be a time when you have no fears and no impatient clarity of mind, and the barrier of power is controlled. But you also want to rest (*Teachings*, 98). Your momentum wanes and seemingly turns back in on itself. He adds that if you can resist your tiredness and live your fate through, there comes a time when clarity, power, and knowledge combine to make all your struggles worthwhile.

## The Seer

Don Juan often used the terms "Toltec" and "seer" interchangeably. While he may have considered second-cycle Toltecs highly indulgent, he noted that they still studied forces affecting perception and sought to expand their knowledge. As a result, some were seers as well.

A seer is one who has mastery over energy-body cohesions, reflecting extreme proficiency in *seeing*. And *seeing*, says don Juan, is the final accomplishment of a person of knowledge (*Journey*, 233). A seer is a connoisseur of perception, a person who easily moves the focal point about the energy body. Placing too many conditions on what a seer is reduces it to a previous level. And more than anything else, this level concerns freedom.

To *see*, don Juan says you must "stop the world" (*Journey*, 233). When you stop the world, all activity around you might freeze-frame, or the world might shatter before your eyes. On different occasions, for example, I've watched a Little League baseball game freeze in mid-action, and I've observed my physical world shake and tear asunder. A luminous world of thick fibers and bright hues then replaces the world of objects. To stop the world, you must find the crack between worlds, a place between thoughts. This awareness occurs from shifting cohesion, which is the mark of a ranger. A Toltec learns to step in and out of it. A person of knowledge skillfully manages it. A seer rules it.

From don Juan's instruction, it is my understanding that by the time you've reached the seer level, you've participated with numerous entirely different worlds. Yet even when you deal with dimensions beyond comprehension, the ability to experience refined states of those dimensions creates the seer's lifestyle. The unexcelled ability to align with various energy fields, therefore, produces proficiency with *seeing*.

To govern the energy body with such skill requires a lifetime of work. But first you must bring the second field to life, to full awareness. Castaneda says that his sole quest is to awaken the energy body. He adds that the energy body is used to dream, to navigate the second field. That's what pulls you to freedom, he says.[2] And an awakened energy body eventually leads to the Fire from Within.

## The Fire from Within

The Fire from Within occurs when you combine your entire physical mass of energy with the energy body (*Dreaming*, 189). Abelar's teacher, Clara, says that to accomplish this maneuver, you must release your entire inventory, including all your human concerns.[3] Yet don Juan says that, even after the human world vanishes, some sense of self remains. He refers to this paradox as "the ultimate bastion of awareness, the one the new seers count on" (*Fire*, 291).

According to the Toltec worldview, the physical body and the physical world form from a specific cohesion. Changing this cohesion to perceive other worlds requires acts of *will*. The differences in the Toltec and person of knowledge stages concern the ability to handle *will*. In the time of a heartbeat, Castaneda observed don Genaro leap from one mountain to another mountain ten miles away. Don Juan says that don Genaro is a person of knowledge, and therefore "he's perfectly capable of transporting himself over great distances" (*Tales*, 48).

In addition, after jumping off a cliff, Castaneda had to shift his cohesion before he hit ground; he had to assemble an entirely new world or die. Remember, don Juan also says that it's in the province of *will*, not rational thought, whether one returns from this leap of perception. If the person does return, and grows to a person of knowledge, the degree of exercising *will* is markedly enhanced.

Resulting from this enhancement is the ability to step in and out of dimensions. On several occasions, I observed don Juan emerge from another dimension into this one. I *saw* him extend his awareness from a luminous field of light. He then suddenly appeared a short distance away from me. Over time, I gained the sense that he had developed into a complete seer. I figured that, as he finished his task with Castaneda, he developed momentum leading out of the person of knowledge level. And I can only surmise that seers so adroitly shift cohesion that they enter and leave dimensions as one would ordinary enter and leave shopping malls.

The Fire from Within, then, is a matter of *willing* yourself to freedom. While activating *will*, we can depart into indulging or into allowing. Second-cycle Toltecs indulged. They ardently pushed their awareness into their energy bodies, pushing their energy bodies out of a natural uniformity. Redressing this approach as aberrant, third-cycle seers sought to cultivate a natural evolution of human awareness. While they used second-cycle practices to speed this process up, they kept the central focus on developing a complete natural field rather than an extremely sophisticated conditional field.

Much to their credit, second-cycle Toltecs instituted death-defier practices. These were the prelude to the modern seers' art of the

Fire from Within. The ancients learned how to change the energy body, but they remained isolated within the overall human band. Retaining the practice but revamping its use, third-cycle seers concerned themselves with entire movements of energy into the third energy field. They equated this movement with freedom. Thus the second cycle related to the Fire from Within as a personal-power skill, whereas the third cycle related to it as attaining a mystifying balance.

Why even attempt the Fire from Within? Don Juan says that the mystery of our totality is revealed at death. Toltecs, he adds, decide to live with that mystery and knowledge (*Tales*, 133). And so they live to stretch their awareness into the land of death and beyond the human condition.

* * *

Another curious feature in all this talk about evolving awareness is that these capacities are meant to be managed, not necessarily understood. In fact, don Juan says that talking about these matters is just for the purpose of pointing out a direction, not for understanding (*Tales*, 120). He says that Castaneda's failures in the Toltec world were often due to his insistence on understanding (*Separate*, 315). Therefore the important part is bringing to life as much awareness as possible. So don't cut yourself short by resting short of your goal. And if your goal is to become a seer, well then, with the complexities, the barriers, the time and devotion required to make the journey, you can well imagine why don Juan says we stand only a chance of a chance for success.

But he made it, as have others. And to enable us to better have that chance, third-cycle seers revamped tracking. Instilling fortitude, forbearance, and finesse was the essence of their work. The resulting integrity is what delivers success. Thus the next section concerns the skills of tracking.

# Part III
# Tracking

# 8
## Steady As You Go

Don Juan says the purpose of tracking is twofold: to move the focal point steadily and safely, and "to imprint its principles at such a deep level that the human inventory is bypassed. . ." (*Fire*, 187). As a result, through tracking you spontaneously cultivate a natural energy field, meaning that you're becoming a person of knowledge. And Toltec teachings are geared, says Castaneda, to doing exactly that (*Teachings*, 218).

Within the margins of shifting the focal point and imprinting principles, tracking takes on multi-faceted approaches and utilizes numerous skills. The forms of tracking eventually give way to tapping the essence of whatever it is you're tracking. This is the quintessential maneuver of becoming the goal itself. Tracking, therefore, requires total realization, not just understanding (*Fire*, 195). This requirement means observing, following, becoming, and living the energy of your objective.

Full realization of a tracking skill includes knowing that the technique works, as well as having the ability to make it work. Since you can always find new explanations for practically anything, you don't necessarily have to know why it works. Realizing the fullness of tracking beyond its individual skills means you have developed personal fortitude to handle focal point shifts. You also have the strength of character to better withstand the constant barrage of forces which pull you from your path.

In essence, tracking prevents complacency. As it hinges on stability, it engenders a unique personal relationship with the world. In order to maintain balance amid the clamor of competing ideas, for instance, it provides guidance for dealing with the world of people (*Fire*, 172). Tracking necessitates learning to be effective, not just willful. In addition, you find that the more you tap the world of *will*, the less support the world of reason offers—no matter how well-constructed. As a result, Toltec guidelines, strategy, and discipline provide a way to leave ordinary human endeavors without sacrificing personal integrity.

# Guidelines for Tracking

In each facet of don Juan's teachings, he addresses common themes. Florida Grau refers to these as tracking precepts (*Gift*, 281). I've come to realize them as guidelines that enable you to remain on track through each of the Mastery of Awareness stages. They are:

1. There is a superior and guiding force for all creation. This force is true Power, or Spirit.
2. Reality is an interpretation of events. How we organize and view the world stems from a reflection within ourselves.
3. We have more to our nature than we presently use, or even suspect.
4. It is our job to develop these capacities for awareness.
5. By merging ourselves with the wellspring of creation, and thus the driving force within us, we may unveil the deepest levels of our nature.
6. The world is, in essence, mysterious. As part of the world, we, too, are mysterious.
7. Whatever we figure out about ourselves and the world forever remains a mystery; otherwise we continue to reflect to ourselves about ourselves.

# Principles

Don Juan and his team presented tracking principles to Castaneda from different angles. In *The Power of Silence*, don Juan says the first principle of tracking is ruthlessness (*Silence*, 138). In *The Eagle's Gift*, Grau says the first principle is that rangers choose their battlegrounds (*Gift*, 280). While these may appear different, the bottom line is that you have to be ruthless in order to choose the conditions of your battleground. A battleground can be your place of residence or work, a wilderness water hole, or the point where you draw the line with another's behavior. It's whatever you choose.

Other principles include relaxing and abandoning yourself to your fate and discarding everything in your life that isn't necessary. The final principle, Grau tells Castaneda, hinges on success with the other maneuvers. It consists of not placing yourself at the forefront of a situation. Thus you rest outside of the circle that presses others. For instance, while healing Grau's leg, a Toltec-curer had another person apply the remedies and teach her how to forge a Toltec path. The curer remained behind the scenes while directing the activity. Thus he gained a more accurate picture of what was taking place. While Grau thought he was the janitor, he actually choreographed her healing and instruction (*Gift*, 288-293).

Castaneda was introduced to these principles early on in his apprenticeship. He later presented them as specific techniques. In his third book, *Journey to Ixtlan*, he even gave them chapter titles. For example, he discovered that "Death Is an Advisor" developed ruthlessness. Through "Erasing Personal History," he learned to cover his tracks. And having "A Worthy Opponent" forced him to keep his resources in check.

In general, these principles consist of the major tenets for handling yourself. The manner in which they are presented is subordinate to the actual practice of managing your resources. Thus we could easily say that the first principle is to develop a natural field. A supporting exercise would be to not expect anything. This would automatically interdict and remold much of our behavior. Rather than continually projecting into the future, we would begin tracking present-centeredness. We would also begin cultivating our core natures. In the process of all of this, we would learn to choose our own battlegrounds.

Furthermore, we could also say that the first barrier of perception is loneliness. In dealing with that, we would have to face fear as well as find our unique way in the world. Therefore, by creating another set of principles and practices, we could achieve similar results.

Basically, then, Toltec principles provide direction in order to avoid taking the brunt of a situation, to relax and not cling to anything, to peak awareness, and to run your own life. But before any of these can be accomplished, don Juan also says, the first principle is tracking yourself (*Silence*, 101). Without the concerted effort to track down and eliminate your foibles, and to recognize and bolster your strengths, you lose sight of the principal purpose of tracking: the pursuit of freedom.

## Strategy

To enact these principles, Toltecs utilize lessons gained from the transition into the third cycle. Don Juan refers to the Toltecs during the Conquest as the unquestionable masters of tracking

(*Fire,* 29). Leaving antiquated, second-cycle practices behind, he says they built a "most effective strategy" which consists of six elements, each interacting with the others. The first five elements are control, discipline, forbearance, timing, and *will.* The sixth element, which don Juan considers the most important, engages the external world. It is the petty tyrant—a person who wields some measure of control over you. And, once again, because this strategy requires a significant expenditure of energy, a significant reduction of self-importance is the key to governing it.

**Control** or **Steadfastness.** This element enables a harmonious containment of energy characteristic of present-centeredness. It also allows energy to flow freely in whatever directions desired. This dynamic is often measured in terms of a constant inner control. Agitation is contrary to it; perseverance and independence are its hallmarks.

**Discipline** or **Vigilance.** This element consists of a marked ability to assess and analyze strong and weak points in the environment, in others, and in yourself. It allows you to harness energy, and it cultivates strength. The discipline of a ranger is the ability to remain vigilant even under the most stressful conditions (*Fire,* 39).

**Patience** or **Forbearance.** This form of holding back permits you to let go of that which belongs to others, claiming only that which belongs to you (*Fire,* 39). Calm endurance marks the commitment to pursue long-range objectives.

**Timing** or **Exquisite Balance.** Timing requires you to tune yourself to the rhythms of Spirit. In doing so, you automatically balance yourself with yourself, with the environment, and with dimensions beyond the ordinary.

**Will** or **Personal Intent.** Success in any endeavor results from the proper accumulation and use of personal energy. The essence of tracking is trimming and shaping your life to the natural currents of Spirit by reducing unnecessary expenditures of energy. Activating your *will* results.

**Petty Tyrant** or **Rigorous Practice.** Having a petty tyrant ensures that you always have plenty of practice to apply the teachings. Due to its importance, it is presented in more detail in the "Practices" section of this chapter.

This strategy offers a program for action. It highlights the essentials of gaining experience, assimilating the results, and practicing to further refine yourself.

## Traits

Presenting the essentials in yet another way, don Juan says there are four basic moods, or traits, of tracking: ruthlessness, cunning, sweetness, and patience. They are levels of intent, or individual currents of energy, meaning that they are also positions of the focal point (*Silence*, 89, 186). In addition, they provide a four-direction orientation for behavior: ruthlessness for the west; cunning for the north; sweetness for the east; and patience for the south. Combining and balancing them in right measure produces the ranger state of *being*.

**Ruthlessness.** Unrestricted determination marks this trait. It is boldness without recklessness, command without arrogance, and is a basic premise of the Toltec Way. Don Juan says it is a main requirement to unseat self-importance and thus restore one's natural ability to perceive the silent knowledge—an immediate "knowing" without ordinary deliberation—of Spirit directly (*Silence*, 169-170).

Don Juan adds that the ancient seers unraveled self-importance and found it to be self-pity in disguise. Hence, success hinges on changing your cohesion to the pattern of "no pity," a focal point location synonymous with ruthlessness (*Silence*, 153). Without this trait, you leave yourself wide open for others to walk all over you. With it, you're more objective, more able to manage your resources, and thus more capable of tracking knowledge.

In his teaching of Castaneda, one of don Juan's unswerving objectives was to get Castaneda to move his focal point. At that time, Castaneda regarded him as eminently rational. Don Juan responded that he only appeared to be so, that his ruthlessness created a disguise of rationality. Through this deception, Castaneda gained enough intellectual security to risk adopting new ways. The main point was getting Castaneda to entrain his energy to don Juan's. This entrainment required unparalleled consistency on don Juan's part and therefore is the reason he says that for a Toltec ruthlessness is not cruelty, but sobriety (*Silence*, 153, 174).

**Cunning**. Cunning involves examining a situation so you may get what you want without warping anyone's energies. Aiming for accuracy, you study the features of a situation and the forces influencing your battleground. You remain prepared and innovative. You need to know where you're headed and what you want to accomplish. Furthermore, cunning involves using the art of deception without being deceitful. Without it, you have to rely on other people's assessments and conclusions. With it, you develop resourcefulness and adaptability.

**Sweetness**. To balance ruthlessness and cunning, you present a likeable facade. However, this sweetness often belies having no pity. Without being condescending, you have cold, calculating eyes. Paradoxically, you are also kind, since wisdom without kindness, says don Juan, is useless (*Fire*, 12). This trait doesn't mean you are constantly dripping with sweetness. In fact, don Juan advises that it's good to show your claws on occasion (*Separate*, 185).

With sweetness, you cultivate a keen sense of humor. You can also let go of your wins and losses, and move on to your next encounters. Without it you might lose balance and become obsessed with your goals, perhaps harassing others on your way to achieving them. With it, you gain the ability to laugh at yourself and at the world.

**Patience**. Patience is forbearance without laxness. You take only what you need, and leave the rest. It also gives you the capacity to listen and wait. Your silence grants access to deeper knowledge, silent knowledge. It provides balance to keep other traits in check. As a result, Spirit moves quietly within and without, smoothly creating the circumstances your intent sets in motion. Without it, you resurface into self-importance and latch onto superficial desires. With it, you find peace.

# Practices

Compared with dreaming, tracking concerns itself with small shifts of the focal point. To the average observer, however, a small shift might seem quite a marvel. To don Juan, for instance, turning into a crow was a small shift. But before any shift can occur, your first energy field must first be de-stabilized, or suspended. To do this, you must break your normal continuity of experience. Exercises such as altering routines, gazing, and erasing personal history are therefore the preliminaries for dislodging the focal point.

You must then move the focal point. While intent is the force which shifts your cohesion, clarity about your goal serves to reduce random interference during the transition. Intent also solidifies, or re-stabilizes, a shift. A nonordinary worldview, learning tasks, and a path with heart all help re-stabilize the focal point at nonordinary locations.

A primary objective of modern Toltec training is to de-stabilize the ordinary world of reason, and stabilize the nonordinary world of *will*. Then the objective is to de-stabilize the nonordinary world in order to stabilize a natural field. It is then that *will* is free.

To accomplish this process, tracking procedures clean your connection with Spirit. Having a guideline that the world is mysterious, for instance, prevents premature closure; and when you do define something, you don't relegate your definition to dogma. You retain options for changing your mind. Moreover, engaging this discipline frees your energy to assess your actions and their results. By tracking Spirit, you find uncommon success in any endeavor. As it permeates everything, your awareness is plugged into something beyond your immediate knowledge. As a result, it leads you better than you can lead yourself. To help you find success in tracking, here are a few applications.

**Controlled Folly**. In *The Power of Silence,* don Juan refers to controlled folly as a technique within tracking. In the same book, he equates it with tracking. Regarding the malleability of terminology, he says that calling a tracker a "controlled folly maker" is too cumbersome. He then tells Castaneda to use any term he wants (*Silence,* 102).

In *The Eagle's Gift,* Castaneda reports that don Juan refers to trackers as practitioners of controlled folly, and dreamers as practitioners of dreaming. Grau adds her instruction, telling Castaneda that controlled folly consists of applying tracking principles to everything (*Gift,* 213, 293). The results, she says, are that trackers are never in a hurry, so they don't fret; they don't take things too seriously; and they freely improvise. In other words, they command their behavior even though they may not understand anything.

Don Juan also says that only those who *see* can control their folly. While seers labor as hard as anyone, they pick and choose with greater fluency because they have more insight regarding the effects of their decisions. Moreover, from their *seeing* they know that they're in over their heads, and that a undefinable force guides their steps. Consequently, they treat "the world as an endless mystery and what people do as endless folly" (*Separate*, 186, ✝ 265). Within the human domain, however, those who *see* can be deliberate about their folly. Choosing a direction, they follow it as though it mattered beyond all else. The principal art of controlled folly is not being attached to anything while remaining a part of everything (*Silence*, 266).

**Adaptability.** Whether in the world of reason or the world of *will*, a ranger must be fluid and adaptable, says don Juan (*Tales*, 110). With those traits, a ranger looks at the world from a variety of angles. To do otherwise stagnates energy into a conditional field.

For example, much of Castaneda's instruction occurred in the wilderness. Indeed, Castaneda always seemed shocked when don Juan took to city streets. On the other hand, practically all of my interaction with don Juan occurred within the city limits of Tucson. As a result, he taught me to turn a city into a hunting ground. Rather than seek allies in mountain forests, he showed how to find them on the local street corner.

Police officers, for instance, are symbols of power. By observing and talking with New York City police, I learned how to stay more alert in that intense environment. It was my experience that the best officers were always relaxed but fully conscious of their surroundings. The more mature officers had a ready smile and took time to offer assistance before returning to a vigilant posture. The younger ones usually side-stepped interaction, preferring to remain watchful to the streets. I also learned that without purpose ⅄ a person is subject to any and all predators roaming the streets or wherever. Purpose moves you through the world. It provides a force which determines your experiences.

In addition, rather than using an owl's hoot or the flight of crows for omens, you can use automobiles' horns and the colors of clothes. Instead of gazing at smoke, you can gaze at steam rushing out of sidewalk vents. You can leaf-gaze at the neighborhood oak tree. In fact, gazing at a street lamp's luminescence as it passes through a tree while you sit on the concrete steps of a brownstone is practically a picture of heaven.

Part of tracking is presenting a coherent image to those around you. In Manhattan, however, you can get away with more non-ordinary behavior since often it isn't out of the ordinary. In that town, it seems the unusual is usual. For example, taking a little time to gaze at the shadows on a building won't have people scurrying about in concern, as it might in a small town.

**Blending**. Since they had to deal with invading armies, blending was a required course for the ancient Toltecs. Blending remains relevant because it offers direct lessons in energy management. It also diverts others' attention away from your pursuits, thereby giving you more freedom. It involves suspending, merging with, and learning about other energies. Indeed, don Juan says that part of tracking is the art of disguise (*Silence*, 85).

Through a disguise, you deliberately project an identity. While walking on a crowded street in downtown Tucson I passed an elderly woman wearing an off-yellow dress. She seemed to roll side to side as she walked, just as a hefty grandmother might walk. It turned out to be don Juan. Julian had him learn that disguise during his apprenticeship. Furthermore, Josefina, an apprentice to don Juan and reportedly an attractive woman, studied to appear as an old woman. As a result, she never attracted the interest of the local villagers (*Second Ring*, 98).

A disguise can be minimal to achieve results. Another apprentice to don Juan, Benigno, bought a camera while in Mexico City and took 425 pictures without film, thereby projecting the image of a tourist (*Gift*, 104).

An experience of mine provides another example. Some years ago, I taught psychology at the high school level. Although I was single I wore a wedding ring. My supervisor had told me about the inclination of some students to make sexual overtures in pursuit of better grades, and I thought that by wearing the ring sexual ploys would be kept to a minimum. Toward the end of the semester, I saw an opportunity to use the situation to educate the class on a common practice within transpersonal psychology. So I seized the "cubic centimeter of chance" and presented a lesson on nonpatterning, or suspending interpretations.

I asked the class who thought I was married. Every student raised a hand. I took the ring off, placed it in my pocket, and told them I was single. We talked about how symbols elicit certain perceptions; in this case, based on a well-recognized symbol, they had closed off their perception by defining my marital status. I said that if they were nonpatterning, they would not have interpreted the ring as anything other than a ring. Only with further investigation would they discover my actual status. They all murmured in agreement. I then asked how many now thought I was single. Most raised a hand. A few smelled something afoot. I returned the ring to my finger just as the bell rang, and enjoyed their quizzical expressions as they filed out the door.

The idea is to give others a particular impression, then let them do work of associating it with what they know. To ensure success, don Juan's teacher stressed knowing the quirks of your disguise so well that no one knows you're disguised (*Silence*, 85). By knowing the ins and outs, you energetically blend into that form. And thus your behavior corresponds with the disguise. Plus, as each disguise represents a minute shift in the focal point, you begin manipulating your energy body.

Also keep in mind that one of the most transformative procedures you can accomplish is to blend with the world to such a marked degree that you become an individual, and thereby know your place in the world. Practicing the art-craft of tracking delivers you to that accomplishment.

**Shapeshifting**. A more rigorous application of blending is shapeshifting, in which your cohesion changes to such a degree that your physical body changes. While giving Castaneda a lesson in no pity, for example, don Juan adjusted his energy to that of an hysterical old man. While don Juan is an elder, he certainly has the strength and stamina of a young man. To me, not once did he ever seem old. But to break Castaneda's reliance on him, he says he actually became old and senile. He also told Castaneda he did it just to see if he could hold that form (*Silence*, 77, 156).

Don Juan adds that becoming an old man registers a very subtle shift. Julian was capable of turning into a myriad of human shapes; he was fluent in this practice. Although considered a small shift, a more drastic change is turning into a crow. Don Juan learned how to do this from the tenant. He then passed on the knowledge to Castaneda (*Teachings*, 188).

Don Juan first gave power plants to Castaneda to facilitate this shift. I've also learned that the dreaming body offers such lessons. Once, while flying about in my dreaming body, I spontaneously turned into a hawk. I lost my human bearings and enjoyed an enchanted flight. Years later, during dreaming I shifted to a rattlesnake. First I saw a snake approach me in the dream. It opened its mouth and extended its fangs. I felt terror but somehow continued to watch. I then saw an image appear in the snake's throat. Focusing on it, I discovered I was looking at myself.

Although initially startled, I relaxed into the dream and then spontaneously began to shift form. Entertaining the shift, I found myself in a nest filled with rattlesnakes. I was amazed at not feeling threatened by them. This confusion cleared when I realized I was one of them. As a snake, I felt as though I were composed of condensed and very powerful energy.

In the larger picture of transformation, these experiences are inconsequential, save for their effect of warming up to the possibilities. I learned from don Juan that by bringing shapeshifting awareness back from dreaming, I could eventually perform the shifts in my physical body. As magnificent as this seemed, he said it was only meant to liberate my energy body. It was simply practice—quickening the process—for the Fire from Within.

By knowing the forces that shape perception (such as association, entrainment, and cognitive dissonance), and then by engaging controlled folly and petty tyrants, you can create a foundation from which to tackle blending. Blending, in turn, becomes a step for shapeshifting. And while understanding may assist these shifts, this skill requires a full-bodied alignment of energy. Unbending intent is therefore the main ingredient. The complete recipe includes learning the specific inventory of what you're shifting into. In other words, learning all the intricacies of that form's peculiarities of perception (*Dreaming*, 78).

**Scouting**. As a scout, you can accomplish many things—mastering basic reconnaissance, becoming adept at leaving nothing to chance, acquiring in-depth knowledge. Some Toltecs even prefer to adopt scouting as their lifestyle. They thrive on solitude and on their ability to withstand the harsh rigors of walking point for their team.

Don Juan says that Toltecs regularly employ scouts, or advanced runners, to "probe our perceptual limits" (*Silence*, 133). He even adapted poetry to this use. Trying this tactic, I found that, by using a verse as a doorway into a new dimension of thought and feeling, it's possible to transport awareness through that door.

Once, while out for an afternoon stroll, I was casually thinking about the difficulties in Somalia. My brother had recently returned from a tour of duty there and I was thinking about our recent conversation. But simply by thinking of Somalia, I entered a waking dream. My physical environment began changing into a savannah. I heard a nearby lion's fierce roar. The subtle, almost lackadaisical, association with Africa had entrained my energy to that environment. In other terms, my thoughts were acting as a scout and my complete energy body was following. I then began feeling physical-body perceptions, as though I were physically near the lion. Realizing that I was transporting to a distant land while my physical body was awake shocked me back to my neighborhood. This wasn't the type of dreaming to which I had grown accustomed. I made a mental note to be more careful of my thoughts.

The most elementary scouting skills include reducing your wants to a bare minimum, traveling light, dispersing a minimum of energy, and blending. A scout also requires ruthlessness to vigorously push ahead, control to withstand the expedition, discipline to measure the journey, cunning to apply all assessments, and patience to calmly continue. As a result, you develop the capacity to enter new terrains and map them out while leaving few traces of yourself. The more knowledge you gather, the more you push beyond barriers of perception. Often the reward is pushing yourself off a flat earth to find that there never were any monsters waiting for a mid-afternoon snack.

**Storytelling**. One form of scouting is storytelling, a traditional and highly respected art-craft. Some Toltecs follow it as a way of life, or a way to Spirit and freedom. Indeed, don Juan says that stories are the best avenue to learn about Toltec ways, perhaps because the best stories come to life and engage several modes of perception simultaneously (*Silence*, 143, 22). Castaneda's books, for example, are in a storytelling format. They're all best sellers.

Storytelling is also a bridge to pure understanding. Again, part of pure understanding is knowing that the story is actually occurring somewhere within the fabric of infinity. When you surrender to the story and follow it as a scout, perception follows. The more your perception follows these magic-making trails, the more the story becomes the reality, and the more reality becomes something else.

**Petty Tyrant**. The ancient seers had fun making an entire category of tyrannical behavior. The primal source of energy was deemed the tyrant, the one and only ruler of the universe. All other authority was given classifications based on the degree of pettiness. Don Juan says that to handle petty tyrants, one need only use the basic elements of strategy: control, discipline, and forbearance. He adds that the other element of strategy, *will*, is used only in dire need, as it involves "a supreme maneuver that cannot be performed on the daily human stage" (*Fire*, 30, 32).

So critical are petty tyrants that don Juan advises his apprentices to deliberately find them, should one not cross their paths. Ideal petty tyrants have authority over you; the more manipulative they are, the better. You get to deal with outright backstabbing, subtle and not-so-subtle bigotry, blind hate, and explosions of rage. But you get to deal with this in the new light of tracking. Having to lose self-importance while keeping yourself intact pushes you past your limits. The only thing for certain in this arena is that you'll lose many battles before you catch on. Then the struggle is sublimely liberating as you learn to find freedom in the midst of oppression.

To find success, learn how to let go of your desires and expectations, and then let go of everything else. Reduce your personal agenda and allow Spirit to flow. Begin throwing out all of your conditioned responses, and strive to remain unaffected at each and every turn of your path. Avoid confrontations, unless you want to generate more heat from your oppressor. Then be willing to take it on the chin. Otherwise, let confrontations diffuse. During your skirmishes, you'll find that your path with heart keeps you focused. It soothes you when your nerves are frayed, and lets you laugh when all seems lost. All the while, though, continually track yourself. Assess strong and weak points, and plug the holes where energy leaks.

Always keep in mind what you're engaging. Know that you're in a petty tyrant relationship. Skirmishes with petty tyrants give you ample practice to regulate your resources. Over time, you feel yourself getting less caught up in the ordinary affairs of the world, and more dedicated to freedom. Remember that you're placing yourself through a mind-numbing obstacle course. The overall effect of engaging petty tyrants is that you continually heighten awareness in order to lessen the irritations, and so the course becomes mind-liberating. In fact, the notion of petty tyrants may be applied to all irritants in your life. The more you push yourself into heightened awareness, the less effect they have.

With time, you also learn that control prevents you from blindly reacting, and discipline enables you to assess what's taking place even through you're feeling pummeled. And you learn that cunning permits you to gradually reverse the situation, while patience allows a deliberate resolution. And, above all, you learn that Toltec strategy and practices prevent *you* from becoming a petty tyrant.

*Will.* Don Juan says that the interplay of all components within the strategy can be accomplished only by a person who has developed *will*. Perhaps an example of this precept is evident in Castaneda's return to Mexico to visit his fellow apprentices. The last time he saw them he had jumped off a cliff, an event that activated his *will*. Upon arriving, he stayed with the Little Sisters, a group of women who had developed remarkable dreaming skills.

As part of don Juan's instructions to spur Castaneda into deeper levels of awareness, on different occasions the women attempted to assassinate Castaneda (*Second Ring*, 60). However, don Juan didn't tell them of Castaneda's "awesome side." In the midst of one battle, Castaneda retained his control and *saw* weak spots in their energy bodies. Kicking those spots, he rendered the women useless to further conflict. In another battle, Castaneda's energy surged, his "double" exited his physical body, and he delivered an extremely powerful blow to dona Soledad, a blow which almost killed her. In both instances, Castaneda's *will* engaged different levels of the second energy field, producing nonordinary results which delivered him from otherwise-certain death.

**Tracking the Second Energy Field.** The stability, direction, and temperance gained from tracking are required to explore the second field. They also provide a way to integrate your findings. But while tracking relates to securing focal-point shifts, dreaming provides many of the options.

There are a variety of ways to open up to the second field. In general, doing so demands stepping beyond ordinary conditional fields. In the following chapters, hosts of tracking and dreaming exercises are provided to assist you. There are also exercises which blend the approaches by hooking together first- and second-field energies. Through her intent, for example, Abelar learned to extend lines of energy out and away from her physical body, forming them into a net or cocoon about her.[1] Thus she was learning to tap the second field and activate her *will*, all the while maintaining an immediate connection with her physical body.

Tracking and dreaming also blend in other ways. Several years ago, I was visiting my place of predilection which is on the northeastern coast of the United States. Don Juan told Castaneda that a place of predilection was used to store energy. It was also the place where his final dance in this world would take place (*Journey*, ch. 13).

Arriving at night, I walked a short distance and stopped. The darkness seemed insurmountable. The very edges of the horizon had a reddish-orange hue, a color that stimulates my dreaming. But a storm was brewing, so the rest of the sky was overcast. There was no light from stars or the moon. Years before when I had visited at night I almost fell in a crevice; such a fall would have resulted in serious injury, possibly death. So I stood still and tried to find my bearings. I then noticed flashes of light shooting out of the rocks. The flashes offered sufficient light to guide my footsteps.

I walked into the forest and sat down in front of a tree and began gazing. While I was doing so, the surrounding area lightened up a bit as is normal with this exercise. I then had a vision in which I *saw* a human figure, bent over an object that reminded me of a tombstone stuck in the ground at an angle. The figure looked as though it were typing. This caused me to change associations. Rather than a tombstone, I associated it with a laptop computer. But I continued to nonpattern the situation. I didn't want to get in the way of this story-omen.

Then the shadow-figure gradually receded and merged into a tree, whereupon the laptop came to life in its own way. I took this as an indication for me to merge with the world and to allow a book I was writing to have its own life. I felt that its purpose was beyond my design. Just as I made that recognition, the clouds temporarily broke open and the constellation Orion—the warrior of the heavens—stood in the western sky. I took this as an omen that I'd correctly interpreted the proceedings.

Tracking skills are also necessary to handle the daily emergence of the second field. During a business meeting, for instance, you might *see* another's aura. But your control keeps you from blurting out what you see. If those with whom you're negotiating aren't aware of auric fields, your behavior may seem quite unstable. And so there goes the deal. On the other hand, if you're very good at reading auras, you can use them to discern the unfolding moods of others. In conjunction with cunning, this ability can make you more proficient at negotiating.

\* \* \*

The greater scope of tracking involves aligning yourself with a goal in order to become the goal. To effect this, tracking principles, strategies, and practices are designed to produce stable shifts in the focal point. Realizing your goal is the equivalent of stabilizing a shift. The pinnacle of tracking is bringing your entire life into line with Spirit. An intense manifestation of this alignment is the Fire from Within. For that degree of living with Spirit, you must measure each and every aspect of your life against that quest.

Don Juan advises that focal point shifts should be done peacefully and performed in harmony with yourself and the world (*Fire*, 216), giving you time to catch up with yourself, to make shifts to and from reason and *will*, and thus to come to your own terms about your endeavors. As a result, tracking helps you foster smooth transitions. So rather than rant and rave about this and that, rather than feeling helpless and afraid, and rather than sit on your haunches hoping deliverance will arrive, you can use tracking to help you steadily and surely forge a path of your own heart's making.

# 9
# A Tool Kit

To withstand a Toltec lifestyle, don Juan says you need inner strength. He also says that sufficient sobriety may actually eliminate the need for a teacher (*Fire*, 182, 178). Sobriety in these terms may be thought of as character, or integrity. Integrity enables a person to develop a link with Spirit, and the link then provides all that is necessary to proceed. Developing this relationship is a primary function of tracking.

Tracking instills character through two principal maneuvers. The first is tempering the first energy field; don Juan refers to such tempering as "cleaning the tonal." The second is tuning down the first field, or "shrinking the tonal." Don Juan says that this training generates sufficient fortitude to handle the second field (*Tales*, 174).

Tempering the first field opens the door to the second field. Then, the more you can tune down your first field, the more you can enter the second field. But your first field has to be strong enough not to wane. Without a strong first field, your experiences in the second field are meaningless and perhaps dangerous.

Tuning down the first field is like turning down the volume of a radio so you can hear someone else talk. Fright, embarrassment, and novel experiences can all tune down the first field. But these are usually random occurrences. Toltecs seek to control the maneuver. Accordingly, while learning to temper your first field, you figure out how to deliberately tune it down without tuning it out. You can measure your first field (whether you are accenting it too much or too little) through feeling.

With increased exposure to the second field comes increased confidence. But don't overestimate your new abilities. While they may enhance your clarity and power, they are not immediately liberating (*Gift*, 188). Indeed, they can easily take you for a ride of self-indulgence. Tempering the first field keeps this tendency in check.

Don Juan says that to reach the energy body, you need energy. He adds that the Toltec Way is a means to reduce energy expenditures, as well as a means to re-deploy existing energy effectively (*Dreaming,* 23, 32-33). The result is strong, fluid energy fields. The following exercises and perspectives assist in strengthening awareness, which includes the ability to de-stabilize, shift, and re-stabilize cohesion. Tracking tools, therefore, allow you to travel past any conditional field and establish the conditions for a natural field. By employing these tools, you also begin reviving your intent, your connecting link with Spirit. *Traveling With Power* offers additional exercises for many of these techniques.

**Accessibility**. By teaching Castaneda how to hunt food, don Juan also taught him how to hunt knowledge. As they roamed the desert, don Juan taught him how to deal with water-hole spirits, omens, and dreaming, just to name a few items on the agenda. As a result, Castaneda learned how to access power. That knowledge, in turn, served as the preliminary for accessing Spirit.

Opening yourself to the unknown can be frightening. But so can walking across a heavily trafficked street if you've never done so. Whether you're tackling the unknown or a busy street, you're increasing your awareness and building your skills. In short, you're learning to handle knowledge and develop personal power. To enter the flow of Spirit, it's necessary to live with it. By living with it, you learn how to abide by it. To access Spirit, then, open the door to it.

**Attitude**. Tempering the first field produces a marked change in a person. It transforms the way you fit into the world. This change is necessary for any chance of success, says don Juan (*Tales,* 227). It is not simply a change in mood or attitude, and yet attitude helps make the change. Whether you're timid or bold, for example, affects your behavior. In addition, the attitude that there are no big or small decisions smoothes out the peaks and valleys of daily life. There are only decisions we make in the light of our death, says don Juan. This makes all decisions of equal weight (*Journey,* ch. 4).

Furthermore, a flexible attitude keeps you from getting entangled in your own pursuits. If you're continually judgmental, for example, you have no time to learn anything new. Assessing a situation is not judging it. A ranger hones clarity of people and events in order to make careful decisions, but does not waste energy on judging. Plus, an attitude of aiming for success while remaining free from the outcome enables you to respond quickly to changing circumstances. Being too tied to an outcome only ties you up in knots.

A memorable line about attitude comes from a Steven Seagal film, *Hard to Kill.* Seagal portrays a police officer versed in martial arts and oriental healing practices. As the result of a murder attempt by corrupt police officers, he spends seven years in a coma. While recovering, he plans retribution with a trusted colleague. In reply to his friend's concern about being outnumbered, Seagal replies that they'll succeed because they have a "superior attitude, superior state of mind."

**Balance**. One effect of Toltec training is attaining a calm assurance while being assured of nothing. This emotional equanimity pays dividends throughout your life, as it reflects a balanced blend of body, mind, and spirit. This balance also parlays into being "centered," allowing new energies to flow freely through you without being thrown too far off your mark.

If we, as a species, were in balance, we would not be destroying the source of our sustenance. We would not deliberately poison our waters, and we would not bludgeon Earth with bullets and bombs thinking that our actions to destroy other humans have no effect on Earth. Hence, we repeatedly demonstrate we are out of balance with ourselves and the world. Therefore, Toltecs start from the premise that they are out of balance, and then work to rectify it.

**Death, the Advisor**. Do you want to think you're alive? Or would you rather feel it? Our death, says don Juan, has been intended since we were born (*Silence,* 66). In other words, it's there—so use it. Bringing awareness of your death into focus gives you leverage to live. It is a potent power to develop presence of mind. Plus it gives you the gumption to follow your dreams.

Using your death as an advisor gives you a wake-up call. If you're not willing to die for your actions, then you're not willing to live for them. In these terms, each moment is equal, regardless of what is occurring. And there is no better or worse type of person. There is only who you are as you were created. Connecting with that essence may well be the hardest part of living; using your death for keen focus helps you do it. To begin aligning yourself with your life, regularly ask yourself:

1. If all I have is this moment, how do I want to use it?
2. Is this the best I can do?

3. Is this activity worthy of my life?
4. If I were to die right now, would my death respect me?

While using death as an advisor provides focus in your daily life, it also propels perception into nonordinary realms. Performing the Fire from Within, for example, is changing your cohesion to an energy pattern in which the intent of death is no longer an active element. According to don Juan, this process sidesteps the ordinary rules of life and death, and thus death may be suspended (*Silence,* 66).

**Diet**. Food is energy. A poor diet distorts your energy fields, making them harder to handle. Castaneda contends that "neuroses are by-products of what we put in our mouths." He adds that sugar is one of our worst enemies.[1] We can also extend diet to cover what we read, talk about, and generally bring into our lives.

Your physical body provides perception. So feed it well. Just ask yourself what you want your diet to accomplish. Is what you're ingesting what you want as fuel to accomplish your goals?

**Inaccessibility**. Being inaccessible means you don't entrain to, and thus needlessly follow, social forces. Indeed, Donner considers it standing outside of social influences.[2] Don Juan adds that it means you don't exhaust yourself or others. He also says that it doesn't mean to hide or be secretive (*Journey,* 94). You remain centered within yourself, rather than losing yourself in another's life. The more inaccessible you are, the more your relation to the world of people changes.

We often give up our personal power to the glamorous, the famous, the rich. By being inaccessible, you can deal with that world of power if necessary without losing yourself in it. Permitting yourself to be governed by Spirit, you maintain your integrity.

Accordingly, part of Toltec discipline is learning how to be alone. Don Juan required Castaneda to rent a dingy, green motel room until he could remain unaffected by being either alone or with someone. Castaneda says he climbed the walls for months until he learned how to be at ease with himself alone.[3] In addition, Clara required Abelar to temporarily break all physical and emotional ties with the world in order to gain unity within herself.[4] The most viable option at this stage is to become inaccessible to the human world, and accessible to Spirit.

Inaccessibility offers a way to streamline your life. It leads to being grounded and practical. It reduces energy consumption and gives the world its life. For example, during a visit in rural Virginia, I was sitting with a friend on a makeshift bench on top of a knoll. On the slope of the hill was an orchard, across a nearby dirt road was a human-made swimming pond, and in the distance were the Blue Ridge Mountains. We talked about Toltec matters and practiced gazing.

Looking off across the land, he remarked that if we cut down a few trees, we would also have a good view of the river. That, I told him, is the wrong kind of access. Being inaccessible means not killing trees just to grant a better view. It involves the same kind of reasoning that don Juan uses with Castaneda when he tells him to touch the world sparingly and not bend it out of shape. You don't act as though you'll never eat again and consume all the food in sight, says don Juan. And, he adds, you don't damage plants just to make a wilderness barbecue pit. He also says that a hunter "must be in perfect balance with everything else." Otherwise hunting becomes "a meaningless chore." And the secret to hunting is making yourself accessible or inaccessible at specific turns in your path (*Journey,* 94-95, 77, 90).

Being inaccessible permits controlled entry into, and exit from, your Toltec travels. As a result, you don't get lost in your discoveries, and you don't permit your quest to develop into a ritual of self-importance. You don't sacrifice your journey simply to become somebody or have something.

**Laughter**. Laughter carries a purging effect. Indeed, don Juan says laughter is necessary to counteract the deleterious effects of the Toltec world (*Tales,* 57). Without humor you become too serious, too morose, too oppressive. Don Juan laughed simply because he enjoyed doing so, even when he was deadly serious (*Journey,* 84). He knew that laughter helps people avoid locking themselves into their own designs.

Accordingly, one of the keys for being well-disciplined is to look for the fun in the world and to actually have fun with it. Don Juan, if you recall, eventually learned to enjoy dealing with petty tyrants (*Fire,* 37). He also taught that, while waiting for something, a ranger should laugh and enjoy the world (*Tales,* 282).

**Listening**. Listen to the world. Listen to yourself. Listen with your ears, your heart, and with your entire being. Listening accesses awareness beyond your normal frame of reference. It's up to you to hear what is there.

**Love.** Love in the Toltec world has little to do with ordinary romantic love. Relentless love, as don Juan calls it, is a pure act of love without looking for anything in return.[5] It is not an investment. There are no guarantees. Nothing can shake you from it. Pure love is an element of a natural, or unconditional, energy field.

Perhaps love is not mentioned all that frequently in Castaneda's books because the topic looms too vast in importance. Don Juan advises Castaneda that the only thing that can truly liberate a person is unswerving love. He also indicates that love is the last lesson. "It is always left for the very last moment," he says just prior to Castaneda leaping off a cliff, "for the moment of ultimate solitude when a man faces his death and his aloneness. Only then does it make sense" (*Tales*, 286).

In addition, this type of rarified affection has little to do with ordinary morality. Rather than establish social guidelines, it keeps energy flowing and thereby keeps perception open. At the same time, it provides a uniform foundation to interact with the world at large, and with the inhabitants of other dimensions. It allows you to stretch out and connect with anything. Therefore, you always have a reference point regarding how to relate with whomever is around, wherever you are and whatever is going on. Affection of this kind is a statement about balance. It is never used as a lure to entice others into following your ways.

**Nonattachment.** Nonattachment, or detachment as it is often termed, does not mean to withdraw or retreat from the world; don Juan regarded such withdrawal meaningless (*Gift*, 142). Neither does it mean you can't be affected, influenced, or touched by another. It is a tool for investigating, and to accurately assess situations. Otherwise you're prone to projection.

It is also a tool for handling your energies. Among the common reactions to a petty tyrant, for example, is tucking the ol' tail between the legs and making a hasty retreat, or locking horns in a mindless struggle to see who comes out on top. Nonattachment lets Spirit flow between the forces of you and the other. As a result, it gives you a break between your behavior and your awareness. It gives you a slight pause for deliberation. Hence, you're less reactive and more capable of handling yourself and the situation.

To build nonattachment:

1. Strive to do your best without concern for the outcome of any activity.

2. If you find yourself too wrapped up in something, or too reactive, let it go. Restore your balance; don't fight yourself over it.

3. Don't block or censor any perceptions. At the same time, have your insights and move on. Don't keep your favorites out of self-interest. That only makes you attached to your current knowledge, thereby preventing new growth.

4. Use your death to advise you on how to proceed rather than by using your normal decision-making procedures.

**Nonpatterning.** This is a principal technique to step beyond any conditional field, be it ordinary or nonordinary. We spend an enormous amount of energy molding our world to our thoughts, thereby creating what we believe to be reality. Nonpatterning consists of deliberately not forming patterns, by, for example, not interpreting your perceptions. Don Juan calls this "not-doing"—not doing what you know how to do (*Journey*, ch. 15). Psychologists refer to it as "deautomatization," or suspending your normal, automatic responses.[6] Whatever you call it, it frees energy. Indeed, don Juan says it is the key to personal power (*Journey*, 217).

We interpret the world by what's on our minds. When our thoughts are challenged we often reply, "But all the books say it's this way." Thus we continually reduce our world to an inflexible point of view. Additional experience with that worldview then enhances that world rather than expanding awareness into uncharted vistas.

Nonpatterning de-stabilizes conditional fields by not plying that cohesion with additional energy. A functional *will* results from nonpatterning the ordinary self. By the time you get to a natural field, you have developed *being* and thus are continuously nonpatterning. To start:

1. Avoid labeling. Every time you label something, you constrict awareness. And when you do label, don't take it too seriously.

2. Suspend your beliefs. Don Juan suggests that the only thing a ranger has to believe is that the world is mysterious (*Tales*, ch. 4). He also taught la Gorda not to believe in anything, as beliefs restrict what can be perceived (*Second Ring*, 46).

3. Hold your conclusions, big or small, in abeyance. Even after

you've formed something into a pattern, you can continue non-patterning by not locking it rigidly into place.

4. Don't anticipate.

5. Use feeling. When you do, you automatically trigger non-patterning as you step aside from the reason and engage the second field.

**Observation.** The first principle of tracking, remember, is tracking yourself. A good way to track yourself is to keep track of yourself. Without doing so, you remain without a clue, as in the joke of the person who slams a fist on the table and shouts, "I'm not angry!" To avoid such pitfalls, self-observation is mandatory.

For this, you need to reduce self-importance, beef up nonattachment, and generally try to remain unbiased. With time, you learn to monitor yourself in all circumstances. You can then rectify imbalances without having someone point them out to you. Self-observation handles projection as well. When you notice yourself criticizing someone, for example, you can examine yourself for those faults. While your perceptions about the other person may be accurate, they also reflect aspects of your cohesion. Furthermore, you find that your degree of reaction often indicates how strong that energy lives within you.

To develop self-observation, imagine watching yourself from a point one to three feet in back of you. Some people like to place this point a foot or two over their heads. Then it's a matter of working to maintain this split awareness. At first, just observe yourself. You need to collect as much information as possible about your behavior before you change it.

In a like manner, the capacity to observe the environment as objectively as possible also helps you learn faster. Rather than argue with the world, observe what's going on, accept it, and conduct yourself accordingly. In general, I've found that women are excellent observers. It's educational to observe women who are in the act of observing because frequently they hardly give a clue that they are observing. The ability to do something without drawing attention is, plain and simple, good tracking. Paying attention to omens is also a great way to begin. They help you notice everything about yourself.

**Personal History.** Your daily habits, including your thoughts about yourself and what you tell others about yourself, establish a specific continuity. Not only do these habits seal your identity in terms of what others expect of you, they also lock your focal point in place. *Seeing* shows that "truth" is based on continuity. It's relative to what is known. To break into the unknown, that continuity must be set aside; hence, erase it. Don Juan says that at a certain point he no longer needed his personal history, so he dropped it entirely (*Journey*, 29).

To erase personal history, Castaneda was told to make up stories to tell people. When Castaneda objected, don Juan replied that lies were lies only if one had personal history (*Journey*, ch. 2). Don Juan stressed that the purpose was not to deceive. Indeed, he advised Castaneda to lead a truthful and deliberate life (*Teachings*, 119). Moreover, he suggested that Castaneda use his death as an advisor to prevent him from becoming shifty (*Tales*, 235). To achieve yet another break in his continuity, Castaneda was also told to strike out anew and leave all his friends (*Journey*, 33).

When don Juan gave me the name Broken Eagle Feather, he achieved a similar effect. He broke the continuity reflected by my previous name while establishing the foundation for a new continuity, a new cohesion. The bedrock for this was instilling a purposeful relation to the world. He did so by telling me the name meant "to serve with detachment" and assigning me the task of teaching. In addition, as the nickname Ken is the second syllable of Broken, it nonpatterns the way nicknames are usually derived.

The oddity of the name still has me wrestling with balance. Part of this struggle comes from not wishing to tread on Native American spirituality. Reflecting the popularity of Native teachings, many people have changed their names to Native designations. While many have done so out of respect and affinity for Native traditions, it seems some have done so just to put money in their pockets. I was therefore reluctant even to appear to usurp another's cultural heritage. But my desire to proceed on the path outweighed all other considerations. I have since grown to see the practicality of don Juan's maneuver. I have a constant reminder for honing my path simply because the name continually jolts my awareness.

Erasing personal history is a powerful technique. Breaking with your past removes you from the social forces that work to keep your energy at a state of rest. Its principal effect is that it delivers shocks to your cohesion. When used with other techniques, the focal point eventually dislodges. You are then at the beginning of forming other cohesions.

As a result, not structuring your identity makes it a preliminary for the arts of blending and shapeshifting. Those skills further teach you the relativity of having an identity. That is, any identity is a focal point position. When you experience a number of different positions, you know that any of them is as valid as another. Each might have become the "you" that you're familiar with. Therefore, lies are lies only if you have personal history.

**Physical Conditioning.** In general, you need a well-conditioned body to handle the increased energy that results from following this path. In order to make awareness the top priority, Clara advises to "avoid anything that is weakening and harmful to your body or your mind."[7] Don Juan prescribes walking to facilitate recollecting your journeys in the second field (*Silence*, 154). He also says that the physical body must be fit for *will* to activate (*Tales*, 86).

He adds that the secret to physical health is in what you don't do, rather than in what you do (*Journey*, 195). Don't obstruct the way your body naturally functions, and it will take care of you. It also seems that maintaining heightened awareness automatically produces a strong body. Castaneda once remarked that a by-product of his dreaming was a more muscular body (*Gift*, 58). Conversely, strengthening your body helps maintain heightened awareness. So stretch regularly and thoroughly without overdoing it. Eat well. And exercise. If you're unsure of your limitations, consult a physician.

**Relaxation.** To explore consciousness, relaxation is a must. If you can't feel calm and pliant, tapping the second field proves difficult, at best. You also find that the second field doesn't have the inherent stress of the first field. I think most stress originates from holding on to conditional energy patterns. We don't want to change, to let go, to step outside our comfort zones. Therefore, the more second-field energy we have, the less stress. As a result, one way to eliminate at least some stress is to steadily and surely develop the second field.

Meditation offers a gentle way to entertain the second field. I've also found that people enjoy the relaxing qualities of gazing. Gazing is a deliberate step to enter the second field, and may be considered a form of meditation (see "Gazing" in the next chapter).

More proficiency in handling the second field doesn't mean you completely escape stress. But how you relate to it is another matter. **Engage** nonattachment and self-observation to isolate causes of the stress. Then aim to remain unaffected by your circumstances.

**Responsibility**. One Toltec-minded person I know told me that his sloppy, less-than-impeccable behavior was beneficial for those around him. He said it made people work harder to deal with him. Well, maybe so. But his attitude definitely reflected his lack of personal responsibility.

Don Juan teaches that once you step on this path, you're no longer responsible for others (*Separate*, 47). This doesn't mean you get to trample people. Nor does it mean you can't render assistance. It does provide leverage to remove you from standardized social requirements which hinder your growth. For example, as an attitude, assuming responsibility gives you control so that you're less susceptible to groupthink. It also means you need not scurry about trying to enlighten everyone on your path. Doing so is just trying to mold the world to your image.

Acknowledging personal responsibility requires honest self-examination. It also requires taking the reins of your life and not yielding to the easy temptation of passing off any blame for your behavior. While you may find the root of a problem stems from your upbringing, for instance, blaming others goes too far. If you find the cause for something, correct it; don't waste energy pulling other people through the dregs of your discovery. For don Juan, assuming responsibility primarily meant one thing: Are you willing to die for your decisions? (*Journey*, 62)

**Rituals**. Rituals are focusing tools. They establish a specific effect of entrainment, and repetition augments it. For this reason, don Juan thinks that rituals can trap attention better than anything (*Silence*, 284). While a ritual may be beneficial to enhance focus, however, it may also hem focus in, leaving perception running about within the ritual rather than freely soaring.

Used properly, rituals set up the conditions which go beyond the ritual. Often the form that a ritual provides is necessary so that the essence behind the form may be comprehended. A ritual creates form through its context of use. It thus adjusts your frame of mind and summons intent, which exists beyond form. For instance, don Juan used rituals when teaching Castaneda about power plants. Doing so invoked the conditions of going to knowledge. The power plants then boosted Castaneda's awareness beyond his normal capacities. But don Juan also regarded the role of a team leader to guide awareness past form and into the abstract. Thus you need to know how to focus without using ritual. In practice, this requirement means, for example, that you have to learn dreaming without the ritualistic exercises that produce dreaming in the first place. This process represents another stage of learning the skill.

While rituals work, be they visualization, chanting, or walking in a pattern, consider them as such. The real work—the real effect—waits right in front of you. Use rituals to spark perception, not to wash it out.

**Routines**. Your habits consolidate your energy fields. They are the conditions which fix the focal point in place and thereby uphold your reality. Your world exists, then, through the habitual position of the focal point, which is governed by your habits, especially habitual thinking.

To establish new cohesions, therefore, we need to introduce new habits. Doing so was the struggle of the third cycle (*Fire,* 124). To break Castaneda's reality-forming habits, don Juan took him on extended hikes through the desert and taught him to hunt (*Tales,* 235). As a result, he rearranged Castaneda's relation with the world. Don Juan also required Castaneda to perform mindless, repetitive tasks in order to teach him how to act without expectation of reward.

In his book *The Psychology of Consciousness,* Robert Ornstein refers to the process of interdicting habits as "dishabituation."[8] Countering your routines offers the general effect of fluffing your energy body, which leads to fluency of thought, and thus breaks fixations.

**Self-Importance**. Don Juan says the most effective way to gain energy is to lose self-importance (*Dreaming,* 37). Our upbringing, however, often instills it—a matter of fact, not of blame. We tend to be raised to be somebody because we know something or possess certain things. And we're told we're better than, or worse than, someone else due simply to material considerations.

As we define ourselves, we create hard boundaries about what comprises ourselves and our world. Thus we develop highly conditional energy fields. Having nonordinary abilities may further accent this. For instance, second-cycle Toltecs could perform marvels but still had tons of self-importance. The drawback, then, is that conditional fields have us spend most of our energy in upholding a sense of self and world. By no longer bolstering our positions, however, we use less energy. This increased energy automatically frees the focal point (*Silence,* 179).

We can split self-importance into two major components: self-enhancement and self-reflection. Self-enhancement consists of accenting yourself, either positively or negatively. Thinking you're too good or not good enough, or that you know more or know less, or that you have more or have less, are all opposite sides of self-enhancement. To rectify self-enhancement means that you neither place yourself above others nor turn your back on yourself. It means that considerations of being worthy or unworthy don't enter the picture. What matters is being neither arrogant nor meek. Your humility stems from being hooked only to yourself, without becoming self-absorbed (*Tales,* 16).

In other words, you don't measure the value of your abilities in relation to others. And you don't exalt yourself in order to motivate yourself. What you have is quiet self-assurance, and the ability to maturely take yourself less seriously. This balance also rectifies feelings of insecurity. For instance, insecurity may cause a person to lash out at the world or to hold emotions too tightly inside. Both conditions reflect imbalance, both demonstrate self-enhancement.

The flip side of self-importance is self-reflection. This concept can be quite perplexing since it relates directly to having an identity and a worldview. An identity defined by society is not who you are. It is an aspect of how you fit in with society. And, since a culture relies on a consensus of opinion about what reality is, it most often equates its worldview with reality. Since having a worldview is a principal means of interacting with the world, our world is therefore based on self-importance. A clever disguise.

This principle applies to worlds of any making. Every time we tell ourselves we are like this, and the world is like that, we generate self-importance. Each and every time we define the world, we only reflect to ourselves about ourselves. Hence, we become entangled in projection of vast proportions. As a result, we spend huge amounts of energy in upholding a picture of the world, rather than finding out that the world is actually beyond imagination.

Don Juan says that we don't completely lose self-importance until we balance the first and second energy fields (*Dreaming,* 161). Accomplishing this, you'd be a person of knowledge. By then you're no longer reflecting on the world, you're *being* the world. In the meantime, you can certainly reduce self-importance. To start, you can:

1. Acknowledge your self-importance.
2. Make the decision that you're tackling your self-importance.
3. Categorize your behavior in terms of self-enhancement or self-reflection, then work to eliminate both. For example, ask yourself if you're pursuing this path to become a Toltec, or to lose self-importance and become one with your world. Following a path to become something or somebody is self-enhancement, and is contrary to don Juan's teaching that a ranger's struggle is against self-importance.
4. Use your death to advise you. Doing so was don Juan's "ticket to impeccability" (*Silence,* 215).
5. Practice *seeing. Seeing* automatically transcends patterns, including the ideas of yourself and your world.

**Service**. Another way to reduce self-importance is through service. Don Juan says that in one sense Toltecs are in it for themselves. He balances this by teaching that some Toltecs have practical goals that are of service to other Toltecs and to humankind at large. Other Toltecs exhibit no self-restraint and have no pragmatic goals. Don Juan says the latter have never come to terms with self-importance (*Fire,* 28). He adds that contact with abstract Spirit erases self-importance, as the self automatically becomes abstract and impersonal (*Silence,* 51-52).

Providing service does not mean piety. Indeed, don Juan regarded piousness, or feeling that we know what is going on, as one of three bad habits, the other two being bigotry and obsessiveness (*Tales,* 58). Nor does it suggest being obsequious. A ranger keeps a clean edge, unfettered from worry about how others view his behavior. By faithfully rendering service, you have the opportunity to extend yourself past your habits. Accordingly, it transports you outside of your normal self. It is not intended to trap others in your web.

Service can take many forms. In the work place, for example, you can overcome the effects of an obnoxious boss by getting in the mood of service to the company. Academy Award winner Olympia Dukakis said she realized her role as an actress was to serve the audience, not to manipulate it. "[Those in] an audience should have whatever experience they want," she said. "Everybody is free to be whatever and whoever they want at that time."[9]

**Traveling Light**. Traveling light means to eliminate the unnecessary, and stay tuned to your purpose. The more you off-load extraneous demands on your energy, the more you have to work with.

\* \* \*

Action, not talk, is the key for Toltec success, says don Juan (*Separate*, 314). Much of your understanding today will change tomorrow as you grow in awareness. Consequently, it's more productive to work with energy rather than with just reason. That's what stretches awareness. When in doubt, or to continue success, stick with the basics as though you were practicing good seamanship. Don't quit just because you're tired. I once practiced a technique for two years to develop a certain aspect of *seeing*. I had no results whatsoever until, clear out of the blue, I could do it.

Each of these exercises in some way develops ranger traits. Indeed, it's not difficult to see how being inaccessible and using death as your advisor bolster ruthlessness; erasing personal history and observation cultivate cunning; laughter and losing self-importance foster sweetness; and nonattachment and traveling light promote patience. Overall, you'll find that a Toltec path is often more tenuous than ordinary roads through life. It always leads into unknown reaches, requiring keen vigilance. Your advantage is that its discipline creates a more balanced, fulfilling life.

# 10
# Power Tools

This chapter continues outlining tracking techniques. Many are more advanced than those in the previous chapter, as they are more complex and thus require more skill. By exercising them, you begin working with energy itself, rather than setting up the conditions to do so. As with all techniques, it's possible to adjust the steps to make the results more personally powerful. At the same time, be careful not to take shortcuts solely because you don't want to make the effort. Before modifying an exercise, it's often best to thoroughly acquaint yourself with it and with the effects it is intended to bring about.

**Body Knowledge.** Life isn't just a mental exercise. We have an entire physical body at our disposal. However, we're normally taught to discount our body as a means of perceiving, and focus on the intellect instead. Perhaps this is why we get lost in the first energy field and neglect the second field.

Don Juan teaches that the second field is comprehended, or handled, by the body. In fact, he considers that all Toltec abilities stem from the body itself (*Gift,* 167). While mental flexibility is beneficial, compared to Toltec endeavors it takes you only a short distance. You can mentally cover all the angles you want, but there comes a time when you have to act.

The deeper you move into awareness, the more your body organizes and translates that energy into meaning. Tapping infinite order, or pure reason, rather than the order of self-arranged reason, automatically speeds up the acquisition of knowledge. It is for this reason that don Juan appeared to Castaneda as so reasonable. Through his *will,* don Juan remained connected with pure reason. Thus his actions always translated as reasonable.

Toward the end of his time with don Juan, Castaneda found he could "listen and watch and sense and recall in all the cells of my body."[1] Doing so produces silent knowledge. Silent knowledge results from direct contact with intent (*Silence,* 124). And it's the body which measures, assesses, and communicates this contact.

To begin using silent knowledge, don't act on your thoughts. They restrain perception and behavior into their own mold. Instead, use feeling. Pay attention to your instinct and intuition. Practice and test your abilities often.

**Energy Dances.** While driving straight through from Tucson to Austin, Texas (an entire day's drive), I decided to try what don Juan called becoming accessible to the wind (*Journey,* 90). A certain dance was supposed to keep you awake all night. So at sunset, just as the last light wavered in the sky, I stood atop a small hill, faced the west horizon, extended my arms with my palms open, and jogged in place.

In a few seconds, I felt energy rush into my palms. My arms extended further and became stiff, almost rigid. I then felt energy flow through my arms and fill my body. A gust of wind hit my face. I stopped the dance, got in my car, and drove off. I remained alert the rest of the night without coffee or artificial stimulants. When I arrived in Austin, I even had sufficient energy to go out to dinner and socialize.

This dance also works well during the day. If you need extra alertness, go off by yourself and perform the dance with your palms open to the sun. Before dancing, ask Spirit to fill you with energy so that you may accomplish the task facing you. By doing so, I've always received beneficial results.

**Energy Passes.** Energy passes are what Taisha Abelar calls sorcery passes. Clara defines them as "movements of the hand that are designed to gather energy for a specific purpose."[2] Clara taught Abelar energy passes for clearing sinuses, removing facial wrinkles, and opening the crack between worlds, just to name a few purposes.

Clara also says that, reflecting a formal method, the ancient Toltecs established the intent of each pass. Thus it's a matter of hooking onto an intent that already exists and letting that energy work through you. A fluid approach, on the other hand, steps outside of rituals and preordained methods. It does, however, require a very astute connection with intent in order to become aware of a pass spontaneously. Furthermore, you must maintain a high level of attention in order to correctly apply hand movements to your energy fields. The advantage here, though, is that you're free to innovate and devise passes for whatever you face at the moment.

Energy passes access the second field and bring its energy to bear in the first field. They massage energy and thus develop suppleness, permitting energy to flow better. Coupling this flow with a specific intent produces the result. Energy passes are also related to using hand movements for curing. For example, don Juan told Castaneda that through intent a stricken friend could push a disease from her body. He added that her intent should correspond with a specific motion of her hand and arm (*Second Ring*, 106).

A while back, a person demonstrated for me an energy pass she used to smooth her skin. Placing her hands with outstretched fingers on top of her head, she pulled down over her face. As she did, I *saw* her energy body part as though she were plowing furrows through it. In another instance, I *saw* that a seminar participant had a murky, grey area in the front of his energy body. I asked him to run his finger through that area while focusing on the goal of clearing his energy. While doing so, he turned a dingy green. I then *saw* that he wasn't drinking enough water to flush his system properly. He said the assessment was correct, and that he knew better but wasn't acting on it.

**Gazing**. Gazing is an avenue to the energy body (*Dreaming*, 124). It de-stabilizes your energy fields and re-focuses your awareness along the lines of your intent. It breaks normal habits or fixations of perceiving the world naturally. It is also an excellent relaxation and concentration tool.

To gaze, first review the steps in the "Seeing" section of Chapter 6. If you have difficulty, don Juan suggests looking at an object and then gently crossing your eyes until you have two identical images (*Journey*, 72). Then direct your perception between them. This nonpatterns the way you normally focus your eyesight. By practicing this method, it then becomes easier to gaze without crossing your eyes. At first, gazing seems to be an optical exercise. However, you eventually expand it so that you gaze with your entire physical body.

Shadow gazing is a good, all-purpose way to begin. While gazing at a shadow, let it change shapes and patterns. As you continue gazing, intend your awareness to enter the shadow. You'll discover shadows have a very rich texture. You can also play with the depth of field. Send your awareness toward the shadow, or allow the shadow to come closer to you without moving your physical body. Then continue gazing until you *see* light emanating from the shadow. At that point, you've established a connection with the second field.

You can gaze at practically anything. Don Juan had the Little Sisters gaze in steps. They went from leaves, to small plants, to trees, to rocks, and then on to another cycle of gazing which included rain and fog (*Second Ring*, 285-287). I've found that rain and fog gazing often produce visions. La Gorda told Castaneda that a true feat of fog gazers is to allow their perception to follow whatever is being revealed in the fog.

In addition, you learn how to separate the properties of the first and second energy fields (*Fire*, 92). For fire gazing, separate the first-field property of heat from the second-field property of flame. For water gazing, separate its wetness from its fluidity. Wetness is a first-field property and fluidity a second-field property. Making this distinction helps you latch onto the second field. As you gaze at water, discount its wetness and connect with its fluidity. Allow that quality to affect and to move your perception. It's really not difficult. The important thing is to gaze, then let your body do the work, as it's not a rational process. Practice, even when you don't think it's working, makes all the difference.

Since gazing can rapidly take you away from your normal world, it's best to gaze with another person when you're water gazing or intending to push yourself well past your limits. For many people, water pulls awareness too far off center. As it solidly engages the second field, it might prove too disconcerting. Therefore, while you're gazing have your partner stand behind you and gaze at your energies. That person should tap you lightly on the shoulder at any hint of you losing your balance or concentration. Your partner might feel you slipping too far away, *see* you succumbing to the second attention, or just have a hunch that you need re-centering. Then switch roles. As you learn to trust your partner, you feel freer to travel further into the second field.

If you're by yourself, you can use a leg tuck (*Separate*, 244-245). Tuck your right foot under your left thigh. Keep your left leg in a squat position; that is, keep the sole of your foot flat on the ground and your bent knee pointing up. You can then spring upward at the first hint of losing your bearings. The sudden change of perception reorients you to your normal manner of perceiving. Furthermore, cupping both hands over your belly just below the navel helps prevent losing energy. Don Juan had Castaneda do this when the gap of his *will* opened too wide, too soon (*Journey*, 250). Cold showers or other methods of stimulating your physical body also work well to re-focus your attention to your known world.

In addition, it's best not to cloud gaze at thunderstorms. La Gorda told Castaneda that gazing had enabled the Little Sisters to hook their second fields to clouds, and they could then travel great distances. However, doing so also establishes a path for the storm's energy to travel toward you. She indicated that Josefina was nearly killed by a thunderbolt while cloud gazing (*Second Ring*, 289).

It is also wise to be sure of your intent. Gazing suspends perception. Whatever intent you hook into the exercise shifts you into that realm. For instance, don Juan once advised Castaneda to quit gazing because he was following second-cycle practices of reducing his perception to concrete form. In this case, Castaneda was starting to lose himself in the energies of the second cycle, rather than use gazing to catapult his awareness into the abstract (*Dreaming*, 124). In general, intending to *see* while gazing offsets going astray.

**Impeccability**. Rather than assess yourself by the yardsticks of others, the singular measuring stick for a Toltec is personal impeccability. There are many facets to this concept, and they all relate to managing personal energy. For example, don Juan says it means "to put your life on the line in order to back up your decisions, and then to do quite a lot more than your best to realize those decisions" (*Dreaming*, 155). He also says it is acting for the benefit of Spirit, not for personal gain. Solutions to problems, then, stem solely from revelations by Spirit. For impeccability beckons the solution, says don Juan. He also says, "Impeccability is simply the best use of our energy level." Above all, the requirement for impeccability is a lack of self-reflection (*Silence*, 99, 248). Thus the main ingredient is losing self-importance.

When Castaneda was attacked by the Little Sisters, he remained impeccable. He wanted to leave, but, following the designs of Spirit, he remained. By the time these incidents occurred he had activated his *will*, his direct connection with Spirit. Abiding by its commands, he reduced his self-reflective urge to run for the hills. And it's not as though good didn't come from the incident. It spurred him to new heights, taught the Sisters a few things, and gave us a memorable story. At the same time, another person in a similar situation might have found impeccability in walking away.

Erasing personal history, dreaming, and other techniques are only aids, says don Juan. Integrity of character is the glue that binds everything in a Toltec's world (*Tales,* 235). This internal strength can be measured as a sense of emotional balance, or equanimity, almost a sense of indifference. It also carries a "natural and profound bent for self-examination, for understanding" (*Fire,* 178). So it's not enough to turn into a crow; it's more important to know how that ability fits into a wider picture.

Much of this character development consists of ridding yourself of indulging. Any excess—be it wallowing in worry or self-pity, staying too long in one place, or wrapping yourself up in emotion, thought, or action—is indulging. At the same time, don Juan warned against denying yourself. Doing so makes us think we are doing great things, he says, when we are only fixated within ourselves (*Separate,* 179). And therefore we again find the need for balance. Neither getting carried away with nor slinking from our challenges reduces indulging and enhances impeccability. Through impeccability we stand a chance of tracking Spirit and evolving to a natural energy field.

**Internal Dialogue**. As we've discussed, your talk upholds your world. The energy body's cohesion entrains to your definitions of the world and fixes the focal point in the location which indicates that world. In other words, talking directs energy and then forms energy fields. Well-integrated thought, such as a worldview, brings coherency to the first field. This worldview then circulates inside your head, creating a unbroken chain of information; from this, you constantly reflect and describe the world back to yourself.

When you stop your internal dialogue, the world changes. The shift from an ordinary to a nonordinary worldview is a significant, yet only partial, achievement. That's because internal dialogue upholds both worlds. The nonordinary world is just more expansive. Quieting and then stopping your thoughts permits perceptions outside both frameworks of reality to enter conscious awareness. You can then step into new worlds and not merely expand your prior set of reflections.

Don Juan says that *seeing* results only when the internal dialogue stops. And remember that *seeing* transports you beyond description and into the heart of things. Don Juan also advises that all tracking exercises facilitate stopping the internal dialogue, and interdicting that flow is a key to Toltec procedures (*Tales,* 34, 233). Dreaming plays a role as well. Indeed, don Juan says the two principal tools for stopping the dialogue are erasing personal history and dreaming. Both jolt the cohesion of ordinary reality, and so the intellect takes a pause from its normal functioning.

In addition, he taught a specific way of walking to stop the internal dialogue. Slightly modified, here is don Juan's "right way of walking" (*Journey,* 38).

1. Walk with your hands in an unusual position that does not attract attention. The novelty directs energy away from the ordinary pattern of attention created by your usual way of walking. But if you hold your hands in a dramatically unusual position, you have to contend with other people sending their energies toward you as they wonder what you're doing.

2. Direct your vision toward the horizon. If you are in a hill or mountain environment, look 10-40 feet in front of you, keeping the same distance between your location and your point of sight as you walk.

3. Unfocus your eyes, allowing your peripheral vision to absorb as much as possible.

4. Listen to and smell the environment. Feel your surroundings. You're trying to get out of your head and into your body.

5. Walk at a normal or slower-than-normal pace.

6. For safety, walk where you don't have to contend with traffic or other obstacles. Otherwise, you have to think about navigating.

**Paradox.** A paradox is a statement of contradiction that may hold truth. People often report, for example, that during a mystical experience they feel as though they've experienced all eternity in less than a second. Or they may experience a fertile wasteland of perception.

You can use paradox to transcend form and arrive at essence. By placing your attention between opposing viewpoints, any set of opposing statements becomes a paradox. You can see the truth of each statement, and finding the middle ground yields an even more expansive truth. A paradox delivers you to an opening that, when coupled with intent, hooks you to Spirit.

To illustrate, find the middle ground in these pairs of Toltec teachings:

1. Self-examination and understanding are vital. Understanding is limiting and can hold you back.

2. Thoughtfulness is needed. Action is what matters.
3. Believe the world is mysterious. Don't believe in anything.

By going between form, you find your actions can be better governed by Spirit. You have all options available to you, but you let Spirit flow through you to determine which is best at any given juncture.

**Path With Heart**. Each person is a conglomerate of energies. Reflecting this conglomeration, we often shift moods and change our minds in a manner that indicates a lack of direction. Some people seem to shift as the wind shifts. Yet we also lean toward certain behavior; we have predilections. We might get a charge out of studying art, business, or diesel mechanics. Or we might tend toward contemplation, while others are always on the go. All too often, however, we find ourselves estranged from our predilections, and thus from ourselves, from others, and from the world.

A path with heart offers a way to restructure your life in order to pull forth your deepest predilections. From this, you find your deepest meaning. You have innate affinities, and when these merge with the world a one-on-one relationship emerges. By finding the dreams you want to dream, you simultaneously develop your first and second energy fields. You strengthen first-field integrity which works to propel you into the second field. Plus, when you lose your sense of meaning by extending yourself too far into the second field, your predilections pull you back, help you integrate your experiences, and make you stronger for your next venture.

Good, purposeful, strong predilections also serve a Toltec as "shields." According to don Juan, shields buffer and filter awareness (*Separate*, 260). As we are constantly bombarded with immense energy, shields buffer the effect and filter out energy which has no meaning. The low side of this is that we continually perceive only our known world as that is the energy which has meaning. The high side is that we can remain focused and not explode as a result of receiving more data than we can handle. Redefining your shields redefines what you perceive and how you behave.

If you lose your shields, you're open to stray influences. Don Juan advocated that Castaneda select a completely new set of shields, as his old ones didn't give him any support in the Toltec world. For example, where once his anger served to keep his energy from dissipating, now it did cause his energy to dissipate.

As a result, Castaneda had to discover several activities which produced profound peace and joy (*Separate*, 182). Ordinary shields, such as the pursuit of money and popularity, were thrown out the window. The sole measurement was that his new shields had to surface from the depths of his heart. Accordingly, Castancda was advised not to pick a path based on fear or ambition (*Teachings*, 121). With several new shields in place, Castaneda had literally formed a new path for himself.

Don Juan also told Castaneda that if shields dominated, they could topple his efforts. To get across the point, don Juan offered Castaneda a challenge regarding his books.[3] Could he maintain impeccability knowing his books might bring notoriety? Would the glitter and glamour of fame pull him away from tracking awareness? Could he remain unfettered in the midst of the turmoil surrounding his path in order to remain calmly and clearly focused within his path? Would his profession overrule his quest for freedom?

Don Juan says this confusion also happens in ordinary reality when we mistake our thoughts and actions for the actual world. "In fact," he says, "I could say that for mankind, what people do is greater and more important than the world itself" (*Separate*, 264). Don Juan considers shields very important, but to be used only to bolster awareness so that treks into the unknown can be accomplished with strength and endurance. Accordingly, shields are supports for your transformation. Focusing on the shields rather than the transformation warps your energies.

A workable shield is a power predilection. It contributes to your well-being while taking you further down the paths of Power. Developing your predilections overrides the harshness produced by the slings and arrows of daily life. Each predilection gives you something that you love doing and provides ample challenges. Each carries its own intent. Like individual branches that combine with a trunk to form a tree, predilections combine to form another intent: the path with heart.

A path with heart gives you direction and purpose. It also offers a sense of power to deal with any concerns. People often feel powerless and find themselves readily upset at social injustice; sexism, bigotry, and other forms of discrimination typically ply awareness into a sense of inadequacy or a sense of outrage. Having a path with heart delivers you beyond normal interests. You don't, however, automatically become indifferent to social problems, although for some people that may be the case. The point is that regardless of how you fit into the social order, you fit into the natural order. You have your own life, and only your death can remove you from it.

Finding your path is a matter of expanding your awareness and thus finding your natural self. You have plenty of assistance for the task. You can disrupt routines to avoid complacency. You can nonpattern to dislodge the focal point. You can use your death as an advisor to trim your life and to enhance your focus. (What does matter to you, anyway?) You can gaze to stretch your awareness. And you can decide without reservation that you want to find your path. And then act impeccably on your decision. In fact, what is needed most for Toltec abilities, says Castaneda, is decision.[4]

Finding your path with heart is a gradual, systematic process. As with anything else, you have to put in the time and energy to realize results. Rest assured, though, that doing so changes your life for the better, and in ways you can't currently imagine. Indeed, a path with heart is a way to fully engage the world and actually derive nourishment from the path itself. Once you've developed your path with heart, you've found patience. It's then that you're a ranger and on your way to *will*.

**Ranger**. Once you've revived your link with Spirit, don Juan says, you're no longer an apprentice (*Silence*, 62). Having gone through exhaustive training, you're well-disciplined and task-oriented. Michael Lee Lanning characterizes Army rangers as having perseverance, extraordinary attention to detail, and absolute professionalism.[5] I'm confident don Juan would attribute those traits to a Toltec ranger as well.

As a ranger, your interest turns to other dimensions. Rather than study basic exercises, you examine the scope of the energy body. Also, as a result of having learned how to shift your cohesion from an ordinary world to a nonordinary world, you now have the skills to handle such exploration. Don Juan says there are fundamental steps to becoming a ranger (*Separate*, 183-184). They are:

1. Developing a sharp sensitivity to your death, markedly increasing your level of concentration.

2. In order to keep this awareness from growing into an obsession, a ranger needs nonattachment—from everything. This nonattachment produces an abstract relation with the world, almost

an indifference to what goes on. A caution here is to not remove yourself from everything. Nonattachment is a relation, not a severance.

3. Enabled by the previous steps, assume complete responsibility for your actions. Indeed, the power of your decisions is your sole advantage.

4. Set your life strategically in order. In other words, forge your power predilections into a path with heart. Such a path, says Castaneda, "requires a degree of abandon that can be terrifying. Only then is it possible to achieve a sparkling metamorphosis."[6] Ranger training both produces and enables you to handle this degree of passion and commitment. It's at this point that don Juan says you've gained patience and know how to wait.

**Recapitulation.** The recapitulation is an exercise to recall, review, release, and recharge energy. It rids you of assumptions and preconceptions. It frees locked energy and restores balance. In addition to losing self-importance, it is the most effective tool Toltecs use. Clara says the apex of a special Toltec art is the "abstract flight," which is jumping from one energy field to another. The recapitulation, she adds, is the key for this shift.[7] Furthermore, don Juan says the recapitulation is necessary for re-deploying energy, which he considers the basis for all Toltec maneuvers (*Dreaming*, 148).

The idea is that all of your experiences have been stored inside your energy fields. As though they are energy cysts produced by stagnant conditional fields, they block the flow of energy, especially those resulting from trauma. They also keep awareness focused within their range of perception, and so prevent transformative shifts of consciousness. Indeed, from day one all of your experiences have in some way molded your cohesion. Therefore, as you perform this exercise you release blocked energy and reduce the fixation of a conditional field, making the energy body more vibrant and able to exercise new options.

For instance, during a dinner conversation my uncle asked me if I remembered a childhood incident. A friend of the family immediately replied for me that I did not, that I was too young at the time to remember. I thought that this was a terrible bit of selective-cueing. The person was teaching that we are incapable of remembering past a certain point. It also kindled a memory of the time I recapitulated my birth. It was as though I were actually being born. As I felt myself exit the womb, I experienced tension etch its way through my being. As it did I felt the stirring of a new awareness. I began to feel physical sensations and entertain the vaguest sense of an ordered world. I felt completely aware, while at the same time completely ignorant. This seemed to corroborate don Juan saying that we are exclusively second-field energy for a short time after birth. The breath of life is what generates the first field (*Tales*, 128).

Don Juan says there are two methods to recapitulate: the formal and the fluid (*Dreaming*, 150). The formal method involves making a list of everyone with whom you've ever associated. You can do it by listing jobs, schools, and relationships. Begin with the most recent and retrace your steps, or vice versa. Clara suggested that Abelar start with sexual liaisons, as they are the most powerful associations.[8] She said males leave their energy inside females, producing an energetic link. In order for a female to restore her natural harmony, she must recapitulate all sex partners and reclaim her own power.

Making the list is an important step of the recapitulation, so don't cut yourself short. While the steps of any technique are subordinate to results, technique offers direction and context. When you have your list, start at the top and work your way to the very bottom. As you do, keep in mind you may spontaneously change your order. You may step into another time or place. This is fine. The important thing is to re-experience the events in detail.[9] At this point, don't think about them. Let your body work with the energy.

In the fluid method, you take the energy at hand, feel what's most important at the moment to review, then recapitulate that. Looking out the window of an airplane, for example, I saw a muddy, winding river which sparked memories of Vietnam. Taking advantage of the moment, I recapitulated my time there. I was fascinated to find how clearly I could review my experiences and how vivid were the memories. I was even more surprised to find I was discharging pent-up energy associated with the war. If you find the same events coming to mind after your recapitulation, as was the case with certain instances in Vietnam, recapitulate them again.

I found the fluid style to be a good way to learn the exercise since I rebelled against having to formally work at something new when my plate was already full with other practices. Later, I made a list using my job history as a guide, and I found the formal route provided another flavor. I also found that I always felt better and more relaxed after a recapitulation regardless of the method.

Plus, I became more proficient with dreaming.

I then divided the recapitulation into two phases. For the first, I recapitulated the people I know or have known. For the second, I worked on and tried to eliminate my needs, expectations, and desires. In addition, I discovered that the recapitulation works well for problem solving. I simply apply the exercise to a problem, work it through as I recapitulate it, then let the solution formulate on its own.

Abelar's book, *The Sorcerers' Crossing,* and Castaneda's book, *The Art of Dreaming,* provide an extensive framework for recapitulating. Based on their work and from my own practice, here is a working outline. Please read all of the steps first in order to know the mechanics of the exercise.

**Recall.** Recall involves the breathing portion of the exercise. The breath is emphasized as a means to fully connect with the energy you're recapitulating.

1. Place your chin near your right shoulder. Now move it in a smooth, sweeping motion to your left shoulder. Then back to your right shoulder.

2. As you repeat step 1, inhale through your nose as you sweep from right to left, and exhale through your mouth as you sweep from left to right.

3. To warm up, perform the first sweep (right to left) as you inhale, and then return your head to a relaxed position looking straight ahead as you exhale. Henceforth, perform both sweeps as indicated in steps 1 and 2.

4. Now as you breathe in, intend your breath to pull in the energy of the event, person, or feeling you're working with. Feel yourself connect with your subject of study, then use your breath to bring that energy into your body.

**Review.** This step concerns fully entering the energy of the recapitulation.

1. As you tap your memories, work from the items surrounding the event, to the people involved, to your feelings.

2. Let your body do the work. Your part is to engage the exercise and, above all, intend the recapitulation to occur.

3. Immerse yourself in your memories without indulging. Allow yourself to fully relive the occurrence.

**Release.** In Release, you let the energy discharge.

1. Now it's time to yield to the energy. Let it work within you

so you enter all the crevices you have forgotten.

2. Allow the energy to dissipate of its own accord. This facilitates realigning your energy fields.

3. Get in the habit of reviewing and releasing anywhere, anytime. Even in the middle of a business conference, you can unobtrusively make one or two breathing sweeps and release energy that spontaneously surfaced. You also find that your intent sets the recapitulation process in motion whether or not you perform the breathing sweeps. What matters most is intending the recapitulation, not the specific manner of doing so. As a result, you may feel energy moving and releasing anytime, anywhere.

**Recharge.** An effect of the exercise is additional vitality.

1. Not only do you have a new relation, a new sense of order regarding the situation, you feel lighter and renewed.

2. Your energy body is cleansed, and you have the previously blocked energy at your disposal. You may then use that energy for Toltec endeavors.

In addition to the practical, cleansing aspects of this technique, don Juan says it moves your focal point back to the position where you first experienced the situation under review. Thus you're gaining valuable experience in producing subtle shifts of cohesion. He adds that in doing so you also create a facsimile of your life. He says that while a person is in the throes of death, the dissolving force of the universe which squelches individual awareness accepts the facsimile and allows the individual's awareness to remain (*Dreaming,* 149). It's as though you have been plucked from the river of eternity by the Eagle. As it carries your energy body through life in its talons, you're aware of life but not of the forces carrying you. Through the recapitulation, by the time the Eagle is ready for its food of live-awareness energy, you have provided a substitute meal and the Eagle doesn't notice your departure.

In other words, while an individual is in the throes of death, human awareness is subject to a force which squelches individual awareness. The recapitulation evens out the energy body, making it fluid and nonreactive to the force. Since the force encounters no resistance, there is nothing for it to act on. Individual awareness thereby remains intact as it passes through the force. Whatever way you look at it, the recapitulation is a preliminary for the Fire from Within.

**Sex**. With regard to energy, Castaneda says that having sex is our most important act.[10] We send our sexual energy off and away, never to retrieve it. Which is why he also says the recapitulation is so important; through recapitulating, energy may be re-acquired.

Don Juan thinks that having sex without having children is a waste of energy, but he adds that having children taxes the energy body. Furthermore, he says that sexual energy is needed to sustain the pressure of extending awareness past its current limits (*Fire*, 72, 150). Because of the need to marshall all of one's resources, Clara flat-out advocated celibacy.[11] In addition, don Juan continues to pass on Elias' teaching that sexual energy governs dreaming. Elias taught that you use your sexual energy either for making love or for dreaming. To make the case, don Juan points out that Castaneda's dreaming is erratic due to a lack of balance with his sexual energy (*Silence*, 55-56).

On the other hand, don Juan says that his teacher, a tracker, was a sexual libertine in and out of ordinary reality (*Silence*, 56). He adds that the rules regarding sexual energy for trackers differ. Then again, while Julian was an extremely masterful Toltec, according to don Juan he couldn't *see* well enough to become a person of knowledge (*Separate*, 182). Is there a tie-in? Is celibacy required to achieve the level of a person of knowledge? If so, what about esoteric tantric practices, where some exercises are designed to channel sexual energy into expanding awareness? What are the limits to this approach?

These are interesting questions begging comprehensive answers. For now, I think the questions that can be readily answered relate to impeccability. For instance, having sex just to fill a void unquestionably squanders energy and reduces esteem. But a person connected with their second field doesn't need sex to feel alive. The energy of that field offers aliveness in full measure. A person also doesn't need to feel connected with another person just to feel connected with the world. The person is connected. And a person doesn't need others just to feel complete because the person has a complete self. Maybe at this point a person can make an impeccable decision regarding having or not having sex. The chosen direction then reflects a path with heart.

**Stopping the World**. You stop the world by suspending conditional energy fields. Gazing, stopping the internal dialogue, and dreaming all work toward this goal. By stopping the normal flow of your attention, you can tune into other worlds. To develop a natural field, you first need to stop your ordinary world, and then stop your nonordinary world. Otherwise, you remain isolated within the conditions that sustain each of those realities. For an additional perspective, please review the "The Seer" section in Chapter 7.

**Trusting Your Personal Power**. Impeccability, says don Juan, is trusting your personal power. He defines personal power as the boost in energy derived from accessing the second field (*Tales*, 161). Castaneda says that he trusts his energy body to navigate the second field and that this process is what pulls a person to freedom.[12]

Unless plugged deeply into Spirit, everyone makes mistakes while learning how to navigate. Therefore, in order to learn the degree of control and abandon associated with freedom, don Juan says the apprentice must learn to trust the team leader (*Dreaming*, 10). Only then can the apprentice be maneuvered into clear associations with Spirit. At all times, however, the person must assume responsibility. Mistakes do occur, says don Juan, but only when personal feelings interfere with the connection to Spirit (*Silence*, 34). For this reason, he taught la Gorda that power would come to her only after she fully accepted her fate (*Second Ring*, 94). For it is by doing so that you find your natural place in the world.

**Waiting**. Patience tempers *will* and offers a quiet balance with the world. It is also a force that produces results. For don Juan, waiting is a way of delightfully holding back as you expect what is rightfully due you (*Fire*, 39). By the time you reach patience, you don't seek ordinary material gains. You're too enmeshed in exploring other worlds and refining your stance in this one.

As a ranger, you wait for your *will* (*Separate*, 178). Don Juan gives guidelines for waiting: know that you're waiting; know what you're waiting for; while waiting, want nothing more than what you're waiting for; while waiting, laugh and enjoy yourself; and when your goal manifests, go with it. You summoned it, it's yours. As you learn to wait, you develop proficiency with the cornerstones of perception, and generally expand your awareness. As a Toltec, you wait to complete your task, an endeavor which don Genaro says requires your "ultimate forbearance" (*Tales*, 280).

\* \* \*

The level-headedness engendered by tracking permits you to enter the wilder sides of a Toltec path. Often the only sense of meaning found after embarking comes from the expedition itself. So you need a strong foundation to withstand the rigors you will surely encounter. As a result, you find that joy and adventure abound as you journey full stride into dreaming.

# Part IV
# Dreaming

# 11
## On the Wild Side

Dreaming can be as pleasant as a gentle catamaran ride on a wind-rippled lake, or as devastating as a sailboat riding rudderless on storm-lashed high seas. Dreaming can open your eyes to what's always been in front of you, and can send you deep into nether-worlds where the substance of ancient memories reveals itself. Its applications are virtually limitless. Its development offers a lifetime of challenges.

Dreaming is a significant part of Toltec teachings. As a method, it has distinct stages for evolving awareness. Don Juan refers to these stages as dreaming "gates" (*Dreaming,* 22), and I refer to them as "levels." The fourth level, for example, is deliberately placing your dreaming body at specific locations. Say that you're sleeping on your bed and you wake up inside your dreaming body which is sitting on your porch. This means that your cohesion has shifted, and now your focal point is at the spot known as "porch." As a ranger, you develop the dreaming body so that such shifts are not only commonplace but controllable. This practice then gears you up for more radical shifts, including that of moving your entire energy body to different locations. This is often termed "teleportation." Teleportation, in turn, gears you up for performing the Fire from Within.

Dreaming, says don Juan, is a door into the second energy field. Thus, it is a key to exploring the Toltec world. In general, it allows us to perceive more than we believe possible (*Dreaming,* 28, 29, 49). For trackers, dreaming provides a chance to refine and elevate their skills. For dreamers, it provides a chance to get into more natural environments. Because of its many applications, it can be used to enhance awareness and to obtain knowledge. Indeed, it provides so many uses and offers so many avenues into the unknown that don Juan calls it a Toltec's jet plane to knowledge (*Silence,* 53).

Because of its power, dreaming should be approached with some trepidation. Don Juan says it's a very serious and sober affair, and should be handled with integrity and confidence, but also with laughter (*Dreaming*, 22). So before you enter the dream world, make sure your priorities are in order and your purposes sound. Then remain light and confident. If this admonition sounds like you need to be well fortified, you're correct. But this is neither a hopeless nor a haphazard situation. For, as don Juan says, the strength to tap dreaming comes from the ranger's path (*Fire*, 178). This approach shapes ordinary dreams into dreaming.

## Applications of Dreaming

Don Juan also defines dreaming as exercising the capacity of cohesion (*Dreaming*, 70). That is, it exercises the ability to form and maintain new energy-body patterns. It's then possible to shift cohesion to pursue any number of options. For instance, dreaming can be used for increasing professional abilities, for interdimensional exploration, and for loads of fun. Even when combined, all of the following applications represent only a thin slice out of the pie of dreaming potential.

**Contemplation.** For those with abstract inclinations, dreaming easily advances philosophy or the study of how we accumulate knowledge. For instance, we've already established that the focal point's location determines what we think and say. In other words, rational knowledge is produced by a particular cohesion; in order to know more, you need to change the conditions of the energy body. Ordinary knowledge is therefore rational and intellectual, whereas Toltec knowledge is cohesional. In true metaphysical fashion, by shifting cohesion Toltecs examine perceptions which are behind the everyday facade of reality.

For those who enjoy the study of human behavior, dreaming shows how personality influences reality. Several years ago, a friend experienced a series of dreaming-body adventures. Lying on his bed, he surrounded his physical body with a mental force field as though he had encapsulated himself in a coffin. He viewed this as protection from outside influences. He then created an opening in the force field and his dreaming body exited his physical body, passed beyond his protective barrier, and sojourned into unknown lands. Consistently, he was met by wicked-looking, hostile entities who engaged him in hand-to-hand combat. Returning to his body, he opened the force field and re-entered his physical body. Invariably, one of the hostile creatures followed and tried to enter his body. As he closed his protective shield, the entity's evil, witch-shaped hand passed through the opening as though it were trying to snatch his heart. He then entered a test of *wills* with the entity to see if he could completely close the force field and triumph. Invariably, he won.

By contrast, with rare exception, my dreaming-body experiences have been fun-filled. And the less-than-pleasant episodes were extremely bland in comparison. So what's the difference?

At the time, my friend was in pre-medical school. He had recently resigned his commission from the Army where he had served as one of the famed Green Beret in the elite Special Forces. To get to that level, he had to volunteer several times for additional combat training. In short, he liked it. He wanted it. Now in college, he no longer had a way to vent that side of his personality. He found, however, that his dreaming-body travels gave him a way to remain a combatant. In turn, my interests never went too far in that direction. I primarily saw the dreaming body as a chance to explore the nature of perception rather than duke it out with other-world creatures.

**Context**. Dreaming offers the opportunity to enhance how we look at the world. From dreaming, we can generate a wealth of new constructs. As a result, the context of our lives continually changes, and so we always have a source of interest and activity. This activity can be as simple as applying dreaming to the definitions of what it may mean to be a dreamer.

For example, friends of mine were working for the summer as volunteers at the Dolphin Research Center in the Florida Keys. While visiting them, I toured the facility. While the tour group was at a pool watching dolphins jump and somersault, I returned to a larger pool that held a couple of dolphins. Earlier I had noticed that when humans approached, the dolphins swam up, rolled over on their sides, and peered at the visitors. Now, however, they kept their distance. I sat down and mentally constructed a question. I wanted to know why, if they were as intelligent as some people claim, did they continue to get caught in fishermen's nets. Why didn't they communicate the trouble among themselves and steer clear of fishing armadas?

I then heard a very distinct voice inside my head: "Because they are dreamers." I immediately knew what that meant. If, indeed, they were dreamers, their forte would not rest with strategy, with understanding the nuances of traps. They would carry a more unified, expansive relation to the world. Just as I realized this, the dolphins swam up and rolled over to look at me. While I'm not saying I believe this experience to be proof positive, I am saying I've filed it for more complete referencing. Its context is provocative.

**Extraterrestrial Exploration.** Beginning in June of 1984, for several years I channeled an energy which identified itself as extraterrestrial (ET) from the star-group Pleiades. I also had numerous occasions when I dreamed of distant, physical planets and witnessed alien lands and cultures. I reported many of these experiences in *Traveling With Power*. It's possible that these may have been a prelude for dreaming-body encounters with ETs.

A short time back, for example, I took a long walk about Manhattan with a Toltec friend. As she is an east dreamer with an avid interest in ETs, we talked mostly about dreaming and extraterrestrials. Upon returning to my apartment, I climbed in bed to meditate. I continued to feel her intense energy coursing through me. In short order, I felt alien energy next to me. Opening my eyes, I *saw* four ET-looking entities surrounding the bed. They had more angular facial features than the Pleiadeans I had grown accustomed to. The Pleiadeans resembled the thin, large-headed ETs in the film *Close Encounters of the Third Kind.* These looked more like the ET on the cover of Whitley Streiber's book *Communion.*[1]

I mentally heard them ask me if I wanted to go out-of-body. I said sure. In unison they reached over and cupped their hands under my body. As they began pulling up, my dreaming body began to lift out. Almost completely separated from my physical body, I recoiled. Since I didn't know these creatures, I suddenly succumbed to doubt. My view of them was thereby distorted and my dreaming body returned. Reflecting on the incident, I realized there was no basis for my doubt other than not having previously dealt with this variety of ET. Talking with my friend, I learned that she frequently had encounters with ETs who resembled the ones about my bed.

**Interdimensional Exploration.** This variety of dreaming relates to entering other dimensions, such as the inorganic world. Once while dreaming, I felt a strong force pulling me deeper into it. I also felt the presence of a person I knew. Since I associated this person with second-cycle, competitive practices, I withdrew from that part of the dream. However, I continued to feel a powerful, magnetic-like force pulling at me. While I didn't withdraw from it, I didn't go with it either. I almost felt as though if I did I would lose my soul. But then I realized that that idea was only an interpretation. My cohesion was shifting and I might lose my sense of the world, but not my soul. I then felt better and more able to assess the force pulling me. While doing so, I felt instinctively repelled by its weirdness. I also knew I was heading into the inorganic world, perhaps the same one that repulsed Castaneda.

I then found myself at a beach. Several varieties of fish swam at the surf's edge. Considering the large size of some of them, I knew they were scouts from the inorganic world. In ordinary reality large fish can't swim in a surf's shallow water. The novelty of them doing so here indicated they were scouts. Don Juan says other-dimensional forces send scouts into our world (*Dreaming*, 29). By isolating them from the rest of the dream, we can follow them back into their world. However, he also advises not to do so unless you know what you're doing.

For many Toltecs, the inorganic world is a testing ground. While it often repels, it also seduces. Castaneda, for instance, was given the opportunity to learn psychokinesis, or the ability to move physical objects with his mind (*Dreaming*, 115). All he had to do was give his allegiance to that world. If he had, he would have been bound for life to that world. Don Juan says such contracts should be avoided. Plus, he says that being pampered in that world may lead to excessive indulgences in this world.

Don Juan also says that "the whole realm of inorganic begins is always poised to teach." Trouble is, it teaches what we already know but have long since forgotten. Not to mention that he says its instruction is geared to our lower selves. Hence, they offer the seduction of powers in order to close the contract for our fidelity. However, don Juan says its value to seers is that it's proof positive that other worlds exist independently of ours. As such, "the existence of inorganic beings is the foremost assailant of our rationality" (*Dreaming*, 66, 67, 98). Crossing into that world breaks the mirror-like reflection of your prior world. You're simply mind-boggled out of ordinary reality. Consequently, if you can handle that world, your cohesion no longer gives allegiance to any world or to anything, save for Spirit.

We are separated from the inorganic world by energy which oscillates at a different speed (*Dreaming*, 47). I've found that when I approach it, I feel as though I hit a wall of energy. What I think and feel echoes right back at me. Crossing over the barrier gives a rush of energy, an occurrence which is common with many dreaming transitions. The energy rush begins upon entering the higher vibrations of dreaming. It ends when the dream has been stabilized. Initial resistance to inorganic worlds is good; it sets the stage for handling its seductiveness and minimizes your entanglements in it. But, personally speaking, to not at least test that world is to seek a bland status quo—for me, the equivalent of death.

Don Juan describes inorganic beings as opaque and resembling candles, whereas organic beings are round and more luminous. He adds that they live far longer than organic beings since they are calmer and their awareness runs deeper. He also maintains that communication with them is possible since they "possess the crucial ingredient for interaction, consciousness" (*Dreaming,* 45).

For additional consideration, don Juan says that inorganic beings may hide in your dreams behind the image of friends and relatives (*Dreaming,* 178-179). So how does this apply to me meeting my deceased father, or to people who meet relatives during near-death experiences (NDEs)? Was my father actually an inorganic scout? What about during an NDE, when people report being visited by long-deceased relatives who tell them their time is not up, that they must return to fulfill some sort of mission, and after which they may return to the good graces of a hereafter—are these scouts? And what if these experiences are simply learning what we already know? What if people subconsciously know they will return from the NDE feeling revitalized with the knowledge of having found their path with heart? If so, since our contemporary worldview doesn't provide for the existence of inorganic worlds, are we interpreting the event in terms of something more palatable? So we bring in loving relatives, a sacred mission, and life-in-the-hereafter—all of which already circulate in our inventories.

A critical aspect in making this kind of determination is that don Juan also says that when a specific form of scout is present, you feel perturbed and ill at ease (*Dreaming,* 178-179). Therefore, there are guidelines based on Toltec seers' experiences to begin assessing interdimensional worlds. By no means, however, should theirs be the last word.

Engaging the inorganic world requires an intricate balance which is automatically developed as part of ranger training. On the one hand, don Juan advises to enter the inorganic world as though you were going into a war zone. It holds dangers just as this world does, and therefore requires astute alertness. But once you pass completely through it into another level, or once you no longer consider it to be a viable resource, its difficulties vanish. On the other hand, don Juan also thinks that world might be the only sanctuary for dreamers who have to contend with an otherwise-hostile universe (*Dreaming,* 110, 96).

**Professional Applications**. Here we apply dreaming to ordinary, practical considerations. For example, don Juan gave Castaneda the learning task of *seeing* his books while dreaming (*Silence,* 14). Castaneda says that he first translates his notes, then goes to sleep, whereupon the content of his book arranges itself. He wakes and writes down what he *sees* in his dreams. The process works well enough that he doesn't rewrite the material.[2]

In another example, a research group working on an AIDS vaccine tested a method deemed unsafe by many scientists when they used a weakened, live form of the virus. They found it provided longer protection for AIDS in primates than previous vaccines. The Harvard University scientist spearheading the research said he tried it because nothing else worked. As part of his research method, he says, "I stay awake at night thinking and dreaming about every angle."[3]

*Seeing* **While Dreaming**. It is possible to *see* while in physical, waking consciousness as well as in dreaming. As previously discussed, the advantage to *seeing* while dreaming is that you're in heightened awareness, reducing stress on your physical body and permitting you to *see* more powerful emanations. Remember, *seeing* is aligning with the energy being *seen.* So without the advantage of heightened awareness, merging with the far reaches of the unknown may present hazards.

Even with heightened awareness, dreaming poses problems. For instance, second-cycle seers found that those who *saw* the Eagle's emanations without benefit of their dreaming bodies died. Moreover, those who *saw* them with their dreaming bodies burned with the Fire from Within. In either case, the knowledge obtained by the seers was lost. These problems were remedied by *seeing* in teams, which meant they dreamed together. Don Juan says there are no procedures for this. Someone takes the lead and the rest find themselves pulled into the same dream. While one person *sees*, the others remain alert to stop the *seeing* if the need arises (*Silence,* 183).

# Levels of Dreaming

Since the winter of 1978, I've experienced hundreds of dreaming-body adventures. That time is significant because it was then that I had my first bilocation, or simultaneous awareness of two distinct physical locations. Over the years, I had let much of Castaneda's talk about inorganic beings go its own way. However, after don Juan outlined the levels of dreaming in Castaneda's *The Art of Dreaming,* I realized I had overlooked a significant part of my training.

Comparing the varied pieces of dreaming I had experienced with the various levels, I found that dreaming levels reflect pronounced shifts in cohesion. Accordingly, they reflect degrees of handling *will.* And while many of my experiences reflected level-three dreaming-body abilities, I saw the value of going back to level one to begin establishing a dream operating system. I figured this would be like a computer disc operating system (DOS), where the DOS provides the foundation to use an extensive variety of application software. By learning to handle dreaming levels from the bottom up, I figured I could use it for a more extensive array of applications.

Don Juan says there are two steps for each level: arriving at the level, and exploring it. Thus there are two maneuvers: entering a level and moving about in it. Learning in the second field, says don Juan, comes as second nature. It's as though we've known what to do all along. Still, each level contains certain obstacles. The critical component of learning any level, says don Juan, is intent. There are no specific steps other than to intend what you're going after. And you intend something "simply by intending it." At the same time, however, he also says it requires "imagination, purpose, and discipline" (*Dreaming,* 142, 18, 23, 26). Only then can intent be experienced and controlled as an energy which is something other than reason.

**Level One: Wakeful Dreaming.** Level one consists of stabilizing your dreaming awareness. Accordingly, you begin to develop autonomy within your dreams. It involves watching yourself fall asleep, and then waking up inside a dream. Knowing you're dreaming while you're dreaming is often termed "lucid" dreaming, or remaining wakeful inside a dream.

Intending yourself to observe yourself falling asleep takes you into a darkness that feels heavy yet pleasant, as though you're wrapped in a heavy down quilt on a cold winter's night. Remaining in this blackness indicates you've reached the threshold of the first level and have learned to watch yourself fall asleep. Later the heaviness lightens as you learn to move about in dreams.

In order to cross into level one, you need to surface from the blackness into a dream. Engaging your intent to do so, you're likely to see images floating just beyond your grasp at the edges of the darkness. Then the objective is to step completely into the dream. Resting in the blackness means you have reduced your focus to the first field. Crossing into a dream indicates your focus has shifted to the second field. By accenting your second field, you begin to identify with the complete energy body rather than with just the physical body.

As a practical task to pass through the door, don Juan suggests finding your hands in a dream (*Dreaming,* 21). Doing so pulls you out of the blackness and into an image-filled dream. You have stabilized level one when you can hold a dream without it shifting. That is, you can flow with the same dream for as long as you want.

For this stage, don Juan also suggests developing the intent of being a dreamer. In other words, by using your imagination and purpose, you establish that you're a dreamer in every cell of your body; thus you feel dreaming energy throughout the recesses of your being. This, says don Juan, produces "an unquestionable bodily knowledge that you are a dreamer" (*Dreaming,* 26). And it gives you unbending intent to remain focused as you dip further into dreaming.

Other supporting techniques include nonattachment and non-patterning. One time, while dreaming, I noticed a large boa constrictor crawling on the floor. Exercising the two tracking techniques, I didn't react; I just watched. As it crawled up my body, I again accepted the scene without holding onto it and without trying to force it away. The snake then slithered into the back of my skull and out my mouth. Nonpatterning became more difficult, but I made the attempt. In a split moment, the snake vanished and my head became glowing white. At that moment, I could direct the dream's content.

As you engage dreaming, you're likely to get lost in the details of your dreams, wonder why you aren't succeeding even though you've tried a hundred times, and fret at all the numerous near-misses. Don Juan advises that the solution is simple: keep persisting. Sooner or later barriers fall and you succeed (*Dreaming,* 36).

**Level Two: Interdimensional Travel**. At this level, you exercise more control within the dream as your lucidity takes on greater proportions. To cross into this level, don Juan says, either you dream that you wake up from the dream, or you use the dream to vault into yet another dream (*Dreaming*, 44). Rather than find your hands, here you isolate a component in the dream and focus on it. You then use your concentration as a springboard to change dreams.

For example, during a dream I was watching a road while standing idly at the side of a house. It was nighttime. I became immersed in watching for the lights of cars before they actually came into view. But then I began listening to wavering tones in my ears. As a result of changing focus, I entered the dream. Since one of my interests is ETs, I spontaneously began feeling ET energy. The dream then changed and an approaching car turned into a flying saucer. I then lost track of myself and grew disoriented. I panicked at not being ready to deal with ETs. I woke up with my heart racing. I knew indecision and fear generated ill effects. But, for most, one of the hardest lessons is getting into your dreams without going out of your mind.

Another major impediment is indulging in the dream's content by either analyzing too much or indulging in your enhanced freedom. You're in for a rude awakening, says don Juan, if you do so for too long (*Dreaming*, 41). The option, then, is to continue evolving within and then beyond the second level.

Once you are over the threshold, the dream ceases to be an ordinary dream. One of your options is interdimensional travel. For whatever reason, Toltecs have isolated the inorganic world as a means to test one's mettle, and use it to learn how to travel in and out of other dimensions. The inorganic world should be approached with confidence and strength, says don Juan, as fear unfavorably compounds the experience (*Dreaming*, 47). Since the energy vibrates at a different speed, a natural barrier forms. So withstanding the transition into that world requires strength and purpose. Moreover, don Juan says second-cycle Toltecs groomed inorganic beings as allies, and garnered their favors for self-important uses. For this reason, he says, you're better off without them. Just stick to your pragmatic purposes and pursuit of freedom (*Second Ring*, 151).

Having a petty tyrant helps you deal with the grand seduction of the inorganic realm. Indeed, what destroyed the second cycle was their assumption that if they could handle the unknown, they could handle people. As a result of their obliteration, seers realized that if they could first handle the world of people, they could then face the unknown, and the unknowable, with impunity (*Fire*, 32).

For those inclined, entering the inorganic universe is an accomplishment. Once there, the task is to discover that it's an independent world with its own predictable rules. As such, an exercise for level two is to discover scouts from that world (*Dreaming*, 108). Don Juan suggests pointing at them in the dream to establish a link of intent. As with any technique, establishing that link is what's important, not how it's done. Sufficient interest, or proficiency with intent, itself, can form the link. By following scouts to their world, you learn dream locomotion. That is, rather than physical-body movement using arms and legs, you learn the basics of traveling through imagination. This knowledge sets the stage for keeping awareness pliable and for moving the energy body across boundaries of perception.

**Level Three: The Dreaming Body**. One of the more interesting aspects of the dreaming body is that it's a natural faculty of human perception. Dreaming-body experiences have been reported as astral projections and out-of-body experiences throughout recorded history. The most skilled practitioners contend that we all use our dreaming bodies regularly, that we just don't remember doing so. And I've found evidence to support that contention.

One morning I woke up feeling tense about the numerous things I had to accomplish that day. I had grown accustomed to following my feelings throughout the course of a normal day rather than following a schedule, and now I felt cornered. For several hours I worked hard to relax as I went from task to task. By mid-afternoon I had restored my sense of freedom. During an afternoon meditation, I found myself in level-one blackness. I decided to play with it and see if I could pass through it into a dream. I then felt the onset of dreaming-body energies. For me, this meant feeling more energized than normal and feeling as though there were a condensed block of energy inside of me.

I thought that I should stop and take notes, perhaps relating the experience to the morning's relaxation efforts. I focused on the kitchen where my clipboard was. I then got up to write and realized I had just come back from the kitchen so that I could get up and go to the kitchen. This jarred me and I knew I had temporarily forgotten being in my dreaming body as it was still outside my daily inventory. Since it didn't fit, I blocked it out.

Don Juan says that at level three you begin to merge dreaming with the daily world. At this stage, he says, the energy body is ready to act. Exercising dreaming leads to a more defined and awake energy body. And so the exercise is to further your skill in moving through imagination (*Dreaming,* 142, 153-154). Developing autonomy of the dreaming body is the vehicle to do this.

A primary obstacle here is getting lost in the details of the environment (*Dreaming,* 142). Don Juan says that in its new-found freedom the energy body latches onto every detail available. To counteract this, he says you need boundless fluidity, beyond any constrictions of reason. This complete abandon is needed to break free from form, from the known. Remain immensely curious, he advises, but not transfixed.

As with all Toltec endeavors, losing self-importance is paramount. To release dreaming energy, don Juan says, you need to re-deploy existing energy. Ranger discipline engenders this process, which also has the effect of revamping your entire life, producing the availability of dreaming energy (*Dreaming,* 37). How you use it depends on your purposes and what kind of model for dreaming you use.

Since the dreaming body is a natural capacity, you don't need to use a Toltec model to become aware of it. However, this model proves quite valuable in outlining steps to it. An additional benefit is that it points the way beyond "simple" dreaming-body perceptions. For instance, don Juan advises that the real purpose of the dreaming body is to *see* (*Dreaming,* 163). In other words, you capitalize on its higher vibratory rate to achieve deeper and more significant energy alignments. By doing so, you stretch your awareness through the entire energy body.

**Level Four: Dreaming-Body Travel.** You're now ready to further harmonize your first and second energy fields. Using your dreaming body, the fourth level consists of traveling to specific, definable locations. As a result, you're gaining marked proficiency in determining your energy body's cohesion (*Dreaming,* 69).

Don Juan says you have three options at level four: traveling to locations in this world, traveling to locations in other worlds, and traveling within the dreams of others. The tenant, for example, pulled Castaneda into a dream which Castaneda mistakenly thought was an actual physical location. But the tenant said the experience was to show Castaneda the mysteries of the second field (*Dreaming,* 200, 232). Crossing into this level requires the skill of intending the second field as you would normally intend your daily activities.

In his books, Castaneda has yet to explicitly label and define dreaming practices for levels five through seven. However, there are references in his books which indicate one possible progression that is consistent with don Juan's teachings. Based on my comparatively limited experience, here is at least a hint of the remaining levels.

**Level Five: The Double**. At times, the term "double" is used to indicate the entire energy body.[4] Other times, it is used to indicate the dreaming body. Here, the double is the dreaming body which has such force behind it that it may be perceived by others as though it were a complete entity independent of your physical body. Indeed, don Juan says that having a double grants the capacity to be in two places simultaneously. He also says that while it's not flesh and blood, it is real. He adds that the double is solid, as solidity stems from the memory of how an event is described. He even suggests that it has been his double that has been associating with Castaneda (*Tales*, 49-56).

Several months ago, I witnessed my double during an airline ride. Keep in mind that being suspended above ground is a tracking tactic to unhinge awareness from normal grounding influences, letting perception take flight. (Grau says that staying in a crate for prolonged periods is used for this purpose as it reduces extraneous stimulation. In addition, don Juan says that remaining suspended in a leather harness cleanses energy from maladies that aren't physical [*Gift*, 290, 187].) Over the years, I've learned to use airplanes for this purpose. This occasion was made to order. I had ten rows on both side of the aisle all to myself; thus I had limited interference from other people. Taking advantage of the opportunity, I gazed throughout the cabin and then out into the clouds. I felt very peaceful and lapsed into dreaming for a couple of minutes. I woke to jot down some notes. I looked to my left and *saw* a luminous version of myself sitting across the aisle but in the same row. It looked straight ahead. The more I focused on it, the more it evaporated.

Also remember that there is evidence regarding danger when you're in the proximity of your double. That danger exists is plausible, so the need for caution exists. Consider, for example, that if your physical body does not have enough energy, does not vibrate at the same speed as your double, touching your double may be analogous to electrocution or to touching antimatter. You may experience a surge of energy which your physical body is not capable of assimilating. If true, an encounter with your double may indeed be deadly.

**Level Six: Teleportation**. Pinpointing complete energy-body travel to physical locations binds the first and second fields. That is, normally if you send your dreaming body to another location, your physical body remains stationary. With teleportation, the physical body travels with the energy body. For example, as don Juan corralled a new apprentice who was to be the next generation's female team leader, he enticed her to cross a line he drew in the dirt. If she did, to don Juan she would then have willingly entered his world. She later recounted to Castaneda that when she crossed the line, don Juan "took a prodigious leap and glided over the roof of the house." As though he were a boomerang, he left her side, sailed over his house, and returned by her side (*Gift*, 229).

The levitation experience I mentioned earlier is only a preliminary for don Juan's degree of control. The Little Sisters had a somewhat better grasp on matters, as they could levitate and fly about their house (*Second Ring*, 244-247).

**Level Seven: The Fire from Within**. By now you have blended and tempered your first and second fields so that, in effect, they act as one. By weaving them completely through the energy body, you arrive at pure awareness unfettered by form or definition. According to don Juan, you arrive at a very specific dreaming position of the focal point known as total freedom (*Fire*, 294).

## Tracking the Second Energy Field

Dreaming, says don Juan, is perfecting the second field (*Dreaming*, 42). The steppingstone progression of levels permits you to track this energy, thereby ensuring strength of purpose and manner—especially applicable for attaining level seven. By then your progression is a matter of completely engaging your totality, rather than engaging self-enhancing objectives.

In general, don Juan says, dreaming exercises the energy body, thereby making it "supple and coherent" and setting the stage for performing acts "that are beyond the possibilities of the physical body" (*Dreaming*, 31). Arriving at level one is the equivalent of reaching the energy body. At levels one, three, and five you focus on going deeper into your energy body, deeper into the unknown.

At levels two, four, and six you learn how to control and move the energy you tapped at the previous level. At level seven, you take leave of this world and take flight into the unknowable.

# 12
# Tracking the Dreaming Body

Dreaming is a forthright step to personal power (*Dreaming,* 21). As such, it has practical daily value, often having more application than physical activities have. The dreaming body represents an intensification of dreaming energies and marks a major step toward consolidating the first and second energy fields. Accordingly, the next two chapters focus primarily on the dreaming body while flushing out more dreaming perspectives in general.

## Definition and Value

The dreaming body has three principal characteristics. First, consciousness has exteriorized beyond the physical body. In other words, if you're centered in your dreaming body on the opposite side of a room from your physical body, you perceive the room, including your physical body, from the perspective of your dreaming body. Second, this exteriorized consciousness has form of some kind. Due to habits of perception, it is often shaped like a physical body. The longer you're in your dreaming body during any one experience, or the more often you enter your dreaming body, the more likely the form shifts. If you have shamanic tendencies, for example, the form may shift to one of your power animals. Quite often the tendency is to shift to a sphere.

Don Juan says third-cycle seers are not interested in creating a form of the dreaming body. Doing so smacks too much of the second cycle. He says they kept the term but defined it as "a surge of energy" which travels to any location corresponding with the movement of the focal point (*Fire,* 182). Thus, it is a coherent shift of perception using the second field. You are aware, but in a different way. I have had a few experiences where it seems yet another energy leaves my dreaming body. It travels in a manner similar to the dreaming body but has no form. It is a point of awareness.

From the majority of my experiences, however, and by researching hundreds of reports, I've found that form typically accompanies dreaming-body experiences. At don Juan's level, perhaps this changes as he and his kind have developed more abstract predilections. But for now, to get the point across that there are other highly recognizable and stable aspects of human perception, I've continued to include form in its definition.

The third characteristic is that the dreaming body carries emotions. It is not a dry experience. In remote viewing, for instance, which is perceiving distant locations through the power of the mind, the experience may be devoid of emotion. Your perceptions may be very accurate, but your emotions are shunted. You perceive the situation as though you're looking at a movie screen inside your head. The dreaming body, on the other hand, often brings experiences to life even more vividly than does the physical body.

You may also duplicate all five of your physical senses. Sight and hearing tend to occur first. However, it is not uncommon to wake inside your dreaming body and not be able to see, or have restricted vision. This difficulty clears on its own. The main obstacle with tactile sensing is that your dreaming body's hands easily pass through material objects. So the lesson here is to touch things delicately. In general, all physical-like senses seem to operate better in the dreaming body than in the physical body, offering a distinct advantage in that dreaming-body experiences relate in some manner to normal experiences. Thus it is easier to learn from dreaming.

An interesting controversy centers around whether the dreaming body always exists, or whether it is created each time. Don Juan says that second-cycle Toltecs created a new body each time they stabilized a dream (*Fire*, 177). Another line of thought is that the double exists continuously and independently of the physical body. This idea has led to numerous *Twilight Zone*-style stories where people meet their doubles. Whether it is created or remains constant, the common denominator is that the integrity and intensity of dreaming energies produce awareness of the dreaming body.

In itself, dreaming is a mode of perception that may be used for good or ill. As don Juan says, it is a "gateway to the light and to the darkness of the universe" (*Dreaming*, 221). Since the dreaming body is an enhanced form of dreaming, it is precarious in that it lends itself to accumulating powers, and perhaps they might be better left alone. This is why don Juan says dreaming retains the mood of the second cycle (*Fire*, 177). With suitable context, however, it gives the strength to bypass the seduction of power and explore the makeup of consciousness. Tracking procedures are therefore intended as the guiding lights of dreaming.

Indeed, tracking and dreaming marry to create a uniform consistency for personal growth. For example, dreaming makes the shifts of tracking—blending, for example—easier. Since dreaming entertains more drastic shifts in cohesion, applying that knowledge to tracking facilitates the smaller shifts. In turn, the stability tracking offers boosts dreaming. This is an important factor since dreaming expands your options. Dreaming assists entering other dimensions and communicating with the inhabitants of those dimensions, for example. The difficulty with enhancing your world is that it's easy to get lost in the marvels of dreaming, and thus lose a deeper connection with Spirit. Tracking, however, enables you to stay in touch with your core. To me, this core feels like a narrow bar of condensed, vibrant energy. It remains constant yet resists definition. Regardless of which world I'm in, when I'm in touch with it I always feel centered. I consider it the Eagle's emanation of myself, the pure Spirit within me. While tracking sustains my awareness of it, dreaming first illuminated its existence.

By remaining centered, you can expand your options while focusing on the principal quest of developing your totality of being. Your experiences then spontaneously and magically unfold. As a result, your experiences emanate from your connection with Spirit. The first field thus prevails without dictating what must be.

An additional value of the dreaming body is that it makes you a part of the experience. As in using virtual reality, you're an integral part of the dream. You may then test your knowledge and assess the results in a more complete and expeditious manner. For example, you can test the plasticity of time and space. While in your dreaming body, you can travel slowly, rapidly, or instantaneously. You can also change your relation to the dreamscape so that the environment speeds up or slows down. For instance, one of my more instructional dreaming-body experiences occurred at night in Tucson. While meditating, I abruptly found myself suspended in mid-air over the downtown streets. I soon found that by shifting my energy I could alter how I observed the traffic's speed. At alternate times, the vehicles zipped about and crawled at a snail's pace. I also found I could slow traffic down or speed it up on command. While the dreaming body allows you to explore such abilities, activating *will* allows you to bring these same capacities back into your daily, physical world. Your daily world then becomes a dream of its own.

# Progression

Don Juan says the ability to control dreams is "no different from the control we have over any situation in our daily lives" (*Dreaming,* 21). Since there are differences in the intents of dreaming and waking control, I think he is referring to how we stabilize cohesion and thus what we perceive. For instance, in a lucid dream you can control the dreamscape. If you want to change a tree into a rubber mat, simply intend it. Or if you want to experience a new location, intend it and the dream changes.

By the time you reach the dreaming body, however, dreams have stabilized. If you want to travel to another location, you don't simply change the dream, you travel from point A to point B. During the progression of levels, you begin blending the first and second energy fields. This blending continues through each level, making the dreamscape more and more objective. At level four, for instance, you travel to precise locations. Doing so represents concrete dreaming. Indeed, I also think don Juan meant that intent is your means of control regardless of your circumstances. So how you affect your dreaming or waking states becomes a similar process. Therefore, control is "no different." What does become radically different is that you eventually evolve beyond tracking and dreaming into a unified whole. By exercising different aspects of the energy body you claim it in its entirety.

Don Juan also says a dreamer's control is like casting a fishing line that goes wherever it wants. A dreamer can, however, keep the line in place where it initially anchors (*Fire,* 177). As a result, the same dream is sustained. But it's obvious a finer control can be had. Castaneda, for instance, repeatedly returned to the same dream of a saber tooth tiger, a tiger that taught him a specific form of breathing (*Gift,* 58). Returning time and time again to the dreams of his books also indicates refined control. Moreover, don Juan's magical boomerang flight over his house demonstrates that the capacity for faultless control exists. In each dreaming level, therefore, you learn to control how and where you cast your fishing line. At the same time, when you first cross into the next level you again find your line sails where it wants.

You may become aware of the dreaming body anytime, anywhere. Excessive fatigue, stress, and even joy may bring about the shift. Quite often it results simply from being relaxed. One afternoon, I was lying on the living room floor, gazing at the ceiling. In less than a heartbeat, it was as though the ceiling jumped at me. I then realized I was in my dreaming body which was floating just below the ceiling.

A very curious aspect of the dreaming body is that you really don't leave your body. The requirement of "going out" stems from the influence of ordinary worldviews. That is, even if we stretch our known world to include the dreaming body, our ordinary inventory insists we must first "get out" of the physical body before we can perceive from another body. From a Toltec inventory, what takes place is that your cohesion shifts, your focal point moves, and you perceive the world from your dreaming body rather than from your physical body. You're still perceiving from within the energy body, just from a different location. The way the sequential, analytical side of us translates this occurrence is that we go out of our bodies. After all, it is even possible to *see* ourselves exit from our physical bodies. What is *seen*, however, is the movement of energy. From another perspective, the perception of movement is a play of mind. And the playground of the mind is the domain of a person of knowledge.

## Preparation

Preparing yourself for dreaming is important. It eliminates some hurdles and eases you over others. Keep in mind that much of what you learn in dreaming occurs on the spot. So don't lock yourself into a standard set of procedures; it's best to acquaint yourself with a variety of perspectives. In addition, knowing why you want to dream focuses energies toward specific results, thereby minimizing stray influences. Then, from level-one exercises, set out to affirm that you are a dreamer. Aiming to convince yourself you're a dreamer and being convinced are complementary facets of dreaming intent (*Dreaming*, 26).

Since dreaming produces natural shifts of the focal point, don Juan says we don't need assistance from others. What we do need is sobriety. And this comes from impeccability in our daily lives (*Fire*, 182-183). Impeccability leads to stronger dreaming and is, therefore, the principal means of preparation.

Other tracking practices also engender sobriety. Applied to dreaming, for example, attitude and balance counter "dreaming moroseness," a condition resulting from stepping in and out of other worlds. It's hard to stay focused and joyful when your world has hinges on it. But following your path with heart remedies this condition. Your path also provides direction and stability for dreaming, as well as the means to apply those results to your daily life. In addition, assuming responsibility enables you to accept and to act on the proposition that you can develop dreaming on your own.

In turn, dreaming, itself, teaches you how to make adjustments. People often tell me, for example, that a big difficulty is their reluctance to enter dreaming in the first place. It seems they've always been told that the bogeyman lives there, so they'd just as soon not make the trip. In the midst of dealing with a similar reluctance myself, I dreamed of a group of black panthers. Surprisingly, as soon as I saw them I felt a strong affinity. I recognized their stealth as quality tracking. And I also associated their spirit with dreaming energy in general. I had the thought that although a panther may not be considered king of the jungle, it certainly was a sleek and powerful prince. Then, in a vision within the dream, I *saw* a panther saunter up to me. I scratched its ears. Then it curled up like a kitten into my heart. I felt rejuvenated and my reluctance to try for a new dreaming level dissipated.

Furthermore, during a time when I was making no progress in dreaming, I found the following *Nova* exercise during meditation, which may be considered a form of dreaming. It goes like this:

1. Extend two beams of light energy a few feet outward and perpendicular to each side of your physical body: one beam out of the right side, one beam out of the left side.

2. Retract these energies to a specific location inside your chest.

3. Again extend two beams of light energy from your body. This time extend one out of the top of your head and one out of the bottoms of your feet.

4. Retract these energies to the same location as in step 2.

5. Form the energy within your chest into a sphere (or other form natural to yourself) and then gently project it away from your physical body.

While *Nova* helped me out of a dreaming slump, part of the problem remained. I still had a lingering malaise. But while resting in the blackness of level one, I intuitively realized I had to back off any preconceived notions of how I wanted dreaming to develop. I also knew I had to dive into it with an attitude combining experimentation and entertainment. These realizations placed me squarely back on the dreaming path.

You also need to prepare yourself for adventures in other

dimensions. For this, you need to strike a balance. On one hand, entering other dimensions is highly instructional. You learn that other worlds are not imagination, that they exist independently of this world. On the other hand, it's easy to become wonderstruck and wander off the path. For this reason, don Juan instructed one of his students, Benigno, not to seek "bizarre visions or worlds outside of his own," as he would find his true source of power in learning about his own world (*Second Ring,* 207). Thus don Juan established for Benigno, a tracker, the reference of "human first." Don Juan's teachings aim to peak the human experience, and dreaming is part of that experience.

## Transitions

For me, the most troublesome aspect of dreaming to date has been the transition from one state of consciousness to another. Years ago, the difficulty expressed itself in dream-time shark attacks. Practically every time I entered dreaming, I was attacked by a shark. When I gave my emotions freer reign, the attacks diminished then disappeared. The difficulty then became getting past the immense surge of energy when going into dreaming or when going from one dreaming level to the next.

This surge of energy also indicates a time when almost anything can happen. During a transition, you're in a high-energy, high-potential zone. It's as though the focal point is in a free-fall state. Until it re-stabilizes, you're susceptible to almost any influence. That is, the slightest fluctuation of your mind as well as any long-standing concern can define the content of the dream. With my shark attacks, I found myself swimming in the ocean, an activity I enjoy tremendously. Off in the distance I saw a dorsal fin. Rather than interpret it as a dolphin, I defined it as a shark. Adrenaline then kicked in, and ostensibly the shark sensed it and headed toward me. This kicked in more adrenaline to which the shark vigorously responded. An actual attack ended the dream. I later realized the shark represented my emotions. And they were coming to get me, ready or not.

When a shift begins you feel movement, anything from floating sensations to high-speed travel. Cultivate those feelings. Breathe easily and stay relaxed. You want the transition; otherwise you don't enter dreaming. Just prepare yourself a little better than I did. Have a clear purpose so you can hook onto a dream. If you slip off track, try again. Then let yourself go. A common tendency is to check yourself and pull back, often due to the unusualness of dreaming. If you pull back, you're likely to pull out of dreaming.

I've also noticed that, prior to entering my dreaming body, I feel as though I have condensed energy inside my body. It's as though there is a warm block of ice inside my chest. Invariably, when I feel this condensed energy, dreaming ensues. A Toltec friend of mine says she knows she will dream when she feels a line of pulsating energy extending from the front of her pubic area to one inch above her navel. She says that while this sensation brings about associations with sexual energy, the pulsating energy is not sexual.

Many times you may not even notice a transition. You simply find yourself in dreaming. If so, you did nothing wrong. But being able to handle all the stages of dreaming, including transitions, might keep you out of trouble. For instance, don Juan told Castaneda that his rapid transitions into the inorganic world were dangerous. He said that ordinarily going into that world consists of a series of slow transitions (*Dreaming*, 196). These transitions strengthen resolve and allow you to learn the lay of the land.

Furthermore, transferring to and from the dreaming body is practice for teleportation, which includes transitions in which you take your physical body along for the ride. Learning to move your physical energy may bring additional concerns, however. Castaneda and the Little Sisters, for example, had difficulty reconstituting their physical bodies when trying to return from a second-field adventure. The male apprentices known as the Genaros had to pour buckets of water on them in order to make them solid. One of the Genaros, Nestor, said that before solidity was restored, Castaneda and crew came out of nowhere and looked "like pieces of fog caught in a web" (*Second Ring*, 310).

To regulate your speed, you need practice. One person told me he enjoyed entering his dreaming body just because he liked the rush of energy during the transition, and didn't give much thought to where he'd end up. That's a little too disorienting for me, so I prefer to have a handle on why I'm entering dreaming and what I want to accomplish, even if the purpose is just to see what will happen. The proper speed can be measured from your core. Staying aware of this deep, inner sense typically results only from experience.

Your commitment to dream also plays a vital role. After I realized my primary goal was committing to Spirit, I found a deeper balance to pursue the dreaming body. For a while, the goal of tracking Spirit seemed so far beyond my resources that I felt drained of energy. As a result, I was having few dreaming excursions. I then recognized that the dreaming body could be used as a step toward the ultimate goal. Everything simplified when I remembered that don Juan defines dreaming as an energy-producing endeavor (*Dreaming*, 174). And maximum energy is needed to release completely into Spirit. Immediately upon making this connection, I felt suspended above my physical body about one foot, although looking down from my dreaming body it seemed my physical body was 20 feet away. I floated around the room and gently ended the event. The point is that just having a few pieces of dreaming intent fall into place produced the shift.

In addition, before a dream stabilizes you might perceive the dream waver, as though it were undulating. It may also seem as though you are spinning. At this point, don't focus on anything within the dream. But do focus on the dream itself. As your cohesion shifts, your perception may not be stable until you master the transition. Until then, take advantage of your natural dreaming shifts and fully enter your dreams. Commitment to dreaming not only produces it, but also smoothes out the transition into it.

Vibrations are also common during a transition. And they, too, might prove unsettling. One woman told me she thought her vibrations meant she was critically ill. After her physician told her she was fine, and after reading about vibrations associated with dreaming, she relaxed and turned her attention to the positive aspects of dreaming.

Furthermore, the content of a dream might also throw you off the mark. During one dream I found myself in a room that had a snake in a terrarium. It looked about three feet long. It was brown with dark brown markings. I checked to see if it had a triangular shaped head which might indicate it was a poisonous pit viper, but it kept moving so I couldn't confirm anything. All at once it was out of its container. I tried to remain calm. I then felt vibrations in my physical body. I realized I was dreaming but the intensity of being with the snake prevented the complete transition. In a flash, the snake's body connected itself to the base of my spine and to the ground. I felt a powerful infusion of energy winding its way up through my body. I began to vibrate again but woke up wondering where the snake was. (Serpentine energy often relates to the kundalini force. In turn, kundalini is often associated with the chakras, or nonphysical energy centers located in proximity to the spine. For more information, please refer to

Chapter 3 in *Traveling With Power,* or other books which outline kundalini and chakra energies.)

You may also discover that the general novelty of dreaming is an obstacle. Dealing with sharks, snakes, vibrations, and a myriad of other perceptions may surprise you back into your physical body. Additionally, just as the woman associated vibrations with illness, other occurrences may conjure equally distasteful illusions. Your body may feel catatonic, or rigid, while you dream. Several people have told me of their horror at finding they could not move their physical bodies shortly before or immediately upon returning from dreaming. It seems, however, this is natural within the scope of what we're addressing. Learning how to handle intent gets you over this hurdle as well. One morning I woke up and realized my physical body was catatonic. I also had a split awareness of being in my dreaming body. From research, I knew it was okay for my body to be immobile. So I just relaxed and enjoyed sensing the acute separation between the two bodies. Taking my time, I gently and slowly intended my awareness to re-focus from within my physical body. In short order, I wiggled my toes and stretched my limbs.

Another anomaly is hearing squeaks, snaps, cracks, pops, and perhaps sounds resembling ocean surf or freight trains. All of these sounds occur naturally as a result of accessing the second field. Indeed, you may experience them while awake and alert if you tap the second field; since dreaming is of the second field, these sounds are part of the package. Again, their unusualness may jar you back into the first field. However, if you're aware that they might occur, you can side-step the knee-jerk reaction to return.

As you work with dreaming, remember that you're dealing with perception, not with hard-and-fast rules. Most borders and barriers are of your own doing. Castaneda kept failing with *seeing,* for example, because he couldn't get past his own thoughts (*Separate,* 164). I had difficulty with dreaming because I wouldn't own up to my emotions. In getting over these kinds of hurdles, people tend to be amazed at how deeply imprinted are thoughts and emotions which they have long since failed to recognize.

## Exercises for Dreaming

Dreaming is a learnable skill. Like studying a foreign language or a musical instrument, it requires time, energy, and abundant practice to master it. Castaneda says that exercising dreaming energies is the essential point in cultivating dreaming. Don Juan likens dreaming to a river which flows into the ocean of the second field. He says that by systematically exercising dreaming energies, barriers to entering the ocean fall away (*Dreaming*, 28-36).

Mental and emotional preparedness and specific dreaming exercises may bring about dreaming, but keep in mind that dreaming is a form of energy distinct from the exercises. So your experiences may vary from how you think they should be. Castaneda says that his breakthroughs always occur suddenly. And it is continued effort, says don Juan, that is the deciding factor for success (*Dreaming*, 49, 36). Under the force of persistence, the energy body's cohesion eventually shifts like a rusty bolt finally giving way to the continuous pressure from a wrench.

**General Approaches.** Typically, you tap deeper levels of your awareness the deeper in dreaming you go. One difficulty is cutting yourself short by interpreting what's going on in accordance with previous definitions. That is, there is a tendency to interpret a level-two experience by what was discovered in level one. If you cling to your newfound world, you keep yourself out of the next world. Just to enter level one, for instance, I found I needed to let go of what had taken me my entire life to understand.

A general approach, therefore, is to continue nonpatterning—all the time. This means you need to remain fluid and not load your waking life or dreaming with expectations about how you think they should unfold. During a dreaming seminar, for example, one of the participants inquired about feeling an unusual heaviness. I told her I would look into it. Before the start of the second day's lessons, I went into another room for privacy. I sat down at the floor and felt a heaviness descend over me. Since I was looking for this, I didn't resist. I let it thicken and move through my body.

The heaviness then left my body and I found myself standing up in my dreaming body, looking down at my physical body. I felt an obscure need to surround myself with light. I did so and felt more relaxed. I asked myself if I should do this before entering my dreaming body. I heard a silent, "No, don't get obsessed. Just after you're out is fine." I then reentered my physical body and proceeded with the seminar. The entire event took less than five minutes. At that time, my bias was not to surround myself in light. Had I fought the proposition, I would have fought the dreaming body itself and not been able to provide some kind of insight to the participant. To her, I specifically mentioned using nonattachment and nonpatterning as a means to flow with the heaviness just to discover where it led.

The following, then, is a general approach.

1. Relax.
    a. Don't push with your first-field, physical energies.
    b. "Sink" deeper into second-field, nonphysical perceptions.
2. Suspend your internal dialogue.
    a. Try not to think—even when you encounter something new or novel.
    b. Let go of expectations and requirements.
3. Exercise nonpatterning.
    a. Don't judge anything, including yourself if you judge something.
    b. Don't identify with anything.
4. Develop different dreaming intents: entering dreams, maneuvering, and goal acquisition, for instance.
    a. Call forth the feeling of a specific destination.
    b. Feel what it's like to move at different speeds, and in different directions.

From this approach, you again find that tracking develops dreaming. Indeed, due to the vastness of dreaming, tracking reduces aberrations. You remain focused and deliberate, and this hones your dreaming energies along purposeful avenues.

**Specific Approaches**. Specific exercises stimulate different facets of dreaming. To get to the dreaming body, for instance, you exercise its various components, such as transitions and maneuvering. The overall intent then comes together on its own, and you find yourself in your dreaming body. You have then progressed beyond the preliminary exercises to the full realization of the goal. At that point, the dreaming body becomes an exercise for yet another goal, another dreaming level.

Preliminary exercises stimulate dreaming by simulating aspects of the dreaming body. While you may not be centered within your dreaming body, you generate feelings and other perceptions associated with it. To look at the world from within your dreaming body, for example, practice opening your eyes while your physical eyelids remain closed. At the beginning, you might find blackness. If so, good. You may be at the threshold of level one.

As another approach, don Juan uses visualization to foster dreaming (*Tales,* 20). Applying this to the dreaming body, you can encourage the transition with this *Split Decision* exercise:

1. Lie down in your bed.
2. Physically get up and slowly walk away from your bed.
3. Repeat steps 1 and 2 several times.
4. Lie down in your bed. Visualize and feel yourself get up out of bed and move about. Your physical body remains in your bed.
5. Repeat step 4 several times.

To engage maneuvering abilities, try *Stepping Out:*

1. Using visual imagery, create a dreaming body. Feel it.
2. Imagine it floating, hovering over your physical body.
3. Imagine it traveling. Feel the movement.
4. Pick a location and go there.

In addition, Castaneda was taught to focus on the tip of his sternum to bring about dreaming (*Gift,* 140). Before I read this, I had been focusing between my eyes, on what many refer to as the "third eye," as a means to bring about dreaming. Now I found that by focusing on my sternum, visual imagery immediately arose from the blackness. It was like touching a greased ball that kept shifting, slipping, and sliding. But it also felt like I was in touch with the dreaming body right from the start rather than building dreaming-body awareness as with third-eye exercises. It turns out that Castaneda was taught that that area of the energy body is where dreaming energy is focused.

While talking with an emissary from the inorganic world, Castaneda was also given additional tips; he was advised, for example, to wear a gold ring or a tight belt or necklace (*Dreaming,* 94). Such devices serve as focusing agents or reminders that facilitate transitions.

With experience, you find that the dreaming-body's core has a natural speed. Whether you're inching along the universe, or catapulting through it, this energy remains constant. Staying in touch with it and letting it determine your speed will produce significant results. For one, it enhances the frequency of dreaming. Indeed, dreaming-body experiences may occur more frequently the more your behavior is regulated by the natural vibration of your core energy. It also feeds over into your daily life, giving you lessons on managing your resources and leading to living a natural life.

Whether you focus on the third eye, the sternum, or other parts of the energy body, the common denominator is that you're focusing on the second field. It is the diligent and systematic exercising of that awareness which produces results. It is for that reason that exercising particular techniques is secondary to exercising dreaming itself.

* * *

By tracking the dreaming body, you cross over the bridge that explains it and exercises it, to its actuality. Once there, you can soar through the clouds, cartwheel through the stars, and dip into a Toltec vat of pure perception. Whether you're playing with traffic, visiting an entity from another dimension, or figuring out how perception works, you can count on ordinary considerations of perception, such as the relationship between time and space, falling to the side as you bend the rules of any and all realities.

# 13
# Scouting the Dreaming Body

In this chapter, we scout the dreaming body. The focus is not only on how to bring about the dreaming body, but on what happens during the experience, as well as on how to end it. By no means is this information the final word. It does, however, acquaint you with the dreaming body so you're better prepared to handle it. Some aspects of the dreaming body, such as form, transitions, and applications, have been covered in preceding chapters.

## Aspects of Dreaming

**Attitude**. Dreaming is not a be-all, end-all tool. But it certainly is a good one. By recognizing that there are new worlds waiting, you apply pressure to step out of your normal habits. Turning your eyes outward gets you out of self-indulgence and leads to knowledge and power. It also lets you cultivate the dreaming body from a sense of positive anticipation. This approach, in turn, helps you make the dreaming body a priority. When you have developing it as a predominant goal and you balance your life around that goal, you place more energy in that direction. This doesn't mean you have to sacrifice your daily life. It means that you're willing to adjust your life to pursue other options.

Dreaming is a serious venture, but the more you remain light-hearted the more dreaming energies surface, and the more they can be controlled. It's also helpful to think of the dreaming body as something natural, even ordinary. Doing so prevents locking your awareness in a spell that says the dreaming body is only for a few masters of sorts, or only for those who seek refined occult states. Accessing your dreaming body is like receiving the gift of a lifetime. Used wisely, it makes your entire life that much more of a gift.

**Breathing**. Unless you're well versed in breathing techniques, simply let your breathing adjust itself. Your body knows how to balance itself if you let it. When anxiety, fear, surprise, or other emotions surface, try to breathe with regular, calm, and even breaths.

While in your dreaming body, breathing isn't necessary. You can remain under water, in the middle of walls, or in deep space without concern for the physical nourishment of air. In fact, the first time you experience the ability to remain under water you'll be delightfully surprised at your newfound ability.

**Commitment**. As you develop your attitudes, you also need to get comfortable with your commitment to develop the dreaming body. Why do you want to do it? For how long will you try? What fears do you have regarding it? Is it a head- or a heart-trip? How do you want to apply it? By detailing your purposes, you find how deep the goal resonates within you. If you find a sincere desire, cultivate your commitment so that nothing can knock you off the trail. Otherwise, you might keep distracting yourself even if you have the best of intentions. In addition, the intensity of a strong, wholesome commitment to dreaming often delivers sufficient force to bring it about without supporting techniques. Still, don't leave it to chance. Work for it.

**Communication**. Most, if not all, communication in the dreaming body is nonverbal. It is telepathic, or directly apprehended in some other way. Teaching Castaneda how to communicate with inorganic beings, don Juan said he was to encode a message within the intent of his communication (*Dreaming,* 48). An encoded message is like sending out intense energy as you would if you were steadfast in telling someone to leave you alone and communicating this by your manner alone.

When communication is accomplished through imagery, you need your intuition clear and sharp to translate. If another entity sends a message, for instance, and if you don't feel the entire gestalt of information, you may *see* geometric symbols tumbling toward you. Rest easy, and ask what they mean. Stop your internal dialogue, nonpattern the symbols, and let the meaning come of its own accord. The same applies if you're asking yourself a question, such as how to proceed in a new environment.

Communication from another entity often sounds and feels as though the entity is right inside your head. One person told me that when he first experienced this phenomenon, he ended his dreaming out of fright because he thought the entity was inside him. If a person were on the receiving end of a telephone conversation for the first time, the experience might be interpreted similarly. With time and experience, dreaming communication comes naturally.

**Concentration.** Single-mindedness is always a plus to attain a goal. The dreaming body is no different. In the beginning, determine a few goals regarding why you want to use your dreaming body. Then let them go so your expectations don't trip you up. Understand that you have goals, but don't hold on so tightly that you miss the steps in achieving them. If you want to go the planet Zanzabu, for instance, you might have to learn how to navigate your own solar system first. Dreaming is a process, so let the process work for you. At the same time, knowing your goals helps you stay centered and deliberate, which produces forces that align your perception to the dreaming body.

Also focus on entering the dream world, for that is the environment of the dreaming body. As with previous dreaming exercises, concentrate on the second energy field. While it takes tremendous pressure to make the shift whenever you want, concentrate gently. There's no need to warp your energies.

**Concerns.** Often people express concerns regarding dreaming. Frequently these concerns stem from physical-world problems. Some people remain bewildered that they have driven several miles and don't remember doing so. "Highway hypnosis," a dreaming-related condition, is common but should not be an excuse for carelessness. Thus paying attention to what you're doing is the order of the day—in both the physical and dream worlds.

Other concerns speak more directly to the dreaming body. Many people experience apnea (a breathing irregularity), nervous tics, and unusual agitation. It's possible that apnea occurs as a result of the shift away from the physical, first energy field. More research is indicated, however. Tics and jolts of energy occur regularly when the second field is stimulated. They are indications of moving energy. In addition, don Juan indicates that Castaneda experienced jolts of fear resulting from energy projected from inorganic beings. The remedy, he says, is to carefully gauge your response and encode a message containing strength and abandon rather than of fear or morbidity (*Dreaming*, 47).

Another common concern is the fear of dying during the experience. I once dreamed of my deceased father telling me not to fear death, to allow it to occur. When I awakened, I realized I was blocking the dreaming body in order to not experience the "little death" it brings about. In other words, part of you dies because your world is no longer the same.

From experience, most concerns have a flimsy basis. They result from lack of experience, inadequate education, or just having had a really bad day, and come with the territory of learning to dream. Don Juan, for example, says that muteness is common when extending yourself past your known world. The more comfortable you become with the unknown, the less you experience speech impediments. He also says there is a safety valve which causes you to surface from a dream should the need arise. In general, he says the way to handle yourself is to develop better and more sober control of your dreaming energies (*Dreaming*, 72, 42). In other words, practice.

**Daily Life**. What you experience in daily life often affects dreaming. These experiences can be as simple as watching television. After watching a special on prisons, I dreamed of being in prison. Lying in my cell bed, I sensed the futility of not having physical freedom. However, I think my desire for freedom sparked the vibrations associated with dreaming transitions.

Recognizing the influence of daily life, it's easy enough to capitalize on it. Since dreams reflect your thoughts, think about dreaming. You can also perform dreaming exercises throughout the day and as often as you can. In fact, integrating your dreaming goals with your daily life is beneficial. You may want to use dreaming to build your business, to write, or to get ideas for your art.

Furthermore, the more balance you have in daily life, the more you exercise awareness in general, automatically feeding over into dreaming. As a stimulus, you can also regard daily life as a dream. As you do, pay attention to elements of your environment without getting lost in them or indulging in your activities. Finally, consider that each and every action either adds to or subtracts from dreaming. Then act accordingly.

**Dimensions**. Entering other dimensions, such as the inorganic world, offers an unparalleled education. To actually witness the existence of other intelligent beings and their world breaks most common barriers of perception. Difficulties may arise, however, when you have no points of reference, no sense of purpose, or no sense of mobility within a new world. Here we go back to a path with heart. To lift you over the hurdle of having no purpose, establish one. Know why you're entering a foreign territory in the first place.

Also, it's good to verse yourself with different maps of dreaming terrains. This keeps you from getting bogged down in a certain point of view. For instance, worrying about the "lower" astral plane is equivalent to worrying excessively about legal concerns in your daily life. Focusing on worries tends to upset your equilibrium. Additionally, they often have no basis. The dreaming world, for example, is not necessarily hierarchical. You don't have to work through lower realms to get to upper realms, unless that way makes sense to you.

In addition, the way you experience entities from other dimensions often relates to your disposition. One person told me she felt a force pulling her away from her physical body and into her dreaming body. Perhaps since she was single woman living in a rough side of town, she automatically interpreted the force as demonic and fought hard against it. Later, when she again experienced the force, she went with it and had a positive dreaming-body experience. In between these episodes, she had re-ordered her life and was taking more control of how she wanted to live.

**Flow.** Castaneda says that a Toltec path is a flow, a process.[1] The same is true for dreaming. While it has no set procedures, it does have energy which carries perception. Going from one level to the next is a matter of handling that flow and of dipping further and further into the intensity of dreaming. To do so, nonattachment and flexibility are required. A short time ago, as I entered dreaming I felt myself spinning out of control. However, I just let it be and allowed the spinning to occur. The spinning energy spontaneously shifted and gained consistency, but now I perceived myself as the blade of a circular saw whizzing down a mountain road. Again, I let it be and went with it. The blade then turned into my dreaming body. As a simultaneous perception, I simply became aware of my dreaming body. Thus I proceeded through the initial stages of dreaming by keeping myself on track with that energy, while another part of me shifted immediately to that awareness.

**Flying Dreams.** It's my opinion that a flying dream is a dreaming-body experience in progress. The person just has not made a complete connection with it, and so the experience remains at a normal dreaming level. Once, for example, I dreamed I was flying a military jet fighter. I was having fun rolling through clouds. A large bomber then came up under my aircraft, producing turbulence. But I soon recognized it was not turbulence, but rather the vibrations associated with a transition. This realization allowed me to make the complete shift into my dreaming body, and I continued to fly through the clouds.

**Frequency of Dreaming**. Since my first bilocation in the late 1970s, I have enjoyed numerous dreaming-body experiences. Most involved studying how to get into my dreaming body, how to move, and how to return. The next major batch dealt with fun, such as flying through clouds. The rest were trips to other planets, other dimensions, and curious states of mind.

At times, I've had three episodes a day for weeks at a time. Other times, I didn't have an experience for months. I think that part of this irregularity comes from the physical body needing time to catch up to what's going on. It needs to integrate new energies and relate to them in a way which promotes well-being. Another aspect of the erratic nature of dreaming comes from a lack of unbending intent. And, once again, this aspect is addressed by having a stable path with heart, knowing why you're engaging dreaming, and having integrated your dreaming purposes through-out your daily life. The times when my life is the most balanced, directed, and calm are the times when I enjoy the greatest frequency of dreaming.

**Goals**. Having dreaming goals offers motivation, focuses energy, provides balance, adds meaning to your life, and thus engages intent. I find it's best to have several purposes. They might include recreation to keep loose and open, studying how to facilitate transitions, problem-solving, and art- or writing-related endeavors. With a variety of goals you harbor no inclinations to rest, or to limit the applications of dreaming. In the meantime, know that you're waiting and what you're waiting for. Then make sure you have fun getting there.

One way to develop intent is to divide dreaming into two parts. The first deals with traveling to specific locations, the second with accomplishing a long-term task. As a result, you learn how to focus and how to build momentum. To achieve either, don Juan's advice is to hold the image of the topic while you turn off your internal dialogue (*Tales*, 20). Thus, the energies of alignment are set in motion. You can also use association to help you feel connected with your goal. If you want to travel to the moon, for instance, reflect on the Apollo moon landing.

Zeroing in on goals is like learning to shoot a bow and arrow. It takes time to hit the bull's-eye. A distinct advantage of pursuing a task is that you become skilled (or at least conversant) in all of the individual elements of the task. To write, for example, you need know the general scope of your topic as well as have proficiency in dreaming. Then you learn how to keep your awareness centered on the topic, how to organize, and how to be fluid enough to let new knowledge come into view. In other words, you can't be shaken by the surprises of how the writing falls into place.

Moreover, while it's enjoyable to deal with the complexities of a skill such as writing, perceiving the goal directly is astute tracking. For instance, dreaming the finished draft of your writing means you have successfully integrated the individual skills of writing even if you've never formally studied it. Knowing the elements of writing, and how to apply them, is tracking. Having all the elements come together in dreaming is tracking at its finest.

For additional perspectives on this and related matters, please see the "Task" section in Chapter 15.

**Intent**. The dreaming body is an intent within the intent of your entire self. It just needs actualization. The down side is that as long as it remains dormant we're missing an important part of us. The up side is that the procedures to awaken the dreaming body are the same procedures used to awaken *will*. Therefore developing the dreaming body is a major step en route to *will*.

Transferring your awareness back and forth from your physical body to your dreaming body teaches you how to handle intent. You must initiate intent to make the transitions, and you must hold intent steady to remain aware of the dreaming body. The main ingredient is getting sufficient energy to make the shift. That increased energy also clues you in on intent itself.

Intent is perceived directly. Once you get the hang of it you can talk about its existence, but talking about it does little to make it work. As you work with dreaming exercises, pay attention to the force which moves and then stabilizes your awareness. That force is intent. The more you exercise it, the more you learn how to handle it.

**Journals**. A standard dreaming exercise is keeping a dream diary. There's no doubt that this activity works. It focuses energy toward the goal and allows you to see patterns in your dreaming. But you also need to ask: where does it keep energy focused? Piddling through regular dreams may offer nice insights from time to time, but it may also keep you focused at elementary levels. You may be having such a good time recording your nightly excursions that you forget about getting on with the program. If this does hold you back and you want to continue your journal, a compromise might be to record only new adventures or new insights.

A journal might also distract you from other quests. Don Juan poked fun at Castaneda when he found Castaneda was keeping a dream journal. Here you are trying to lose self-importance, says don Juan, and you have an elaborate, very personal diary called *My Dreams* (*Dreaming*, 37). Another way to address a desire to keep a journal is to store notes in your body without usual note-taking. In other words, create a nonpatterning journal. This route is what don Genaro was suggesting when he advised Castaneda to take notes by writing with a finger instead of a pencil (*Gift*, 26).

**Maneuvering Intent**. Once you're in your dreaming body, you again engage intent to travel. As with any intent, you intend by intending. In other words, you have to do it. Learning to maneuver in dreaming is like learning to walk. It's instinctive. You try, fall, try again, fall, try again, and then succeed. You know you want to travel so you intend it.

Perhaps the hardest part is releasing yourself to forces beyond your control. Here you are in another world and you don't know the rules of the road. But neither did you know the rules when you were first learning to walk and risked leaving your mother's arms.

**Negative Situations**. Once I've fully entered the dreaming body, almost all of my experiences have been positive. (The shark attacks were during the transition to it.) My worst dreaming-body experience ever occurred when I was scouting a foreign country and was pulled against my desire toward a river. As a result, I simply ended the episode. From time to time, however, I hear tales of horror. Upon close scrutiny most can be attributed to a poor state of mind. That is, they resulted from the projection of mental or emotional imbalances.

Remember, focal point shifts themselves can produce terror. But once you catch on to the shifts, you begin to look forward to discovering whatever it is that waits for you. In fact, this attitude lifts you over most obstacles. You don't get bogged down in a dream world where negative entities have to exist. And even if you do meet an entity you deem negative, stop and ask yourself what's going on and how you should react. Don't surrender your command just because you heard or read that you are at the mercy of dream forces.

To me, the most negative aspect of dreaming is that it can be used to generate second-cycle practices. That is, it can be used to harness energy and then that energy can be applied against others. Just as there are disreputable physicians, lawyers, and politicians—all of whom are regarded as being in public service—there is the chance of finding disreputable Toltecs. There are guidelines, however, to assist you in staying out of trouble. Since the winds of darkness and light are always blowing, the levels of dreaming outline a way to keep on track to freedom, and out of the dregs of dreaming lusts.

**Position of the Physical Body.** The main point here is to nonpattern your normal habits of using your body. To exercise nonpatterning, one of the Genaros, Pablito, walked backwards. He later built a harness with rear-view mirrors so he could walk uninterrupted for extended periods. La Gorda says that don Juan told her the best posture for women is to sit with legs crossed and let the body fall forward, as one's attention centers on dreaming (*Gift,* 141, 142). Castaneda also had success with this posture.

I tend to lie on my back. The longer I remain on my back without rolling over onto my side, the more my dreaming progresses. I have, however, also had dreaming-body experiences while lying on either side, sitting in a chair, and, on a few occasions, standing up. While posture may facilitate dreaming, catching the intent of dreaming is the main concern.

Simultaneously relaxing and latching onto a dreaming intent is what to aim for while you're dozing off. Try to resolve any disputes or misgivings before you do so they won't distract you or eat away at your energy. Practicing a couple of dreaming exercises before sleeping also focuses your energies.

**Projection.** Whatever you've experienced during the day to some degree affects your energy body. If you hold onto attitudes or energies because you favor them, or even because you are disgusted by them, you plant that energy a little deeper than you do the experiences which don't affect you. This energy carries over into dreaming. As a result, your experiences may reflect your biases, fears, joys, or anything else that has taken root. The more you nonpattern, the more you sweep away projection. Remember that the recapitulation also cleanses perception.

**Protection.** A traditional form of dreaming-body protection involves surrounding oneself in white light. People often use an affirmation concerning protection in conjunction with light. Only two or three times in all of my travels have I felt compelled to summon white light. And even then I did so out of uncertainty rather than from a sense of danger. As mentioned in a previous anecdote, however, immersing oneself in light does promote relaxation if nothing else. That alone is sufficient reason to use it.

I don't think that engaging light places a person inside an envelop of protection as much as it realigns perception away from the trouble spot. When people use white light in dreaming, they tend to be highly motivated. After all, trouble may be afoot. Extricating themselves from trouble does not mean they've been saved. It could mean that their concern focused energy in a different direction. As white light is associated with "all that is good," it readily lends itself to re-focusing awareness into desirable environments. Therefore, when used prior to entering the dreaming body, white light focuses positive energy right off the bat.

Overall, I regard protection as another way of saying you have some control over what happens to you. Since your daily life influences your dreaming, if you have a strong, deliberate, wholesome life, your dreaming follows suit.

**Returning.** Another frequent concern is the fear of not being able to return from the dreaming body. The fact is, you're likely to return before you want to due to a full bladder. Also, the slightest discomfort in the physical body usually pulls awareness back to it. And even when you can stay away for extended periods, thinking about and feeling your connection with your physical body realigns you with it. In essence, then, focusing your intent on your physical body restores that awareness.

At the same time, there may be instances where you feel you can't return. On each occasion where I've heard about or experienced something of this nature, it has been the result of needing to wait just a little longer for a lesson to be revealed. If you find yourself seemingly trapped, relax and ask yourself why. If you interpret the situation as negative, you automatically generate energy that may fulfill your prophecy. If you give yourself room to maneuver, you have more maneuverability.

As you return, intend a smooth, gentle transition. If you snap back, I don't think you'll harm yourself, but you may feel out of sorts for a few days. Tell yourself to return with all your energies aligned and in harmony. Ease back in and you're likely to wake up feeling refreshed and invigorated. There may be times, however, when you feel as though you've been digging in a quarry all night and you return feeling very tired. If so, you've probably tackled a new dreaming situation and have worked hard, and you're feeling the effects. In this sense, it's no different than waking up stiff and sore after having strenuously hiked the previous day.

**Silver Cord**. There have been many stories about a silver cord which connects the dreaming body to the physical body. Most often, the cord is *seen* while a person is in their dreaming body. Legend has it that if the cord breaks, the person dies. In her book *Out-of-Body Experiences: A Handbook,* Janet Lee Mitchell, Ph.D., states that reports of the silver cord have diminished over the years. She adds that the cord may be only a symbol which grants a sense of security.[2]

This possibility makes sense. Perhaps perceiving the cord is like astronauts being tethered to their space capsules during the first space walks. As knowledge and experience grew, the need for the lifeline was eliminated. They now carry their propulsion systems with them. Accordingly, as our species' experience with dreaming grows, perhaps the need for a safety cord is being eliminated.

**Sounds**. During the transition into the dreaming body, you may hear a variety of sounds. Ocean surf, bells, and freight trains all seem to make their appearance sooner or later. As you progress through the transition, they fade away.

You may also have a steady tone or ringing in your ears. While this is often considered an effect of ear damage, it may also reflect audio perception of other energies or dimensions. I always have a steady tone in my ears. Often the frequency changes, shifting from high to low or vice versa. I've had my hearing checked by a physician and it checks out as above average across the board. In recent months, I've learned to use the ringing to enter dreaming. When I focus my entire attention on the tones, dreaming ensues. I have identified a straight, simple, and quick way to enter dreaming.

**Stabilization of Intent**. Before your dreaming becomes workable, it usually is erratic. Dreams might waver or spin. Or you may feel only half connected with the dream. To correct this wavering connection, you need to get over the hurdle of uncertainty. So summon your reserves and concentrate on the dream. You need to know what you want to accomplish, and that you're capable. To stabilize dreaming, then, work through your purposes and then practice. Get more experience. Just as you stabilize your daily world, you stabilize dreaming.

**Waking Up**. Dreaming lends itself to a variety of moods. Coming out of dreaming, you experience most of them. At times you may bound out of bed energized and ready for a new day. Other times, you may want to reflect on your dreaming, letting it simmer and work its way through you. In the first instance, the challenge lies in not letting the mood get the best of you. In the second, set your schedule to avoid the frustration of not having time to reflect.

In addition, the time between wakefulness and sleep and between sleep and wakefulness is ripe for dreaming. During this timeless zone, you can consolidate prior dreaming, or use dreaming to map out the day. Furthermore, by constructively using your dream time you always wake up to a world full of adventure, challenge, knowledge, and positive anticipation.

# Part V
# Intent

# 14
## Tracking Intent

To understand a Toltec path, it's best to know that it does not stem from a world of ideas, but from a world of intent. It does not deal with a world that is formulated and bound by reason; it does reflect a world that hinges on *will*. Its practices yield only to the domain of silent knowledge, which don Juan simultaneously defines as intent, Spirit, or the abstract, and thus descriptions always seem inadequate (*Silence*, 167).

Don Juan thinks that in the course of human evolution, our ancestors became too fixated on trying to know intent objectively, as though it could be studied as something separate from human awareness. The more they tried, the more elusive it became. Please keep this in mind as we continue to poke around the edges of intent in order to gain a better sense of it.

### Defining the Undefinable

At the core of intent is silent power; indeed, Power itself. It has no movement, no form. And yet it produces movement and form. It is an immeasurable, indescribable force. It is also the force which causes us to perceive. Don Juan further defines intent as pure energy. And he says it is "the universal feature shared by everything there is" (*Silence*, 16, 121, 244). Clara adds that intent lies beyond thoughts and feelings, but can be used. You intend, she says, not by having intentions but by using intent.[1] Thus, while intent may be colorless, odorless, and tasteless, handling it is a skill of its own.

While everything is connected to intent, by intent, everything has its own intent. Just as there is an intent known as "human," for example, there are intents within that intent. There is an intent for gender, for race, for culture, and for each individual. In addition, each and every person is connected to the pure intent of Spirit. The job at hand, therefore, is not to make the connection but to remember it. In terms of Toltec training, restoring awareness of that link is the work of an apprentice. Shining it is the work of a ranger. Handling it is the work of a Toltec. And managing it is the work of a person of knowledge.

In general, don Juan refers to *will* as the force responsible for holding alignments of energy in place, while intent produces shifts of alignment (*Fire,* 218). In this light, intent is the purposeful guiding of *will*; in other words, the deliberate molding of energy. Yet don Juan also relates intent to both the shifting of alignments and holding alignments stationary (*Dreaming,* 161). What you might consider here, then, is that *will* represents the raw force of the Eagle's emanations. These emanations are woven throughout existence. From a storyteller's understanding, we discovered that everything already exists within the emanations. Accordingly, intent is the deliberate application of *will* to manifest whatever you seek.

In one instance, don Juan says that through impeccability Toltecs turn the force of *will* into the force of intent (*Fire,* 295). Thus they achieve conscious, individual awareness of the emanations, leading to control of intent. By fully stretching their awareness, they accomplish a remarkable alignment of energy which lights up all of the emanations within their energy bodies. This process results in gaining total awareness of the human condition, a feat corresponding with total freedom.

Making actual shifts of alignment is the mark of success in Toltec training. And since the shifts require handling energy directly, talking about what takes place doesn't matter all that much. Thus, don Juan says that contradictions in the Toltecs' world are with the terms, and not with the actual practices (*Silence,* 179). In the practice of silent knowledge, there is only the matter of learning about and handling intent, a practice which transcends form. As it is universal energy, defining intent automatically removes you from it. But defining it can point out that something exists beyond the normal senses. The remote chance of gaining freedom, says don Juan, rests with this awareness.

## Unbending Intent

Anything can cause a focal point shift, says don Juan: hunger, fear, love, ambition, war, even mysticism. The preferred method of Toltecs, however, is unbending intent (*Silence,* 240-241). He likens unbending intent to single-mindedness, to having an ex- ceedingly well-defined purpose where there is no interference from distracting desires. He adds that it is also the force produced by stabilizing the focal point in a nonordinary position. Hence unbending intent shifts the focal point into new positions, and these positions further generate unbending intent.

To implement unbending intent, your ruthlessness must be disguised, says don Juan. You don't want your cutting edges showing, so tracking is essential. Social manners, for example, offset the roughness humans so often exhibit. But disguising your ruthlessness, continues don Juan, is not done as an act of kindness, but as a part of a ranger's training. A ranger should be magical and ruthless with well-sharpened edges, he says, but always on the alert not to advertise (*Silence,* 126).

A "fierce purpose" is needed for an apprentice to begin awakening intent (*Silence,* 62). Initially, however, team leaders supply energy to their apprentices, eventually weaning them away from the external source by teaching how to manage personal resources. To help their apprentices generate their own energy, leaders use ploys ranging from petty tyrants to learning tasks. There is more on teaching methods in the next chapter.

## Awakening Intent

Don Juan says that the average person's intent is practically dead. Realizing that they begin with a nonfunctional intent, Toltecs begin awakening it by performing a single action that is "deliberate, precise, and sustained." Repeating the act long enough produces unbending intent (*Fire,* 179).

Accessing intent occurs in heightened awareness (*Silence,* 104). And proficiency with tracking and dreaming leads to heightened awareness. Thus a good way to start your awakening is to practice a variety of exercises. Then allow intent to lead you in the proper directions. Furthermore, Castaneda advises that you should move toward intent without understanding.[2] Doing so gives you time to explore. Without wasting time, take your time to learn the intricacies of intent. Don't wrap up your knowledge too soon, or you will have to spend even more time trying to get it right. As don Juan says, command your knowledge before you try to figure out what's what (*Silence,* 106). Also keep in mind that you're going deeper and deeper in awareness. The understandings you have today often fade as you round the next bend.

Also stay alert for the glimmerings of something waiting to unfold. The further you travel, the more you're going to sense something looming, something waiting to break into full awareness. This is the unknown ready to become known. So that you don't misinterpret, misdirect, or otherwise interfere with your soon-to-be knowledge, get interested in what intent really is, rather than what you want it to be. This directive applies to every intent, especially the purest form of intent, Spirit. The more you reduce self-importance, the more you perceive; thus the more you bring the Spirit within you to life.

# Manifesting

By latching onto an intent, you bring that intent into view. Often this is termed "manifesting," or bringing something—an idea, a goal, an object—into conscious awareness. From a Toltec perspective, manifesting concerns aligning your energy with the energy of the goal. This alignment produces the perception of it. In all phases of energy alignment, intent is the key.

Manifesting is a moment-to-moment process. In each moment we balance between the known and unknown. Ordinarily, this relation is so flimsy that we perceive new potentials only if they fit with our current, known world. And so we automatically reduce most potential. For this reason, an unyielding purpose is necessary to shift the focal point outside of its comfort zone. That is, only with such purpose can you deliberately step beyond your normal thoughts and habits which keep the focal point in place in order to arrive at new, transformative perceptions.

With unbending intent, your commands become one with the commands of the Eagle. Second-cycle Toltecs, says don Juan, issued commands by talking about their ways, creating energy reflecting their thoughts, and thereby enhancing their self-reflection. Rather than incantations and superfluous dialogue, third-cycle Toltecs learned to issue directives by using intent itself (*Fire,* 293-294). By wishing without wishing, and doing without doing, they latched onto intent directly (*Dreaming,* 23-25). As a result of their inner silence, their commands were free to match those of the Eagle. Whenever this match occurs, you've manifested your goal.

Don Juan also says that intent is available to everyone, but its command belongs only to those who explore it (*Silence,* 105). Accordingly, the following views are offered to help you scout and track aspects of intent. Each of these is applicable to manifesting anything, but the bias concerns manifesting deeper connections with Spirit. Success requires giving Spirit complete control of your life without losing control of yourself.

There are a variety of markers which indicate you're on track. You may feel as though something fell into place. Or you may have a sense of energy coagulating. At the beginning your quest may seem vague. You might feel as though you can't relate to any of this. But at each turn of your path, you cultivate more strength of manner and purpose.

## Aspects of Manifesting

We all face numerous influences which govern how and what we manifest. Here are a few:

**Decisions.** When people make decisions, says don Juan, they merely acquiesce to a far greater power. Decisions are therefore a matter of allowing the first energy field to adjust to what's already occurring in the second field (*Tales*, 243). In other terms, as awareness filters through into conscious awareness, you make a choice which echoes an Eagle's command. To surrender the illusion of personal decision-making takes quite an effort. But with sufficient time exploring the world of Spirit, you realize that personal control doesn't amount to much. You find that all of your gains reflect how well you have merged with the directives of Spirit. This might be why don Juan considers Spirit to be the real player, and himself as only its agent (*Dreaming*, 200-205). It's also in this regard that he considers team leaders as intermediaries of Spirit (*Silence*, 178).

Learning to give yourself to Spirit is not done in a helter-skelter fashion. Don Juan offers guidance. One bit of advice is that you make your decisions so carefully that you're not surprised by what unfolds (*Tales*, 155). Another is that by applying personal responsibility, a ranger makes decisions that leave no time for regrets and are always strategically the best (*Separate*, 184). Making decisions in this manner brings about a tracker's control. And this kind of control is what enables you to track Spirit.

Don Juan also says your body knows when you've made the right decision. Make the wrong one and you feel tense, or ill at ease. With the right decision the body relaxes and stands ready for the next decision (*Tales*, 214). And remember to remove yourself from personal thoughts and feelings. Mistakes occur only when personal considerations interfere with your direct link to intent.

Unless your body knows you've made a mistake, stick with your decisions. Your decisions result from having accumulated more personal power, and thus you have a more solid connection with intent. When you backslide and deviate from a decision, you reduce your power and extend the time required to bring about the complete manifestation.

A decision unleashes energy. If you want to shift cohesion and make a new alignment, you need to apply steady, even pressure. When you can maintain strong, well-directed pressure, you have created unbending intent. As you learn to acquiesce to Spirit and remove personal wishes from decision-making, manifesting occurs as a result of becoming more aware. At the ranger stage, this means you build your life one day at a time. And to do this, you must trust your personal power.

**Desires and Expectations.** Referring to seers' interactions with people, don Juan says that seers desire nothing even though they can get anything they want. By *seeing* into anything, seers can easily track and obtain anything. But by accepting their fate, however, they let Spirit unveil their paths. Their form of desire, then, is to tap their core natures. To do this, Spirit must rule, as ordinary desires block the flow of Spirit. Don Juan adds that personal desires produce unhappiness, and that if we trim our lives so that we have no wants, the smallest item is the largest gift (*Separate*, 186, 173). As a result, don Juan says that to not want anything is a ranger's highest attainment (*Tales*, 242).

Even with a casual look, it's obvious that our desires herd us along through life. Wanting this, demanding that, we're in a constant struggle just to fulfill our fleeting wishes. Yet don Juan also applies this force to Toltec instruction. He tells Castaneda, for example, that just the desire to erase personal history can provide the force to make it so (*Journey*, 29). In addition, finding the desires which are imprinted within your path with heart delivers you to the ranger stage. Once there, however, the guidelines change. For the ranger waits and wants naught. The desire for knowledge is not included on the hit list, as don Juan considers learning natural to humans, and thus learning fulfills the purpose of life.

As discussed in Chapter 5, expectation acts in a similar manner, as it channels awareness along its own paths. If you expect to find something, you most likely will. While this produces one kind of result, it diminishes another. By having expectations, you reduce the possibility of finding something new, something that fits outside your known world. Expectations often interfere with a natural order. If you want something to occur, you reduce your chances of aligning with a greater, possibly more fulfilling, outcome. Thus you block your natural energy field and thereby block your connection with Spirit. The challenge is balancing the pros and cons of desire and expectation in a manner that effectively produces results.

**Emotions**. Your emotional posture is a major influence regarding how others relate to you and how you experience the world. If you're afraid of doing something, you're likely to avoid it or be timid doing it. On the other hand, your fear may actually set up the precise conditions for which you're fearful. If you're afraid of muggers, more often than not your energy attracts such predators. They're continually on the alert for fear and if they sense it, they track you down.

At the same time, if you don't acknowledge negative feelings, you allow them to fester and thus diminish physical, mental, and emotional health. Worry, for example, warps energy. Enmeshed in the furrows of worry, people constantly struggle with, and tear apart, stabilizing energies such as control, patience, and timing. Thus the people become accessible and lose their balance and their wits.

On the positive side, emotions allow you to track the qualities, sensations, and other energies of your goal. Indeed, by knowing your feelings inside and out, by molding them about your goal, and by refining them so you have no contradictory feelings, you can use your feelings as a bridge to unbending intent (*Silence*, 244).

**Focus**. Like a water-filled balloon placed in the ocean, you are one with, yet separate from, your world. How and where you direct your energies determines where you travel and what you experience. Manifesting, then, is basically a matter of focusing energy. Typically, however, we're unaware of many of the influences affecting our focus. We all have habits and attitudes whose full effects we don't realize or of which we aren't even aware. To remedy this, self-observation is essential. Throughout the day, notice what draws your attention and where you aim your energy. Remembering that how and where you place your energy determines what you experience, ask yourself if what you're doing is what you really want.

Furthermore, having a purpose focuses energy along specific

avenues. The more intense the purpose, the greater the movement of energy. Accordingly, focus on the energy of your purpose from within your body. Sense it, guide it, live it. Hence, the primary focus is on gaining more awareness. When you can perceive the world without the artificial barrier of self-importance, and do so while maintaining the integrity of your personal energies, you've manifested a natural field. The balloon in the water ceases to exist, so to speak, but the energy within the balloon retains its own integrity and so a sense of individuality remains.

**Geographic Location.** A familiar concept today is the existence of vortices, power spots, and other locations where power is thought to be abundant. Don Juan teaches how to find your beneficial area so you can have a place to rest on wilderness outings, a technique which is easily adapted to urban environments.

Don Juan expands this notion of a location influencing the focal point to include entire regions. For example, he considers that the Sonoran desert pulls the focal point downward, to the place of the beast. This region of the energy body is deemed most suitable for shapeshifting into animals as well as for second-cycle practices traditionally associated with sorcery (*Fire*, 146). I wonder, then, if shifting the focal point upward would produce shapeshifting to a type of extraterrestrial who has evolved past the human form. At any rate, please consider that, while shapeshifting may be exhilarating, if it isn't applied to furthering growth it can trap you in nonordinary practices rather than liberate you to Spirit.

From my time living in southern Arizona, I appreciate how that rugged, harsh environment can affect a person's outlook and manner, just as living in the mountains or on a beach adds flavor to perception. The idea is to pay attention to how your environment influences you. You can then flow with that energy to produce different effects throughout your life.

As with shapeshifting, the principal difficulty with some locations is that it's easier to get lost in second-cycle practices than to use those experiences as a reference to build yet other worlds. Don Juan's world, for instance, was fluid and highly malleable. He interacted with the world not as a world of solid objects, but as a world molded by the interaction of energy fields (*Fire*, 49). Since the world is then no longer rigid and solid, this shift in outlook opens the door to manifesting the improbable, if not the impossible.

**Imagination and Visualization.** One of Donner's instructors, Esperanza, says that freedom means you have the ability to manifest the impossible, to produce something which has no reference or foundation in everyday life. To do this, she says, imagination is necessary.[3] Don Juan, in turn, cultivated Castaneda's imagination by advising Castaneda to think of all he could accomplish through dreaming (*Journey,* 127).

In conjunction with imagination, visualization plays an important role. One of the premier exercises for dreaming, for example, is to find your hands in a dream. To set the stage, don Juan says to practice visualizing your hands prior to dozing off. Moreover, the tenant advised Castaneda that whole civilizations disappeared into new dimensions by repeatedly visualizing the same scenery (*Dreaming,* 232). So imagination opens doors, and visualization lets you step through them.

The impact of these tools carries over to enhancing eyesight. Don Juan explains that our eyes have been trained by the first energy field, and therefore perceive only the physical world. To perceive auras, elementals, and other second-field manifestations, the eyes have to be retrained. One way to spur this retraining along is to convince yourself that other worlds exist (*Tales,* 172-173). With a sufficient amount of gazing, dreaming, and *seeing,* convincing yourself is not a problem. Imagination and visualization tap these abilities.

Don Juan also says that the shine in your eyes reflects intent (*Silence,* 146). Whether you're showing affection for a loved one, keeping your eye on the ball during golf, or sizing up a business deal, in each instance your eyes shine in a way that indicates your intent. Furthermore, he says that not only do your eyes reflect your intent, but they summon intent. When your eyes are caused to focus in a different way, they latch onto an intent and thus bring it into play. Practice focusing on different intents and it's not too hard to see this principle at work. Think about and visualize going out to dinner, for instance. Then check your feelings. Or reflect inwardly on visiting a friend. Notice how your attention focuses, and how your eyes feel. Woven throughout of all of these perceptions is intent.

**Interpretations.** How you initially interpret something often influences the final outcome. If you *see* an elemental climbing a tree, and you interpret it as a play of shadows, for instance, you're keeping your perception trained within an ordinary inventory.

If elementals are not in your inventory, it's quite a feat to accurately perceive them. And even if you have an extensive inventory, you still can't account for everything in the universe. Expectations, and thus interpretations, stem from your inventory. This is why Toltecs make detailed inventories, then throw them away. In doing so, they give themselves the freedom to expand the possibilities.

**Kinesthetics.** In many cultures, strong emphasis is given to perceiving in visual ways. You are told to imagine this, visualize that; and meditations are dubbed "guided-imagery" exercises. There's nothing wrong with this approach, providing you bring the rest of your body along for the ride.

Some people's strong suit is their kinesthetic sensing; that is, they rely more on the perceptions found in their muscles, tendons, and joints. Through the degree of tension in their body, kinesthetically-oriented people discover what's going on. For instance, a discomfort in the right side of the body may mean you are unbalanced in your daily life. Using a Toltec schematic, the right side of the body relates to the physical world, and the left side relates to the dream world. By inwardly asking what the discomfort indicates, you sense the answer. The answer may be intuitive, another kinesthetic perception, visual, or a combination of all.

In addition, measuring right and wrong decisions requires staying in touch with the full body. Furthermore, by changing your posture, you can change your mood, and thereby manifest different outcomes. Plus, for the arts of blending and shapeshifting, you change features of the body. Thus you must be fully attentive to what's going on in your body. At the same time, visualization may help you initiate any of these changes. Thus it's not a matter of whether visualization or kinesthetics is better, but rather of developing both.

**Letting Go.** To open up and allow an intent to work its way, you need to let go. Let go of desires, expectations, and inventories. Otherwise you remain confined within a conditional energy field by upholding all of the conditions you think are appropriate, and thereby removing yourself from the flow of Spirit.

To let Spirit flow, don Juan says, you must be unconcerned with the outcome of your endeavors (*Tales,* 283). This attitude doesn't mean to be reckless or mindless. He says it means that after you've made your calculations, and have decided on a course of action, let go and abandon yourself to your path (*Journey,* 150).

The art of letting go weaves its way through all aspects of a ranger's life. Since anxiety often results from shifts in cohesion, you must let go and ride the anxiety out in order to settle down. In other words, surf the wave of anxiety—don't push it away or hold onto it—and feel yourself gaining more awareness about the details surrounding the anxiety. All the while, allow the shift to occur and re-form into another cohesion. As it does, anxiety dissipates.

Esperanza says that women are better dreamers than men simply because they have a better ability to let go.[4] Furthermore, dona Soledad says that one of don Juan's apprentices, Eligio, didn't have to jump off a precipice to conclude his apprenticeship. Like don Genaro, he left this world while standing in a field of dirt. Dona Soledad says he was one of the best because he knew how to let go, and his jump resulted from him entirely letting go of this world (*Second Ring,* 46).

**Thoughts**. "Thoughts are like scouts," says Clara. "They cause the body to move along a certain path."[5] If you think your lot in life is to marry, raise children, and grow old in the comfort of your spouse, then there you go. While this may be part of a path with heart, Toltecs give themselves additional options. Tracking, dreaming, and stepping into other worlds are but a few. By changing their thoughts, they've changed their world.

As a form of energy, thoughts are as real as anything else. Their power enables them to funnel energy along their own corridors. However, while thoughts give direction and form to energy, they are not the main issue. They can deliver you to the threshold of intent, but are not, themselves, intent. Don Juan says it takes years before a person learns "that knowledge and language can exist independent of each other." He adds that a major difficulty in connecting with Spirit stems from refusing to accept that we can know something without words or thoughts (*Silence,* 57).

**Timing**. Proper timing occurs when you're aware of the forces about you and are in tune with them. You allow your world to unfold, while trying not to get in the way. You have the patience to do it right, go for the full manifestation, and not be swayed by your desire to make it happen just so.

When you see a pattern begin to take form—be it in a relationship, at work, or the first quarter of a football game—the natural barrier of clarity exerts a force to close off the pattern, giving a false sense of power that the world can be easily predicted and controlled. If you don't continue nonpatterning, you end the blossoming order too soon, and deprive yourself of the full, natural order. Because the difficulty of remaining nonattached is so great, don Juan relegated timing to the province of a person of knowledge.

The discipline of waiting provides a steppingstone for handling clarity. Having learned how to wait, patience is yours. You let go and allow Spirit to flow. You can afford to do so since you know where you're heading and what you want from life. You're more flexible since you attend to omens and other manifestations of intent. Remaining balanced and impeccable, you foster a natural energy field.

Waiting is also a force, bringing all your manifesting efforts into alignment. As your thoughts, feelings, and exercises tumble into place, you're that much closer to your goal.

*Will.* With patience and *will*, you can build anything, says don Juan (*Separate*, 177). But first you have to activate *will*. Impeccability, according to don Juan, is all you need. To generate this, a Toltec path implements ranger discipline. To become rangers, apprentices focus on their learning tasks. Committed to such tasks, they dip deeper into their core natures, which are governed by intent. As a result, they align themselves more and more with intent. Achieving a sufficient alignment produces a functional *will*.

A personal *will* means you have the capacity to intend. To get there, however, you have to learn how to intend. Again, an apprentice task facilitates this. As part of this discipline, you wait for your *will*. Waiting for your *will* provides the timing, the circumstances, and the knowledge of how to bring *will* to life. Once activated, you embark on a new task. This task, your Toltec task, gives you lessons on how to handle *will*. Trackers *will* new directions in life; dreamers *will* new dreams of life.

You also find that your individuality wanes the more abstract you become. Accordingly, desires lessen the more you spread yourself through the abstract. Grooming a natural field eventually places you completely within the abstract. By then, you no longer reflect because you *are* what you once reflected on. You vanish, yet remain (*Separate*, 186).

* * *

Toltec seers hold that we're all created by Spirit. Therefore, manifesting our core natures is manifesting Spirit's creation—a true act of Power. It then follows that we have everything within us to lead full, complete lives. In this light, our ultimate task is learning how to tap the deepest levels of our being. Doing so simultaneously brings to life our uniqueness, and renders individuality obsolete. This delicate balance results from educating ourselves on the intricacies of intent.

# 15
## Educating for Intent

"Everything I've put you through," don Juan told Castaneda, "each of the things I've shown you was only a device to convince you that there's more to us than meets the eye." He went on, saying that at some point all those who traverse a Toltec path think they are learning Toltec maneuvers or sorcery. In fact, he maintained, they're learning about the hidden power within all humans and that power can be reached (*Silence*, 10-11).

Learning involves a change in behavior. In order to uncover what is natural to the human condition, Toltec methods structure behavior to reach that goal. It's not enough to accumulate new thoughts; you must be able to act, to do. Thus, by participating with its structure, your behavior changes in ways that increase the likelihood that you can attain your goals. As with any educational model, its teachings are biased toward what its proponents regard as important. Accordingly, to promote freedom by better understanding the Toltec manner of education, this chapter provides an overview of Toltec curriculum.

## The System

The Toltec Way is an energy-based system. The universe is comprised of energy and each world in that universe has its own energy fields. Success in utilizing these fields hinges on the amount of energy, or personal power, a person has. For example, don Juan says that his benefactor, Elias, and his teacher, Julian, were both remarkable men, but neither acquired the status of person of knowledge (*Tales*, 239). Elias got trapped in the inorganic world, and Julian, in addition to losing himself in the liberties of the second energy field, had to fend off tuberculosis (*Dreaming*, 105; *Silence*, 112-113). Consequently, both had to expend enormous energy to make any headway whatsoever. Thus they had less energy to explore their totality. Perhaps these limitations caused don Juan to say that while both peeked into the full nature of themselves, the entire mystery had to wait until their deaths to be revealed (*Tales*, 239-240). From one perspective, while both men greatly enlarged their views of the world, they remained in a nonordinary conditional field.

In ancient times, don Juan says, teachers moved their apprentices' focal points through dark practices of spells, rituals, and subjugation. To experience more of their totality, students had to rely on the temperament of the teacher. Don Juan adds that modern-day teachers insist that their students perceive energy on their own. Doing so is then a matter of personal attainment, rather than of receiving a blessing from the teacher (*Dreaming*, 205). As a result, an overriding intent of modern Toltec instruction is ensuring apprentices learn how to clean their links with Spirit by themselves.

## The Teacher

Don Juan says that a teacher's first step is to introduce to the student that the world is only an idea. From there, the apprentice learns that any reality is only the veneer of an energy which no worldview adequately describes. Then, by building the Toltec world the student learns to jump back and forth between ordinary and nonordinary realities. The trick here is to impart enough of the Toltec inventory so that the apprentice may discern that other worlds exist, but not give so much that the apprentice gets lost in another world (*Tales*, 231, 240). Thus building a Toltec world is practice for stepping away from any conditional reality and into a world of pure, abstract perception. At that point, the person has sufficient internal integrity to let all the rules go out the window. As don Juan says, it's then a matter of life to be lived.

While the same lessons are imparted to each apprentice, the order of the lessons vary according to the student (*Tales*, 239). Lessons also vary according to the personality and style of the teacher. Don Juan, for example, does not consider it efficient to wait for his wards to catch on, or to decide on their own if they want to proceed. He prefers to give them a push by placing them in situations where they had to implement the teachings. On the other hand, he says that Julian, while quite stern, never acted directly to turn the course of events. He figured that there was no such thing as a free lunch, so you'd better help yourself. At the same time, don Juan says Julian freely helped everyone help himself (*Gift*, 184-185). In fact, he says that while Julian missed the boat to freedom, he remained impeccable and let don Juan be himself (*Dreaming*, 206).

With the exception of those gifted with impeccability, a teacher is needed to convince the student of personal power (*Silence*, 10-11). The teacher lends energy so the student gets a first-hand taste (*Dreaming*, 25). All the while, the focus is on empowering the student. One of my favorite features of Toltec method is that students are always groomed for freedom. The teacher thoroughly trains students, then leaves them to fend for themselves. Thus the method echoes the teachings. For instance, ingraining personal responsibility is both taught, expected, and required. Hence, the teacher teaches how to learn so students may lay claim to their own knowledge and be permitted to evolve beyond the teachings.

The best teachers tailor their lessons, including how they describe their world, to fit their students' mentalities. Don Juan made his teachings relevant to Castaneda, and Castaneda says he did so with us (*Dreaming*, ix). For example, in the midst of teaching Castaneda how to hunt, don Juan reminded Castaneda that he was constantly subject to forces beyond his control (*Journey*, 115). Don Juan also taught Castaneda bizarre sorcery practices such as sewing the eyes of lizards shut (*Separate*, 124). In both instances, don Juan so intrigued Castaneda that he had no problem keeping Castaneda's attention. When Castaneda did revolt, don Juan performed a minor marvel such as turning immobile for hours on end. Castaneda then had to own up to don Juan's abilities, and decide whether or not to continue (*Journey*, 81-82).

By making their instruction functional, don Juan and Castaneda demonstrated that they are nonattached to their teachings, yet impeccable in doing their utmost to educate. If mistakes are made, such as don Juan's team's inaccurate reading of the number of compartments in Castaneda's energy body, they're chalked up to personal education. To worry about mistakes would make them accessible, and would be contrary to their own teachings. Throughout it all, don Juan adds that teachers must not clamp down too hard. To do so only brings about obsession and morbidity (*Tales*, 22).

As team leaders, both don Juan and Castaneda had an impact on more than the next generation of Toltecs. Don Juan's style of teaching was also reflected in the way he dealt with his team, as evidenced in, for example, his attempt to dissuade team members from entering the inorganic world. And it seems that Castaneda takes a tack of his own. Donner says he offers no directives regarding daily life but guides his team through dreaming.[1] Should

Castaneda ever assume the role of directly passing the teachings to another generation, it should prove an interesting story.

Don Juan says a team leader's presence alone provides sufficient force to shift another's focal point (*Dreaming,* 144). He adds that one of the team leader's roles is to shatter a person's mirror of self-reflection, a natural effect of shifting another's focal point. When this shift occurs, people tend to get fidgety, even hostile, since their known world takes a back seat. Even though it may be inefficient, hostility acts as a means for people to keep track of themselves. Optimally, this type of shield is replaced by power predilections which allow the focal point to shift freely.

## The Apprentice

Teachers don't go looking for students, and people can't automatically sign up for a teacher (*Tales,* 229). In fact, volunteers are shunned. They bring with them their own purposes, says don Juan, so they're unwilling to lose their sense of self. As a result, if the Toltec world places demands on the volunteers which are contrary to their purposes, they refuse to go along (*Silence,* 62). As you might imagine, this refusal might place an entire team in a quagmire of inaction at best or destructive action at worst.

The decision, then, of whether a person enters a Toltec path rests entirely with Spirit. A Toltec capable of teaching acts on omens regarding whether or not a person is enlisted, so to speak. Castaneda's, Donner's, and Abelar's books suggest that a new team is organized in time for the previous generation to exit through the Fire from Within. This process doesn't mean that it's an exclusive club, however. Don Juan says that if a person seriously practices the techniques of erasing personal history, losing self-importance, using death as an advisor, and assuming responsibility, the person eventually gains enough personal power to find a teacher. Finding a teacher, therefore, is not so much a matter of solicitation, as it is an effect of storing energy. That's part of the Rule, says don Juan (*Tales,* 235-238).

In my case, I found that by practicing tracking techniques, I relieved the distress of a bleeding ulcer. By the time I had eliminated medication, I saw the worth of the Toltec world and committed myself to it. Within a year, I was living in Tucson where I met don Juan. Similarly, don Juan remarks that one day he realized his life wasn't worth living, so he changed to earn his self-respect (*Journey,* 80).

The theme of being pushed or pulled into the Toltec world is common. Florinda Grau was at the mercy of a healer until she acquiesced to a Toltec lifestyle. In addition, while healing don Juan of a gunshot wound, Julian pulled don Juan into his world. At the same time, there are those who immediately recognize it as their world once Spirit ushers them to the threshold. One of the Little Sisters, Rosa, for example, entered the Toltec world without coercion (*Second Ring*, 59).

It's difficult to start along the path to the pure abstractions of Spirit by oneself, cautions don Juan. He adds that very few people listen, fewer act, and even fewer yet learn from their actions (*Tales*, 221-227). Thus teachers plow their students' energy fields, offer them direction, and supply context for their pursuits.

When you deal with such immense power, independence is a hard-won skill. At the beginning of an apprenticeship innovation is frowned upon. Until you learn what it is you're innovating, second-guessing just adds confusion and extends the time to learn. Thus don Juan told Castaneda that he must abide by hard-and-fast rules, and Clara told Abelar that the intent of energy passes had already been established. But, as Grau says, down the road innovation is required. Otherwise, you have virtually no chance of becoming a person of knowledge. To stay within a framework keeps you pinned down inside a conditional field. To develop a natural field, you must learn to flow freely and easily with Spirit, action which requires being so highly disciplined that you can step outside of form without losing direction. Garnering this discipline is the advantage found from following a metaphysical path and is what generates the ability to innovate.

## Right- and Left-Side Teachings

For male apprentices, don Juan says that two main teachers are required. Don Juan was Castaneda's teacher and don Genaro was his benefactor. The Genaros—Pablito, Nestor, and Benigno—had don Genaro as their teacher and don Juan as their benefactor (*Tales*, 249). Don Juan says that the teacher imparts the system's structure and grooms the apprentice for impeccability. In doing so, the teacher deals with tracking. The benefactor's role is to acquaint the apprentice with the second field and thus deals with dreaming.

Castaneda says that don Juan emphasized that how an apprentice relates to the Toltec world is governed by the personality of the benefactor. Pablito was motivated by fear stemming from don Juan's authoritarianism, while Castaneda was ruled by affection because don Genaro was sweet and affectionate. The pairing between student and teacher results from the personality of the student. Castaneda, says don Juan, needed a strong teacher and a gentle benefactor, whereas Pablito required the opposite (*Tales*, 264).

Don Juan highlights his teachings by likening perception to a bubble. He says we continually reflect to ourselves about the conditions which exist inside the bubble. The teacher's job is to sweep the inside of the bubble clean, thereby minimizing reflection and generating integrity. The benefactor breaks the bubble from the outside, thereby opening the way to perceiving something beyond the reflections (*Tales*, 248).

This two-pronged emphasis may not necessarily be evident for females. Whereas males must learn to connect themselves with the world, females have pre-established, natural connections. Thus, in keeping with natural variations, the method may vary. What remains constant is the instruction for right- and left-side procedures—for tracking and dreaming, respectively, referring to the right and left sides of the energy body. This instruction may also be considered tutelage for handling the known and the unknown.

Don Juan regards women as natural trackers or dreamers, depending on their predilections. His associate, Florinda Grau, thinks that a man can command both tracking and dreaming, but not excel in either to the level that a woman can attain in her respective art (*Gift*, 290). Again, women therefore form the crucial components for a team. Four women trackers, one from each direction, and four women dreamers, one from each direction, ensure that the team can fully avail itself of tracking and dreaming intents.

By having a full complement of trackers and dreamers, the entire team may also perceive everything within the human domain. As an electron jumps into another orbit about a nucleus due to excessive excitation, when you experience the fullness of being human, the focal point jumps outside of this domain. Thus you have tracking to temper the first field, and dreaming to temper the second field.

Another way of looking at this is that right-side instruction concerns everyday life with the goal of cleaning your link with intent. In some instances, the process is disguised. In Castaneda's case, for example, he was taught under the ruse of hunting and sorcery. Left-side instruction occurs through intent itself, and without the intermediary of the spoken word (*Silence,* 12). In other words, don Juan and don Genaro applied pressure to Castaneda's energy body, thereby entraining it to new cohesions.

His right-side teachings occurred when he was in ordinary awareness, and left-side instruction occurred when he was in heightened awareness. Since Castaneda is a team leader, tracking also took place through his left side. Team leaders must learn tracking principles while their focal points are deep within the left side of their energy bodies and well past their human inventories, says don Juan. Since they're leaders, they must be able to act without first thinking about what to do (*Fire,* 9, 172).

This procedure also applies to individual learning. For instance, long before Castaneda's *The Art of Dreaming* was published, I was practicing the fluid, spontaneous form of the recapitulation. I don't remember discussing this with don Juan or anyone else. And I remembered reading about only the formal method in Castaneda's previous books. I knew I was getting results, but I also felt a twang of guilt in thinking I was too lax. Yet I could never bring myself to use the formal method of making lists. I felt relieved when I read about the fluid style. I realized I had been practicing a standard tracking technique without remembering any instruction concerning it.

Since left-side teachings occur in heightened awareness, the apprentice remembers only a scant portion, if anything at all. But each lesson has been stored in the energy body and is marked by a specific focal point location (*Dreaming,* 145). The objective, therefore, is to elevate perception into a constant state of heightened awareness. During this journey, the forgotten pieces of instruction are reclaimed. Part of the method is that after the training a person is left to figure it all out under the steam of personal power alone. The teachers have exited and so the neophyte Toltec must employ everything to move the focal point back to the numerous locations where each lesson occurred. Castaneda, for example, forgot most of what he experienced in heightened awareness. Through his task, however, he recollected those teachings. I think *The Fire from Within* and *The Power of Silence* most accurately reflect his ability to remember don Juan's left-side instruction.

Moreover, the principal post-apprenticeship task is to re-accumulate all of the teachings and in doing so acquire your totality of being (*Fire,* 129). This process is often referred to as "remembering." Remembering is done through the body, not the intellect.

Consequently, tracking and dreaming enable the focal point to move and stabilize at a number of locations so that remembering may occur.

Shortly after one recapitulation session, I entered dreaming. A few minutes later I remembered a lesson from one of don Juan's team members. She went on and on about the role of women in Toltec circles. I debated some of her points by saying that perhaps much of don Juan's emphasis on women was due to Castaneda's chauvinism, and so don Juan had to over-emphasize the point to get it to register with Castaneda. I added that while I agreed that women had the edge in most Toltec matters, I also knew men who were more than up to the task. Then I told her it was sexist to arbitrarily exclude men from consideration of great accomplishment. She listened to me, then went on about the across-the-board superiority of women. When I got to the point of just listening, she stopped talking.

Then I *saw* the most curious thing. She didn't give a hoot about what she was saying. She only wanted me to free my thoughts and not hold on to any point of view. I then felt extremely close to her, as though we were the closest of friends. From out of the blue I remembered that she, more than any other of don Juan's team, permitted me to feel as though we were equals. I also remembered that she frequently gave long discourses on almost any topic. The constant element was that she never cared whether she was right or wrong. Her philosophical discourses were fertilizer for perception. She pushed an idea to its limit, especially if it went against another's thinking. She cared only about the freedom, not about the content.

## The Split

As part of right- and left-side teachings, splitting a person in two is high on the agenda. Hence, the emphasis is on splitting apart right- and left-side energies. Emilito told Abelar that the split is accomplished so that energy may flow freely between the energy fields. While he downplays the value of ritual and breathing exercises, he adds that the recapitulation and energy passes serve to promote the split.[2]

Don Juan says the split is dangerous because it requires breaking apart the unity of one's world and doing so without harming one's being. In addition, if a person who is newly split cannot maintain energetic integrity, the person is likely to wane away (*Tales,*

191-193). Thus we find another benefit of having a teacher: having someone to guide you through such intricacies.

An effect of the split is that the person is no longer bound by chronology. Thus, don Juan says that a ranger can perceive two places simultaneously (*Tales*, 53). Put another way, the ranger perceives through reason and silent knowledge at the same time (*Silence*, 259). It's like you can be here, now, and simultaneously be there, now. This split perception enables you to gain more awareness. By assessing an environment through two different avenues of awareness, you come up with more data and glean more knowledge.

There are also other forces which generate a split. Tracking and dreaming, for instance, reflect different energies. For tracking, the controlled-folly skill of pretending to be fully involved in your activities, or being in the world but not of it, reflects a split awareness. In dreaming, having your awareness split allows a full acceptance of the double. After his split, don Juan could remain in his ordinary self or in his double for days on end. He also had the option of being in both, but found this state caused his perception to be too vague to have practical merit (*Silence*, 265).

Other procedures reflect a two-sided split as well. Gazing properties within nature, for example, are divided into two sets. For water you have the first- and second-field properties of wetness and fluidity, respectively (see "Gazing" in Chapter 10). This split also highlights the second energy field within nature, making you more sensitive to its existence. In addition, self-observation produces a split awareness between observing oneself and what is taking place. Moreover, at a certain point don Juan presented Castaneda with two choices: either follow the ordinary world of reason where other worlds do not exist, or follow the Toltec world where other worlds abound (*Dreaming*, 74). Don Juan thereby emphasized the split between reason and *will*.

As a friend once said, "There are two kinds of people: those who separate everything into two, and those who don't." The point is to remember that this is method, not a bunch of hard-and-fast rules. While it's a practical method that generates results, it is method and style nonetheless.

## Learning for Mastery

The principal goal of the Toltec method is to produce fundamental changes in the way a person perceives the world. In doing so, don Juan says it's a matter of what's emphasized more than actually changing. In other words, you may stabilize a new cohesion, but the old cohesion remains at rest within your energy body. By emphasizing a new cohesion, you no longer focus on the old one (*Tales*, 236). For example, he tells Castaneda to focus on the "wonders of *seeing*" rather than on his fears (*Separate*, 39).

One indication of the utility of this method is that its results are constant. Accordingly, don Juan says that while the steps may vary, the results of aligning energy with new worlds are always the same. That is, the person perceives new worlds (*Fire*, 213).

In one sense, Toltec training is a way to remember your complete self. While teaching Castaneda how to communicate with plants, don Juan says, "How can the little plant tell me now what I've known all my life" (*Journey*, 44). And when discussing communication with inorganic beings, don Juan says, "What the emissary did was merely repeat what you already knew." Furthermore, when talking about his effect on Castaneda, the tenant says, "You already know what I know. All you needed was another jolt in order to claim what you already know" (*Dreaming*, 65, 227). Hence, Toltec method is intended to deliver you to yourself.

Along the way, a person learns for mastery. Don Juan decided to teach Castaneda an example of second-cycle practices by having him pull an inorganic being out of a mirror. While doing so, he says, "Someday you yourself will also know how the technique works; you will understand what's behind all this." And, when discussing Toltec travels, don Juan declares, "When you solve this riddle, you'll be ready for the definitive journey." Moreover, don Juan tells Castaneda that all team leaders must reorganize the teachings, figure out everything that has happened, and do so on their own (*Fire*, 94, 105, 213). In each example, the responsibility for learning rests with the student.

## Terminology

In addition, there are other features which regularly surface. The use of terminology is one of them. For example, Castaneda in one case equated "sorcerers" with "warriors," whereas in other cases the terms indicated different levels of awareness. While remembering his left-side teachings, for another example, Castaneda realized he wasn't being taught sorcery; he was learning about awareness, tracking, and intent. And he wasn't dealing with sorcerers, he was dealing with seers (*Silence,* 12, 10).

While inconsistencies such as these may pose a problem in certain instances—such as in academia—the impact terms have diminishes the more you learn to handle silent knowledge. In this light, the instability of terminology often yields positive effects. Indeed, shifting terms helps pave the way to silent knowledge.

For instance, with right-side teachings, the four barriers to perception are outlined in a normal, easy-to-relate-to manner. You have fear, clarity, power, and old age. With the left-side instruction, the meanings change and relate to handling intent. Rather than fear as ordinarily considered, fear means that the energy body is encrusted, stagnant. So you experience a lack of momentum. This inability to connect with intent and thereby move perception translates to ordinary awareness as fear. In turn, clarity results from cleaning intent, power from manipulating it, and old age from learning to move with the more refined and delicate designs of Spirit (*Silence,* 247).

Another example concerns the first, second, and third fields. In Chapter 6, I mentioned how shifting the definition of the first field from indicating physical energy to the known world opens the door to the Fire from Within. Here, let's look at how the change further impacts learning.

While each energy field is independent and infinite, from another perspective each is intertwined with the others and all unite as one force. So whether you define something as physical or nonphysical results from perspective rather than from actuality. The implications don't stop there. Since all energy fields are as one, the division among them reflects a method to bring about the awareness of different types of energy. Now then, since the unknowable is within the known, everything in your known world is, therefore, inherently unknowable. Accordingly, you never really know anything. You know only the reflections of your known world.

The beauty of this is at least three-fold. First, since you know your world results from self-reflection, you bring more energy to bear on losing self-importance. Second, it makes it easier to laugh at your inventories and dismiss them. Third, by knowing that you really don't know, you keep your awareness open. In all instances, you have successfully interdicted a natural force of human perception that tries to bring awareness to a state of closure. As a result, you're always in an attentive learning posture, and always in a wide-open world.

# Tasks

Until a student can clean the link with intent, the team leader supplies purpose and thus supplies unbending intent. Don Juan says this is often the most difficult part of an apprenticeship because the student must relinquish personal identity to the teacher (*Silence,* 62). I know that by myself I would never have initiated the tasks don Juan gave me. It seemed that they ranged from the too farfetched to the "That's really not me." Over the years, however, in each instance they've proven to be enlivening, challenging, inspiring, and packed with dividends of new knowledge. Furthermore, each task has ushered me a little further along the path. Don Juan's ability to match tasks with the undiscovered predilections of his students and with the world at large is one of his more remarkable accomplishments.

Each task is more difficult than the last, but all focus energy toward intent. During his orientation stage, for example, Castaneda had to find his beneficial spot in front of don Juan's house before don Juan launched into the apprenticeship. Don Juan regarded Castaneda's success as an omen that also indicated what manner of instruction Castaneda required (*Tales,* 238). Writing books about don Juan's tutelage was another of Castaneda's tasks (*Silence,* 14). And the task of remembering is a universal task requiring a lifetime of effort (*Dreaming,* 17).

Don Genaro told Castaneda and the Genaros that if they returned after jumping off a cliff, each person should focus all of his energies toward completing his task. Upon completion, each would receive the "promise of power," which would be a unique gift (*Tales,* 279).

Castaneda says that after he jumped he experienced seventeen elastic bounces between the first and second fields. Completely attuned to the first field, he had "visions of order." Focused within the second field, he says he "perceived [his] body disintegrating," and although he was aware, his thoughts and feelings weren't coherent or unified as they usually were (*Second Ring,* 7). He says he later woke up in his Los Angeles office. Referring to his split perception, he adds, "Whatever woke up in that office, could not be the 'me' that I knew linearly." He considers that his ability to achieve that break in continuity is an indication of why he's a team leader.[3]

Don Juan says that team leaders carry the additional task of lighting up their entire energy bodies. Once they do so, he says, the rest of the team entrains to the Fire from Within, and will "all be gone in an instant" (*Fire,* 185). And true enough, at the end of *The Eagle's Gift,* Castaneda dramatically depicts don Juan's team turning into pure energy and leaving this dimension. In *The Art of Dreaming,* however, don Juan says that while most of his team would leave with him, Florinda Grau would stay behind in order to direct Castaneda and the rest of don Juan's apprentices (*Dreaming,* 60). So again we find that the first rule is that there are no rules. And most of what don Juan says is intended to impact the moment, not to deliver carved-in-granite dogma.

Regardless of a person's stage of awareness, all tasks in some way stimulate and balance the first and second fields. The first field is bolstered through reason, and the second field through action until one supports the other. At that point, their harmony shifts perception into heightened awareness and a new task blends them further. The person of knowledge, says don Juan, has joined the two sides of tracking and dreaming, of the first and second fields, of reason and silent knowledge (*Tales,* 160-161, 88). I have concluded that this capacity is not only what enabled don Juan to execute the Fire from Within, but is also what enabled him to return in order to teach others.

## Trickery

Don Juan says that, due to the reluctance of humans to learn, Spirit established trickery as an essential part of a Toltec path (*Silence,* 26). While many are drawn to spiritual vocations, it seems that few keep their energy peaked to continually break new ground. Quite often we find comfort in our new knowledge and refuse to give it up in order to pursue the more radical stages of mastery.

In mild practice, trickery means that teachers often de-emphasize main issues to avoid obsessions. For example, don Juan says he restored Castaneda's warrior spirit through the trickery of teaching him how to hunt (*Journey,* 257). From time to time, he also surreptitiously hung a piece of cloth over a bush, and had Castaneda gaze at it as a means to shift Castaneda into another frame of reference (*Second Ring,* 293). One time, Castaneda perceived the cloth as having a life of its own. To the dismay of don Juan, however, he then recognized what it was and restored his ordinary reality instead of following the initial shift into another world. Furthermore, don Juan had Castaneda yelling in his dreams not because that was a required technique to enter dreaming, but because don Juan used Castaneda to have a little fun with the tenant (*Dreaming,* 234-235).

Not all tricks are so subtle. For example, a common feature of an apprenticeship is that sooner or later the person withdraws. Don Juan regards this withdrawal as a natural, even level-headed, reaction. Castaneda backed out thinking he had succumbed to fear (*Teachings,* 214). He later realized that the strenuous nature of the path posed a serious threat to his "idea of the world" (*Separate,* 16). To offset this energy impasse, don Juan tricked Castaneda into a duel with a "worthy opponent," a variation of the petty tyrant (*Tales,* 241).

Castaneda's first worthy opponent was la Catalina. Don Juan coaxed Castaneda into believing she was out to do him in. Although her onslaughts were real enough, she was an associate of don Juan. He employed the maneuver to ensure Castaneda remained on his Toltec path. Since Castaneda had to summon his resources to handle la Catalina's intense energy, the ploy worked. Don Juan says he used her as a worthy opponent because Castaneda trusted women, and that trust had to be disarranged so Castaneda could avail himself of worlds beyond his established habits (*Tales,* 241-242).

Later, the Little Sisters carried the worthy opponent banner and boosted Castaneda along the path. Apparently Castaneda tended to have women as worthy opponents also because he ignored them. For instance, he was oblivious to the Little Sisters as don Juan's apprentices all the while he was an apprentice. Walking into a den of well-trained females must have given Castaneda the jolt of a lifetime—a real attention-getter—which is straight to the point of why trickery is used.

Trickery is not unique to Toltecs. In *Teachings from the American Earth,* Barbara Tedlock writes about "sacred clowns." Sacred clowns, or contraries, act contrary to prevailing cultural values. They may run naked through camp, or laugh in the middle of a sacred ritual. They are tolerated, and even encouraged, since they help keep perception open and thus reduce groupthink.[4]

Toltec trickery is used only when necessary. Castaneda offers several examples of where it was not required. Elias didn't use it with don Juan. Julian's counterpart, Talia, strode freely into the Toltec world. And the Little Sister, Rosa, didn't need to be tricked (*Fire,* 151; *Silence,* 43; *Second Ring,* 58).

The overall effect of this strategy, says don Juan, is that the student learns to act solely for the heck of it, to act without expectation of any reward whatsoever (*Tales,* 233). This approach sets the stage for having a "romance with knowledge."

## Power Plants

Rather than for mind-tripping, for recreation, or for escape, power plants are used for education and to rectify imbalances of the mind. As such, they aided me in glimpsing heightened awareness. Had it not been for don Juan's instruction, however, I might never have learned how to reach that awareness without using them. While I now consider them very valuable for catapulting awareness outside of ordinary reality, I also recognize their inherent limitations. Primarily, as don Juan says, their drawback is that they cause "untold damage to the body" (*Tales,* 238).

Don Juan administered at least three types to Castaneda: mushrooms, peyote, and datura. Each carries a different form of power; therefore, each embodies a different intent. The mushroom, or "little smoke," says don Juan, is peerless. It is used to *see.* However, he says it also blinds you with fear as it forces perception beyond all boundaries (*Teachings,* 78, 183).

Peyote, or "mescalito," is a protector and teacher. Its energy provides lessons, especially lessons about what it means to be human (*Teachings,* 102, 174). It was after don Juan started using peyote that he reduced his power practices. Don Juan's grandson, Lucio, says that don Juan was once a great Toltec, perhaps the best around, until he "took to peyote and became a nobody" (*Separate,* 88). Perhaps it was the influence of peyote which pushed don Juan down the road of losing self-importance.

Don Juan relegated datura, or the "devil's weed," to second-cycle power practices. Indeed, he says under its influence he easily tossed boulders and jumped higher than trees. However, he thinks datura more than the other plants weakens the mind and body; it distorts people and does not fortify their hearts. It also blinds a person with ambition. And it makes people think that its avenue to knowledge is the only way. At the same time, he considers following this path a supreme challenge for a person of knowledge (*Teachings,* 75, 62, 183, 182, 63).

The effect of power plants on behavior cannot be overemphasized. I knew a couple who were quite serious in their Toltec studies. I'll call them Alice and David. Both favored extensive use of marijuana, and they had a datura plant growing in their back yard which they said they did not consume.

On one occasion, David and I strongly disagreed about the use of power plants. At one point during the conversation he jumped up and shouted, "Alice and I agree on this and so we're more powerful than you!" On another occasion, I proposed an experiment to *see* the effects of marijuana on the energy body. After initially agreeing to it, Alice later backed out. She told me that she and David had agreed that it was my self-importance that set up the experiment in the first place. After assessing the self-importance that I did bring into the situation, I still found that they responded in terms of personal power plays. And thinking in such a manner is, according to don Juan, a side effect of datura.

In addition, months later during a dinner conversation with David, I associated datura with the second cycle. He responded that he didn't have one second-cycle bone in his body. From my reckoning, I regarded this as him being blinded to his behavior, an effect don Juan also attributes to datura. I also found this to be an especially curious statement since he regarded himself a staunch Toltec, and as such he'd be subject to the influences of the entire lineage, including the second cycle. When I then mentioned the datura in his yard, David replied with a snide affectation that he and Alice grew it "for its beauty." I took this as him defending the plant, just as Castaneda had done (*Teachings,* 74).

The binding point is that I *saw* energy tentacles from their datura plant permeating their apartment. The whole place was jam-packed with datura energy. I *saw* it as thick, root-like filaments. It was as though the inside of their apartment was a healthy potted plant with so many roots that it was ready for a larger pot. Without them recognizing it, and without them actually ingesting datura, they were consumed by it. To me this was a vivid example of how environment shapes behavior and why modern Toltecs de-emphasize the use of power plants.

## Trajectory

Don Juan says that learning to use awareness as an aspect of the environment is at the core of Toltec teachings. Since awareness is everywhere, it can be used as a medium for perception to travel. He says there are three steps in doing so (*Dreaming,* 185-186). First, a person learns to free existing energy. This step is accomplished through impeccability, and impeccability is learned by following the path. Second, the newly acquired energy is used to develop dreaming and therefore to develop the energy body. Third, this knowledge is used to place the entire physical mass into the energy body, thereby completely entering other worlds. These steps reflect tightening your life, letting go of your known world and exploring the unknown, and then fully integrating your findings.

Thus the trajectory reflects learning tracking, dreaming, and intent. Optimally, each stage guides awareness toward Spirit. The more you're connected with Spirit, the more you're connected with your inner mysteries and power.

* * *

While the emphasis is on tilling your innate abilities, what might actually happen is anybody's guess. Don Juan learned to burn with the Fire from Within and then return. One of his apprentices, however, Eligio, left with don Juan's team, perhaps never to return (*Second Ring,* 210-212). With the stakes so high, it's not surprising that people back out once they've traveled a distance. For others, it all seems like a real-life fantasy, and they hop aboard too easily. But the realities of bringing about such a fundamental and radical change are not that easily considered. So it's no wonder volunteers show up looking for a quick ticket to enlightenment.

While I don't think following a Toltec path is for everyone, I do think that the Toltec method has some measure of value for everyone. It can crystalize your predilections, further illuminate your path, and help you generate an intimate relationship with life. Toltec structures are solid, and yet they yield. They are consistent, and yet they continually change. And whether this path is experienced as a gentle stream or a raging river, its flow delivers you to the mysteries and adventures of human awareness.

# 16
# Hot on the Trail

Since don Juan's teachings focus on how to become a person of knowledge, this chapter emphasizes developing a natural energy field. Development of a natural field is an optimum condition of human awareness. A principal effect of having a natural field is that you experience the state of *being*. And getting there requires stepping aside from ordinary and nonordinary conditional fields. When you have a stabilized natural field, you will have succeeded in becoming a person of knowledge.

I believe this correlation is the reason don Juan considers the modern ranger to be a ranger of the third energy field (*Gift*, 23). Orienting yourself to the third field enables you to jump the hurdles of any conditional field. You're then more concerned with pursuing abstract freedom than with accumulating powers. And your interests rest more with unfolding perception than with cultivating a worldview. As a result, you actively seek to align your energies with Spirit. Doing so is what subordinates your *will* to the creative force's *will*, yet simultaneously bestows your complete individuality. You live with and within your personal intent, your personal connection with creation.

## Being

While the word *being* may seem like only a form of the passive verb "to be," its practice is quite dynamic. Having arrived at *being*, your life manifests moment to moment. Nothing is taken for granted. Everything is experienced through and through. Your journey is what's at hand. And what's at hand is your life. You also recognize each form of consciousness as a work of art. To do otherwise deprives humans and other forms of consciousness the value of their existence.

While *being*, you're in a quiet flow of awareness. Instead of forcing your way through life, your efforts center on maintaining a constant, natural field. The rest unfolds naturally and according to your natural self.

You're also aware of your immersion within infinite creation. All you need to do to begin waking up to this fact is stand in place and turn around in a complete circle. A circle is an infinite number of points which are connected. As you turn, realize that you have an infinite number of options at each and every moment. Governed by a worldview, we automatically and drastically reduce the number of these options. The result is that we feel as though we've exhausted our lives. While *being*, you're aware that there is nothing to exhaust. As a result, you have one power-filled moment after another.

The following elements are often associated with *being*. You may experience:

- immediate attention to the here and now;
- a sense of newness in all your activities, no matter how repetitive;
- peacefulness;
- your perception accenting the environment more, and focusing on yourself less;
- a sense of rightness or perfection about everything;
- little or no thought;
- touching, or at least getting closer to, your core nature;
- a strong, clear connection with the world;
- reality as only a reflection of yourself;
- an innate sense of purpose;
- complete abandon or surrender;
- nonattachment;
- balanced energies;
- unconditional love;
- joy and/or bliss;
- patience;
- the sense of residing in a timeless present that stretches throughout eternity.

Furthermore, as your life unfolds, you become more aware of multiple levels of perception working simultaneously. In one respect, therefore, the more you learn, the more you can apply your knowledge. The more adept at application you are, the more you can innovate and produce original applications. The more you innovate, the more you can *be*. *Being*, itself, simultaneously incorporates learning, application, and innovation.

## Developing the Art of *Being*

*Being* is tracking the flow of Spirit proficiently. One common difficulty in doing so is that as soon as people recognize this flow, they begin to think about it. How did it happen? What did they do to get there? After all, constant reflection is an ingrained habit. But excessive reflection is what removes awareness of the flow in the first place. The work, then, is to remain with the flow. Doing so activates *will*. Accordingly, how to remain with the flow is where tracking enters.

For instance, while *being* you're continuously nonpatterning. By not creating patterns, you don't trip over yourself; you therefore more easily maintain a natural field, which acts as a conduit for Spirit. Nonpatterning is also a natural effect of aligning with Spirit. That is, as you abandon yourself to Spirit you nonpattern naturally since your behavior is governed by Spirit. To follow Spirit, you must set all preconceptions, all patterns, aside.

Indeed, by tracking Spirit you automatically perform almost all of the basic tracking exercises. You disrupt routines since Spirit is fluid. You lose self-importance since you no longer reflect on the world. And you erase personal history because you're part of everything, an abstract energy that has retained awareness of itself without retaining a specific identity. Seers, therefore, use tracking exercises to awaken to the possibilities and to generate the initial connection with Spirit. Hence, the exercises stimulate an awareness which already exists. Once there, you're in a different ball game and so you no longer need the system. You need only your impeccability.

Don Juan gives other perspectives to track Spirit. For example, he advises not to expect anything. This allows everything in your life to fall gracefully into place (*Tales*, 155). Letting go of desires and expectations eliminates the binding effects of a worldview since you're not forcing your world to unfold in accordance with that view. Remaining open, you stand to become aware of other energies. Thus you are placed hot on the trail of uncovering your personal intent.

Furthermore, a person of knowledge doesn't think, says don Juan (*Separate*, 114). He isn't suggesting that such a person is a dolt; rather, don Juan proposes an alternate way of thinking. The idea, he says, is to think clearly by not thinking (*Silence*, 143). In this way you become aware of a more expansive order, and thereby have more options available than through tapping reason alone. You flow with a natural order rather than with a human-made order.

For females, the quest to *be* involves merging their natural cycles with the rhythms of heaven and earth, allowing a supernatural alignment to unfold. As a result, females become everything by becoming nothing, the same prescription don Juan gives for *seeing*. Males need to go with their strong point, gut-level feelings. They then expand the process to use the entire body. And to do so, they're wise to take lessons from Toltec females on tuning awareness to a natural order.

As you track Spirit, there are times when all of your new perceptions build up too much. You feel pressure since they have not settled down to a workable order. To settle them, don Juan says that you need to track yourself in a ruthless and cunning manner. As one method, he advises using death as an advisor, as a way of giving yourself jolts to shake up your energy. By using the leverage of your death, you quit indulging and regain focus. You again size up your life, easing strain and allowing you to regain composure. He also says you can give yourself a jolt from beauty, such as from the impact of a poem (*Silence*, 128-129, 131). And let's not forget the sure avenue of learning to handle your energies: the petty tyrant. A petty tyrant helps you track the abstract by having you work extra hard entraining to the flow of Spirit rather than entraining to external forces. In other words, a petty tyrant helps you sidestep the conditional energies humans most often exhibit, and plug into the creative force.

## *Being* and *Becoming*

*Being* is meditating twenty-four hours a day, seven days a week. Behavior as it is normally defined no longer exists. Your first and second fields run smoothly and in harmony with each other. Accordingly, *being* is an optimal state. Plus, you're not just passively hanging around, letting things happen to you; you have momentum. And this momentum is a key ingredient of *being*; it is the process of *becoming*. That is, while *being* you're continuously *becoming* your core nature.

A key to *becoming* is using your impulse power. Just as a spacecraft relies on impulse power to fine-tune its flight attitude and trajectory, you must rely on highly sensitive, intuitive adjustments to adequately keep your energy aligned with Spirit. To accurately do so, you must pay attention to what your body tells you. Tracking and dreaming got you out of your thoughts and into your body. Now those skills must be further tuned and aimed to produce even more intensity, or depth of awareness. So you use your complete body to focus energy, and leave the thinking about it behind. As a result, you perceive exclusively through *will*.

*Being* incorporates all that exists, as it exists. It taps the fullness of the world that's already created. *Becoming* is traveling through the conditions of going to knowledge, through predilections and a path with heart, and through the Mastery of Awareness stages. Handling this combination is the quintessential skill of energy management. Applying the elements of Toltec strategy, we find that with control, you're able to feel a continuous flow of energy. With discipline, you make the necessary adjustments to maintain the flow. With patience, you don't get carried away by it. With a petty tyrant, you stretch further into it and regain it when you lose it. With timing, you astutely follow it. With *will*, you marvel at it.

*Being* and *becoming* result from unparalleled tracking of self. As a form of discipline, tracking has given you the tools for successful energy management. Dreaming, in turn, has supplied the stretching, the raw energy, the necessary forays into awareness that make transformative leaps in consciousness possible. *Being* occurs when tracking and dreaming energies merge and create a transcendent heightened awareness. In other words, your first and second fields have now been refined and work together as one. Then, through *becoming,* you face constant renewal. You possess a magical consistency in the face of an ever-changing world. *Becoming* is a force, like sap rising through a tree. Matching this force with the force of time produces *being*.

## Time and Timing

As you proceed through the Mastery of Awareness stages, you experience time in different ways. As a matter of basic discipline, you relate more and more to the day at hand, then condense time further to the hour, then to the moment. In addition to this evolution, you also witness time from a direction 180 degrees different. Typically, we watch it recede. Put another way, we perceive its effects after it passes. Then we put the pieces together. That is, we make sense out of our world by studying the after-effects of our behavior, and then by outlining a worldview based on how we understand those effects.

There is another way to experience time: face it, or approach it. When you approach time, you are in the midst of time as it unfolds. It's almost as though you watch it stream toward you. You remove yourself from mental, conceptual relations of time and immerse yourself within it. This maneuver is a way to center yourself in the here and now. Each moment feels new and contains life untainted by expectations of how it should unfold. You're no longer building a world based on prior effects, but on creative potential.

Florinda Grau says that only trackers perform this shift (*Gift*, 296). She says this is due to the way trackers and dreamers use the world around them. Trackers hone in on goals. They finely tune their energy in order to produce a precise alignment with the energy of their objective. Dreamers, in turn, produce dreams which incorporate the goal. As don Juan says, dreamers mold the world around them to fit their needs precisely (*Dreaming*, 33). I've observed that either approach leads to *being*.

Approaching time is an ingredient of *becoming* in the way *becoming* is an ingredient of *being*. As such, *being* is perceiving an unfolding universe and realizing your connection with it. You are attentive to the moment of creation, and your discipline guides you toward realizing the greatest potential of that moment. This realization permits you to enter worlds which are beyond reason. It also radically alters the way you behave. For instance, Castaneda says that don Juan was a team leader who did everything of importance on the spur of the moment (*Dreaming*, 221). The times I was with him taught me that he did everything on the spur of the moment. He was effective at doing so because he was proficient at tracking Spirit. He had learned to *be*.

Over the years, I've spontaneously entered *being*-like states a number of times, often for days at a time. One time, I felt obliged to take notes. I wrote that my life was on autopilot. The procedures I normally attended to such as assessing situations and making decisions occurred on their own. My normal thought processes had ceased, and I didn't try to figure out anything. At the same time, I possessed an inner knowing, an intuitive sense that guided me in any situation and transcended the need for deliberation. My attention rested in the present and all my actions stemmed from that awareness. I observed the energy of time flowing to me, rather than watching it after it passed by. I simply recognized all these processes, let any attachment to them go, and then became aware of the results, to which I at once surrendered. I tried to remain attentive and aware, and then my thoughts and actions occurred as though I were an actor playing a part. The difference between these experiences and complete *being* is that I was only glimpsing what someday might become fully realized.

Approaching time requires adept timing. And timing, remember, is in the province of a person of knowledge. But since all stages are within us, we can begin right now orienting ourselves in that direction. In between laziness and hurry, for example, is timing. If you're neither lazy nor in a hurry, you stand a better chance of feeling your balance with the world. Therefore, you're more likely to tap timing. Since each of us has our own rhythms, each has an innate sense of timing. If we are too accessible to the demands of society and follow its time schedule, we lose sense of ourselves. Concurrently, if we don't recognize our place in relation to society, we also lose our timing since we haven't stimulated ourselves sufficiently. In other words, by not tackling the forces of society we forgo the strenuous discipline required to step beyond our ordinary selves. And we need to do this in order to tackle the unknown. Thus timing also rests between the first and second energy fields. Harmonizing the two fields produces timing, just as harmonizing the pistons in an automobile's engine produces good timing.

An additional skill for refining timing is relaxation. Relaxation is necessary in order to track yourself rather than continually tell yourself who you are. You need to feel your body, its needs, and its directions. Tracking yourself is living who you are without knowing who you are. For this, you feel your way to your core. Once there, you're in the midst of all time, right now. If you're too tense, there's no way you can make such a sophisticated discernment.

Furthermore, seers typically regard time as paradoxical. For instance, the Eagle's emanations are considered constant. They are eternal and unchanging. Yet they are always in a state of flux. Nothing is preordained, yet everything is always occurring. It follows that how you match your energy with the emanations determines the nature of your timing.

## The Human Form and Formlessness

The human form is a tension, an aspect of cohesion that channels perception along highly specific avenues. It is a primary feature of projection; thus, don Juan says that as long as you have the human form, whatever you perceive automatically reflects that form. The form, then, is a force that governs how and what you perceive. Inorganic beings, for instance, often appear to have human shapes until the human form dissipates. La Gorda says she *saw* inorganic beings as monsters until she lost her form, after which she felt them only as a helping presence (*Second Ring*, 153, 152). In addition, upon losing the form these beings are often experienced as abstractions of light. Indeed, don Juan says the essential nature of inorganic beings is that they're formless energy fields (*Silence*, 75).

There is no doubt that form carries power. Medicine, for example, has evolved into a very complex form. And it delivers results. In a like manner, the form of physics has enabled humans to walk on the moon. Even considering these powerful results, Toltecs consider losing the human form essential for growth. For one thing, don Juan says it's the only way to unify the first and second fields. And unifying the two fields is the avenue to *being*. Nonattached, being-in-the-world-but-not-of-it behavior, for instance, results from losing the form (*Second Ring*, 284, 55).

The pure abstract contains all possibilities and thus contains all form, and yet it's not restricted by form. Since the human form continuously filters out much of these possibilities, it relegates perception to its own order. Thus we continually perceive in human terms, based on human qualities. We even reduce God to a human image. In short, the form maintains a highly conditional energy field. Once this mirror is lost, however, you're free to behave in nonordinary ways since ordinary behavior doesn't necessarily relate to anything meaningful in your life. Therefore, you're that much freer to pursue nonordinary possibilities. Don Juan says, for example, that you can try your hand at lightning-bolt gazing and not worry about getting hit if you lose your form. On a more expansive scale, you've taken a firm step toward losing your idea of the self, a necessary condition of losing self-importance. Thus, as la Gorda says, real change is impossible until the form dissipates (*Second Ring*, 289, 157).

As with all growth along a Toltec path, losing the form hinges on impeccability. Impeccability relinquishes the foothold of the human form (*Second Ring*, 274). Thus tracking paves the way. Don't force an issue is one bit of advice la Gorda gives. And don't cling to anything is another (*Gift*, 34, 40). Moreover, the Little Sisters and the Genaros were all given specific learning tasks to help them eliminate their respective forms (*Second Ring*, 256).

While it is a part of the curriculum, losing the form isn't a ticket to paradise. La Gorda had to struggle with emotional upheavals (*Gift*, 129). Also, in the process of losing her form, she felt as though she suffered a heart attack and was weak for days afterward (*Second Ring*, 256). Losing the form may also open you up to stray influences, even if they're benign. You might entrain to another's energy, for example, and follow that person's wishes too easily. The remedy is to continue being impeccable. And there are no shortcuts. You must open up in order to find out who you are. Sooner or later you settle down to a new order, a new way of dealing with the world. And those lessons must be learned through on-the-job training.

Part of the difficulty with losing the form is that formlessness means the focal point moves more easily than before. Fluid focal point shifts mean you can no longer base your life on a predictable future because you have no concrete reference for what the future can or will be. On the one hand, this helps you to be here, now. On the other hand, it may reduce focus. To deal with this state, sticking with a task keeps you on track.

Part of the blessing of formlessness is that an easily movable focal point means you can *see* better. That is, you can align with other energies with less difficulty. In this light, losing your form gives you practice to handle radical shifts, such as occurs when you lose all sense of meaning. As don Juan says, *seeing* detaches you from "absolutely everything" you knew before (*Separate*, 186).

## The Human Mold

Everything has a specific mold, says la Gorda, relaying to Castaneda a lesson from don Juan (*Second Ring*, 153). The human mold is like a template that binds emanations into a specific pattern: the pattern known as "human" (*Fire*, 261). To further illustrate, the human form may be likened to cohesion, to a pattern of energy. The human mold, then, may be likened to uniformity, to the overall container. For example, humans around the globe share a uniformity. Regardless of location, it's a simple matter to identify humans. They have a standard shape or mold. Due to race, culture, and other factors, their cohesions vary. They exhibit variations within their general shape. But these variations are consistent with humanness; hence, the human form.

A step in gaining formlessness, and breaking the confines of ordinary human perception, is *seeing* the mold. Doing so breaks the fixation of the focal point. Don Juan says the mold may be *seen* two ways: as a human, or as light. *Seeing* it as light reflects a deeper shift, a shift toward your core (*Fire,* 256, 266).

Don Juan also says that, historically, chance *seeings* of the mold have been interpreted as meeting God. When Castaneda *saw* the mold, for example, he experienced a field of radiant light filled with beatific abundance. He says he knew beyond doubt he had met God, and that God loved him. *Seeing* further into the light, he met a shiny man who exuded love, understanding, and truth. It was after he fell on his knees to worship the man that don Juan ended the visit, then poked fun at Castaneda, saying he could now pass as a spiritual leader who had *seen* God. Accounting for projection, don Juan also told Castaneda that if he were a woman he would most likely have *seen* the mold as a woman (*Fire,* 259-265).

Thus projection is perceiving more from superficial levels of your energy body than from your core. The reactiveness often associated with projection doesn't occur when you're centered since you have a solid foundation; hence, nonattachment occurs on its own. Furthermore, a natural field harmoniously resonates with core energies. While a person of knowledge has bridged the core, a seer resides in it.

To don Juan's reckoning, we interpret our experiences with the mold of man as meeting God because the mold holds all that is human. In meeting the completeness of ourselves, we expand the experience tremendously and call it God. Don Juan thinks experiences reported by mystics throughout history are distorted. They are flawed by the error of thinking they have met an omniscient creator. Seers, in turn, *see* the mold whenever they wish. Therefore, they have gone beyond the initial infusion of power the meeting generates, have lessened the resulting distortions, and have more fully examined the experience. In a like manner, Castaneda reports that the more he *saw* the mold, the less affected he was by it. As a result of repeated visits, seers have discovered that the mold is a group of emanations within the energy body. Thus it is the portion of the Eagle's emanations which may be *seen* without concern, and without the intense preparation needed to *see* beyond human emanations, such as gazing at the Eagle (*Fire,* 264, 257).

Perhaps "God" and "Eagle" are different words for the same singular source of creation. If so then, like the Eagle and its emanations, God is everywhere and nowhere, and certainly can't be confined solely to the nuances of human perception.

## Metaphysical Fundamentalism

Reality is a conglomerate of thoughts forming a complete, recognizable world. One theme of this book is that this principle not only has utilitarian value, but also hems in perception. At least until you become a person of knowledge, you need a worldview to have a world. Quite frequently, however, a reality blocks further growth by defining Spirit and thus limiting the options.

Like any metaphysical system, the Toltec Way harbors such limitations. Following a Toltec path is like being a wizard straight out of a fantasy novel. While it's a real world, complete with fairies, shapeshifting, and dreaming flight, it may hold perception too rigidly in place. This is the trap of it. And this is why don Juan fed Castaneda enough of the Toltec view to demonstrate that other realities exist, but not enough so Castaneda would get bogged down in yet another description of the world (*Tales*, 240). With this approach, the emphasis remains on freedom.

Second-cycle Toltecs, to don Juan's reckoning, lost themselves in their worldview. They could not escape their own paintings. Their focal points were confined within certain boundaries. Without sufficient margin for the focal point to shift, don Juan says a person becomes either hysterical or self-righteous (*Dreaming*, 75). As a result, fundamentalism is born. And others must follow a prescribed way, or suffer the wrath of those who do follow it and know the "real" truth.

Applied to contemporary philosophical trends, it's easy to find this dynamic at work. As more and more people agree on "new consciousness" or "new age" views and customs, for instance, more and more people are calcifying their perception into dogma. You can be spiritual only if you abide by a certain outlook and manner. As this outlook is far more expansive than their previous, ordinary reality, it's even easier to get lost in. By settling into this new reality, we find the failings of the second cycle re-emerging as groupthink takes hold.

People interested in metaphysics, for example, often speak in terms of "That was *supposed* to happen." Or "Your current difficulties are the result of past-life troubles." While these perspectives may hold truth, to relegate them to a definitive cause and effect is heading for trouble. The possible grains of truth these phrases contain bend perception into pre-established categories, and set the stage for fundamentalism.

Any viable metaphysical system—be it shamanism, yoga, Christianity, or Hinduism—involves working with Spirit. The seers of these disciplines teach that the designs of Spirit are incomprehensible. The advantage of a system is that it provides direction. It provides a boost, an intermediate step to Spirit. But through natural properties of human consciousness (such as association, entrainment, closure, and groupthink), people may mistake the enhanced and expansive energies of the new reality for direct contact with Spirit. While you may be working with a system that incorporates Spirit, you may not necessarily be working with Spirit.

The cohesion of an ordinary reality, for instance, permits space flight. The cohesion of a nonordinary reality permits dreaming-body flight. The respective cohesions carry immense power. In terms of tapping metaphysical currents, you can develop psychic abilities, experience past lives, and converse with elemental spirits, just to give a few examples. According to Toltec teachings, these kinds of enhanced potentials remain within human borders of the first and second fields. But they do not, by themselves, liberate perception beyond form and into Spirit. As much power as form carries, there's even more power beyond form. It's the power of awakening to all creation and to your niche within it.

## Ethics

When dealing with the abstract, you're acutely aware that you can't fully account for much of anything; everything is abstract and putting your life into some kind of form removes you from it. Yet to arrive at the abstract, people tend to reflect on what they're experiencing and to generate some kind of form. This self-reflection is necessary, up to a point. Progressing through the Mastery of Awareness stages, you reflect on different things. During the orientation stage, for example, you figure out what path to walk. During the training stage, you figure out how and where you fit in the scheme of life as you refine your path with heart. At each stage, however, you increasingly work to reflect less. You lose self-importance, disrupt routines, and use death as your advisor. As you gain more awareness, performing these exercises may cause you to reflect more. But you also gain the understanding that self-reflection eventually gets in the way. By the time you become a person of knowledge, you're no longer reflecting; you're *being*.

As you progress through each stage, the attitude of "human first" keeps things in perspective. "Human first" doesn't negate the superior influence of Spirit over humans. What it does do is give you a baseline reference to assess your growth.

At each Mastery stage, the abstract becomes more pronounced, making it easier to lose yourself in abstractions. You might then rationalize any sort of behavior without regard for the concrete effect of that behavior. If you think about it long enough, for example, it's possible to arrive at a conclusion that harming someone is just another expression of Spirit. By nonpatterning ethical standards, you open the door to such thinking. But fluency of thought does not equate with fluency of cohesion, fluency of the entire energy body. To arrive at that level of adeptness, action—not just thinking—is required. Third-cycle seers recognized that having an anything-goes attitude interferes with the push to continually go deeper in awareness. Thus ethical guidelines usher you past thought energy to the complete energy body. Having a reference of "human first" grounds the abstract and connects you with your life.

"Human first" also gives you a way to find a ranger's humbleness in occupying such a tiny niche in all creation. That is, rangers neither lower their eyes to another, nor require others to lower their eyes to them. Essentially, their humbleness is derived from impeccability rather than from having knowledge (*Tales*, 27, 16). Acting in such a manner enables you to find additional balance with the world. But even though you may play a small role, you're still part of creation, and so there's no trouble summoning gusto for your travels. Gusto often parlays into error, however. Second-cycle Toltecs had lots of gusto, for example, but they were misguided in the application of their knowledge. As part of the third cycle's reformation, therefore, ethics were introduced.

A black magician, according to don Juan, is anyone who knowingly or otherwise tries to limit your perception. Second-cycle Toltecs used their awareness and power to unduly influence people. They knew how to entrain, or fixate, the awareness of their victims (*Fire*, 15-16). Thus they could bend others to their wishes. On a larger scale, Castaneda says evil exists only as a result of the mind being overwhelmed by the interlocking structures of a worldview. The complexity of a reality keeps the focal point locked rigidly into place (*Dreaming*, 239). The imbalances created by locking perception in a straitjacket distort your connection with Spirit and produce a good-evil dichotomy.

Don Juan says that quite a few people fall into the category of black magicians because they are hooked to a certain path and work to prevent others from deviating from that path (*Tales,* 28-29). Hindering freedom is thus the defining feature of dark-side practices. Fundamentalists, for example, unwittingly oppose freedom. They actively work to restrain perception to their accepted form. Addressing this, third-cycle seers sought to develop core predilections so a person might better align with formless Spirit. When you have your own power predilections, you're self-fulfilled. Since you have your own it's easier to grant others what's theirs, making the path to *being* all the more enlivening.

What separates seers from fundamentalists, says don Juan, is growing away from pettiness and into a lifestyle governed by beauty and morality (*Silence,* 102). Such a lifestyle doesn't require a syrupy-sweet, doe-eyed demeanor. It means a seer, rather than seeking a competitive edge, seeks to find the grace in life. And grace stems from your relation with the world. If you're first a human, you can regard your fellow humans with respect. Respect eliminates exploitation. If you're first a human, you may explore all spiritual approaches to God, Spirit, or the abstract, with respect. You can then allow that creative force to flow through you with respect. And this flow ushers you past form and into freedom.

\* \* \*

As don Juan says, a Toltec path is for those who seek to lose self-importance. Like anything else, if you want to be good at it, you have to devote your life to it. While developing the intellect is part of the path, Castaneda offers sound advice to move toward intent without trying to understand. In this way, you learn the ins and outs of systems and worldviews as mental constructs. You also realize that there is always more, always the mystery that can't be touched by understanding. Thus you always find any worldview possesses inherent limitations. And there are always revelations which render any worldview obsolete. The intellect can take you far, but only so far. For total freedom the entire energy body must be developed, and for this action carries the day.

By losing self-importance, you stand a chance of stepping beyond structure, beyond your self-reflection, and into full participation with intent. Passing out of self-enhancement and through self-reflection is the journey to Spirit. The power of making such a journey available is the power of the Toltecs.

Of course, Toltecs do not have exclusive rights on Spirit. There are many other paths to help you make this journey. The common denominator of these paths is that they consist of form. They blend theory, method, and practice. And the best ones are very clear that their form is best used as a foundation to boost awareness beyond form and into formless, abstract Spirit.

Less bound by worldview, you're freer to fully live the adventure of your life. The rigors of the path may not produce wealth and worldly goods. But, as Castaneda says, there are those who simply "live to prove we are sublime."[1] Don Juan adds that life is a gesture, a gesture that requires acts of true abandon, generosity, and humor. With such gestures, a person summons his best and silently offers it to Spirit (*Silence,* 262).

It seems that the more a Spirit-related agenda manifests in mainstream endeavors, the more people are able to gain control of their lives. Yet often we want to impose the conditions of our success on Spirit, rather than let Spirit continue delivering our education. We focus on how we want things to be, rather than giving ourselves to Spirit in order to find out how to *be*. So we remain shackled by attachments to economic levels or to social status. Not that we must shun money or accomplishment—but if these things are to be a part of our lives, let them come as an effect of following Spirit rather than of following a path of monetary accumulation. In this way, Spirit becomes the foundation to support all aspects of life. If your path reflects your God-given nature, if it is a path with heart, it doesn't matter where you are, who you are, how much you know, or how much you have. You *are* the fabric in the art of all creation. That, in itself, makes the journey worthwhile.

Whatever your path to Spirit, I wish you well.

# Notes

## Chapter 1:  Stepping Off a Flat Earth

1. Ken Eagle Feather, *Traveling With Power* (Norfolk, VA: Hampton Roads, 1992).
2. Quotations from Carlos Castaneda's works are cited in the text using the following abbreviations:

    *Teachings:*   *The Teachings of don Juan: A Yaqui Way of Knowledge* (New York: Simon & Schuster, 1968).

    *Separate:*   *A Separate Reality: Further Conversations with don Juan* (New York: Simon & Schuster, 1971).

    *Journey:*   *Journey to Ixtlan: The Lessons of Don Juan* (New York: Simon & Schuster, 1972).

    *Tales:*   *Tales of Power* (New York: Simon & Schuster, 1974).

    *Second Ring:* *The Second Ring of Power* (New York: Simon & Schuster, 1977).

    *Gift:*   *The Eagle's Gift* (New York: Simon & Schuster, 1981).

    *Fire:*   *The Fire from Within* (New York: Simon & Schuster, 1984).

    *Silence:*   *The Power of Silence: Further Lessons of Don Juan* (New York: Simon & Schuster, 1987).

    *Dreaming:*   *The Art of Dreaming* (New York: HarperCollins, 1993).
3. Clarissa Pinkola Estes, Ph.D., *Women Who Run With the Wolves: Myths and Stories of the Wild Woman Archetype* (New York: Ballantine Books, 1992), 9.
4. Florinda Donner, *Being-in-Dreaming: An Initiation into the Sorcerer's World* (New York: HarperCollins, 1991); Taisha Abelar, *The Sorcerers' Crossing: A Woman's Journey* (New York: Viking, 1992).
5. *Dissertation Abstracts International,* Xerox University Microfilms, 33B (May-June 1973): 5625-B.
6. David Hunter and Phillip Whitten, eds., *Encyclopedia of Anthropology* (New York: Harper & Row, 1976).
7. Steve Aukstakalnis and David Blatner, *Silicon Mirage: The Art and Science of Virtual Reality* (Berkeley, CA: Peachpit Press, 1992), ch. 1.

## Chapter 2:  Places in Time, Places in Mind

1. Julian Jaynes, *The Origin of Consciousness in the Breakdown of the Bicameral Mind* (Boston: Houghton Mifflin, 1977).

2. J.C. Cooper, *Taoism: The Way of the Mystic* (York Beach, ME: Samuel Weiser, Inc., 1972), 89.
3. Sam Keen, *Fire in the Belly: On Being a Man* (New York: Bantam Books, 1991), 14.
4. Alexander Blair-Ewart, "Being-in-Dreaming," *Dimensions*, 7, No. 2 (Feb. 1992): 21.
5. *Nagualist Newsletter*, Issue 4 (Dec. 1994/Jan. 1995): 13.
6. Norbert Classen, *Das Wissen der Tolteken (The Knowledge of the Toltecs)* (Eurasburg, Germany: edition tonal, 1992).

## Chapter 3: Toltecs Have Their Way

1. W.L Reese, *Dictionary of Philosophy and Religion: Eastern and Western Thought* (Atlantic Highlands, NJ: Humanities Press, 1980).
2. Donner, 167.
3. Robert Monroe, *Journeys Out of the Body* (New York: Doubleday, 1971) and *Ultimate Journey* (New York: Doubleday, 1994).
4. Abelar, ch. 10.
5. Donner, ch. 3.
6. Abelar, 229.
7. Ken Eagle Feather and Carol Kramer, "Being-in-Dreaming," *Body, Mind & Spirit*, Nov./Dec. 1992, 45.

## Chapter 4: A Toltec Team

1. Brian S. Cohen, "Being-in-Dreaming," *Magical Blend*, April 1992, 24.
2. Blair-Ewart, 24.
3. Abelar, xii.
4. Bruce Wagner, "You Only Live Twice," *Details*, March 1994, 218.
5. Abelar, vii.
6. Michael Lee Lanning, *Inside the LRRPS: Rangers in Vietnam* (New York: Ivy Books, 1989), 147.
7. Arthur J. Deikman, M.D., *The Wrong Way Home: Uncovering the Patterns of Cult Behavior in America* (Boston: Beacon Press, 1990), 72.
8. Feather and Kramer, 47.
9. Warren Bennis, *On Becoming a Leader* (Reading, MA: Addison-Wesley Publishing Company, Inc., 1989).
10. Donner, 186.
11. Donner, 107-108.

## Chapter 5: The Shape of Things to Come

1. J.P. Chaplin, *Dictionary of Psychology* (New York: Dell Publishing, 1975).
2. Donner, 300-301.
3. Chaplin, *Dictionary*.

4. Chaplin, *Dictionary.*
5. Cohen, 83.
6. William James, *The Varieties of Religious Experience* (New York: Macmillan, 1961), 297.
7. Chaplin, *Dictionary.*
8. Wagner, 218.

## Chapter 6: Awareness of the Self Beyond

1. Abelar, 133.
2. Michael Talbot, *The Holographic Universe* (New York: HarperCollins, 1991), 174.
3. Adapted from:  Classen, *Das Wissen*, 112.
4. Donner, 219.
5. Donner, 237.

## Chapter 7: Ready, Aim, Fire from Within

1. Keith Thompson, "Portrait of a Sorcerer,"  *New Age Journal*, March/April 1994, 70.
2. Wagner, 218.
3. Abelar, 65.

## Chapter 8: Steady As You Go

1. Abelar, 142.

## Chapter 9: A Tool Kit

1. Wagner,  213.
2. Cohen, 82.
3. Wagner, 215.
4. Abelar, 42.
5. Wagner, 213.
6. Arthur J. Deikman, M.D., "Deautomatization and the Mystic Experience" in *Altered States of Consciousness*, Charles T. Tart, ed. (New York: John Wiley & Sons, Inc., 1969).
7. Abelar, 42.
8. Robert Ornstein, *The Psychology of Consciousness* (New York: Penguin Books, 1972).
9. Sharon Kirby Lamm, "Olympia Dukakis to Women: Face the challenge to evolve," *St. Petersburg Times*, North Pinellas Edition, March 9, 1994, 1, 3.

## Chapter 10: Power Tools

1. Thompson, 156.

2. Abelar, 105-107.
3. Wagner, 214.
4. Wagner, 219.
5. Lanning, *LRRPS*.
6. Thompson, 154.
7. Abelar, 133.
8. Abelar, 57.
9. Abelar, 47.
10. Wagner, 214.
11. Abelar, 42.
12. Wagner, 217.

## Chapter 11: On the Wild Side

1. Whitley Streiber, *Communion* (New York: Beech Tree Books, 1987).
2. Thompson, 156.
3. "Vaccine hailed as AIDS landmark," *St. Petersburg Times*, from Times Wires, Dec. 18, 1992, 1, 3A.
4. Wagner, 217.

## Chapter 13: Scouting the Dreaming Body

1. Wagner, 171.
2. Janet Lee Mitchell, Ph.D., *Out-of-Body Experiences: A Handbook* (New York: Ballantine Books, 1981), 136.

## Chapter 14: Tracking Intent

1. Abelar, 142.
2. Wagner, 216.
3. Donner, 48.
4. Donner, 46.
5. Abelar, 72.

## Chapter 15: Educating for Intent

1. Wagner, 214.
2. Abelar, 236.
3. Wagner, 217-218.
4. Barbara Tedlock, "The Clown's Way" in *Teachings From the American Earth: Indian Religion and Philosophy*, Dennis Tedlock Dennis and Barbara Tedlock, eds. (New York: Liveright, 1975).

## Chapter 16: Hot on the Trail

1. Wagner, 169.

# Bibliography

Abelar, Taisha. *The Sorcerers' Crossing: A Woman's Journey.* New York: Viking, 1992.

Aukstakalnis, Steve, and David Blatner. *Silicon Mirage: The Art and Science of Virtual Reality.* Berkeley, CA: Peachpit Press, 1992.

Bennis, Warren. *On Becoming a Leader.* Reading, MA: Addison-Wesley Publishing Company, Inc., 1989.

Castaneda, Carlos. *The Art of Dreaming.* New York: HarperCollins, 1993.

———. *The Eagle's Gift.* New York: Simon & Schuster, 1981.

———. *The Fire From Within.* New York: Simon & Schuster, 1984.

———. *Journey to Ixtlan: The Lessons of Don Juan.* New York: Simon & Schuster, 1972.

———. *The Power of Silence: Further Lessons of Don Juan.* New York: Simon & Schuster, 1987.

———. *The Second Ring of Power.* New York: Simon & Schuster, 1977.

———. *A Separate Reality: Further Conversations with Don Juan.* New York: Simon & Schuster, 1971.

———. *Tales of Power.* New York: Simon & Schuster, 1974.

———. *The Teachings of don Juan: A Yaqui Way of Knowledge.* New York: Simon & Schuster, 1968.

Chaplin, J.P. *Dictionary of Psychology.* New York: Dell Publishing, 1975.

Classen, Norbert. *Das Wissen der Tolteken (The Knowledge of the Toltecs).* Eurasburg, Germany: edition tonal, 1992.

Cooper, J.C. *Taoism: The Way of the Mystic.* York Beach, ME: Samuel Weiser, Inc., 1972.

Deikman, Arthur J., M.D. *The Wrong Way Home: Uncovering the Patterns of Cult Behavior in America.* Boston: Beacon Press, 1990.

Donner, Florinda. *Being-in-Dreaming: An Initiation into the Sorcerer's World.* New York: HarperCollins, 1991.

Estes, Clarissa Pinkola, Ph.D. *Women Who Run With the Wolves: Myths and Stories of the Wild Woman Archetype.* New York: Ballantine Books, 1992.

Feather, Ken Eagle. *Traveling With Power: The Exploration and Development of Perception.* Norfolk, VA: Hampton Roads, 1992.

Hunter, David, and Phillip Whitten, eds. *Encyclopedia of Anthropology.* New York: Harper & Row, 1976.

James, William. *The Varieties of Religious Experience.* New York: Macmillan, 1961.

Jaynes, Julian. *The Origin of Consciousness in the Breakdown of the Bicameral Mind.* Boston: Houghton Mifflin, 1977.

Keen, Sam. *Fire in the Belly: On Being a Man.* New York: Bantam Books, 1991.

Lanning, Michael Lee. *Inside the LRRPS: Rangers in Vietnam.* New York: Ivy Books, 1989.

Mitchell, Janet Lee, Ph.D. *Out-of-Body Experiences: A Handbook.* New York: Ballantine Books, 1981.

Monroe, Robert. *Journeys Out of the Body.* New York: Doubleday, 1971.
————. *Ultimate Journey.* New York: Doubleday, 1994.

Ornstein, Robert. *The Psychology of Consciousness.* New York: Penguin Books, 1972.

Reese, W.L. *Dictionary of Philosophy and Religion: Eastern and Western Thought.* Atlantic Highlands, NJ: Humanities Press, 1980.

Streiber, Whitley. *Communion.* New York: Beech Tree Books, 1987.

Talbot, Michael. *The Holographic Universe.* New York: HarperCollins, 1991.

Tart, Charles T., ed. *Altered States of Consciousness.* New York: John Wiley & Sons, Inc., 1969.

Tedlock, Dennis, and Barbara Tedlock, eds. *Teachings From the American Earth: Indian Religion and Philosophy.* New York: Liveright, 1975.

# Index

Chapter subheadings, charts, and diagrams.

## Charts

## Diagrams

# About the Author

*A Toltec Path* is Ken Eagle Feather's second book detailing the teachings of the Toltec seer don Juan Matus. Concurrent with his apprenticeship to don Juan, Ken obtained degrees in education and mass communications. He later served on staff at The Association for Research and Enlightenment, which is part of the Edgar Cayce legacy, and at The Monroe Institute, founded by Robert Monroe, a pioneer in using sound technology to facilitate the exploration of consciousness. Ken's first book, *Traveling With Power*, provides, in addition to Toltec teachings, a glimpse into the Edgar Cayce psychic readings regarding astral projection and offers an overview of The Monroe Institute's brain-wave synchronization process.

Ken has taught metaphysics for more than 17 years, and in recent years has traveled internationally presenting lectures and seminars on the topics in his books. In addition, he has created an educational performance-arts presentation, "Shapeshifting Through Time and Space," which blends shapeshifting, storytelling, and traditional instruction. He is currently writing a science fiction screenplay, and is continuing his Toltec-related investigations for a third book, *Lessons from Toltec Travels*.

If you are interested in sponsoring his work, please contact Ken at:

Eagle Dynamics, Inc.
P.O. Box 1311
Dunedin, FL 34697

Hampton Roads publishes books on
metaphysical, spiritual, health-related, and
general interest subjects. Would you like to be notified
as we publish new books in your area of interest?
If you would like a copy of our latest catalog, just call toll-free,
(800) 766-8009, or send your name and address to:

Hampton Roads Publishing Company, Inc.
976 Norfolk Square
Norfolk, VA 23502